T0384394

Ever since the trades unions were defeated in the 1980s, alienated work, unbearable inequality and disappearing quality jobs have become the order of the day. Andrew Brady's new book focuses on the unfashionable but crucial role of trades unions as a break on this never-ending decline and as a source of hope for the future.

—Yanis Varoufakis

Andrew Brady has produced an important and original new study of the changing ways through which British trade unions have exercised national political influence through the Labour Party over the past fifty years, which draws on detailed interviews with leading Labour and trade union figures. The 'insider views' of the Union-Party relationships during the New Labour period, in particular, are a major contribution to our political and historical understanding. The book is very timely, as Labour enters a new political phase and union influence over policy appears to be growing.

—Peter Ackers—Visiting Professor in the History of
Industrial Relations, Loughborough University

Andrew Brady has the skills of the academic, the guile of a street politician, and the negotiating noose of the trade unionist. He needed all three of these traits in writing this book of unravelling the almost schizophrenic relationship between the New Labour and the UK Trade Union Leaderships. He has succeeded brilliantly.

—Sir Ian McCartney—former Labour Government
Minster and Chairman of the Labour Party

Using a unique dataset drawn from interviews with leading players from the trade unions and Labour, Andrew Brady's book allows us to rethink key events such as the struggle for the National Minimum Wage and the Employment Relations Act in new and insightful ways.

—Paul Thompson—Professor of Employment Studies,
University of Stirling

The mass re-engagement of voters with the radical left in Britain has its roots in a political turn by trade unions in the early 21st century. Andrew Brady's timely book traces the change in strategy that has led to unions taking overt political action to represent their members, and to a wave of unionisation struggles by precarious workers. Brady's rigorous overview of these developments will stimulate debate among academics, HR professionals and the wider labour and trade union movement itself.

—**Paul Mason**

Unions and Employment in a Market Economy

Due to the sharp declines in trade union density and collective bargaining coverage post-1979, the shift by trade unions towards political action has had significant implications for employment relations regulation in contemporary Britain. Yet there remains insufficient discussion of the factors of influence affecting changes in the political action process from a historical and contemporary perspective. *Unions and Employment in a Market Economy* will evidence how trade unions were able to offset environmental constraints through a progressive focus on political action, despite diminished power in the Labour Party's structures and the wider economy. The book presents four legislative events categorised as functional equivalents enacted in two different periods of Labour governance (1974–79 and 1997–2010). The selected events are the Social Contract (1974–79), National Minimum Wage (1998), Employment Relations Act (1999) and the Warwick Agreement (2004). The book's findings lend credence to the proposition that in a liberal market economy there is a valuable dividend associated with trade union political exchange through the Labour Party.

Andrew Brady is an academic with a PhD from the University of Strathclyde and works in the British labour movement.

Routledge Research in Employment Relations

Series editors: Rick Delbridge and Edmund Heery
Cardiff Business School, UK.

Aspects of the employment relationship are central to numerous courses at both undergraduate and postgraduate level.

Drawing from insights from industrial relations, human resource management and industrial sociology, this series provides an alternative source of research-based materials and texts, reviewing key developments in employment research.

Books published in this series are works of high academic merit, drawn from a wide range of academic studies in the social sciences.

Unions and Employment in a Market Economy

Strategy, Influence and Power in Contemporary Britain

Andrew Brady

Routledge
Taylor & Francis Group

LONDON AND NEW YORK

First published 2019 by Routledge

2 Park Square, Milton Park, Abingdon, Oxon, OX14 4RN
605 Third Avenue, New York, NY 10017

*Routledge is an imprint of the Taylor & Francis Group, an
informa business*

First issued in paperback 2020

Library of Congress Cataloging-in-Publication Data
A catalog record for this book has been requested

ISBN: 978-1-138-48987-5 (hbk)
ISBN: 978-0-367-78679-3 (pbk)

Typeset in Sabon
by Apex CoVantage, LLC

Difficult but not impossible.

Contents

Tables

Boxes

Preface

The book will present a deeper understanding and examination of the role performed by the trade union bureaucratic centre—the Trades Union Congress (TUC)—and the largest affiliated Labour Party trade unions to achieve employment relations outcomes at junctures of Labour governance. Trade unions affiliated to the Labour Party theoretically have a more effective channel for political action due to the institutional role and leverage held inside the party's structures. The conceptual underpinning of political action as a method for attaining employment relations outcomes is contained in Webb and Webb (1913, 1920). In essence, if the enforcement of Common Rules (i.e. the determination of the standard minimum wages and conditions throughout each industry) could not be achieved through the Method of Collective Bargaining, then it could be through the Method of Legal Enactment. The latter would be achieved through political action.

Yet there remains insufficient discussion of the factors of influence affecting changes in the political action process from a historical and contemporary perspective. The book will evidence how trade unions were able to offset environmental constraints through a progressive focus on political action, despite diminished power in the Labour Party's structures and the wider economy. The findings lend credence to the proposition that in a liberal market economy there is a valuable dividend associated with trade union political exchange through the Labour Party channel. The book presents four legislative events categorised as functional equivalents, which are the Social Contract (1974–79), National Minimum Wage (1998), Employment Relations Act (1999) and the Warwick Agreement (2004). Admittedly, there are inevitable drawbacks in categorising the events as equivalents, with each having displayed a series of multifaceted dimensions. The rationale for selection was based on each event performing a macro-economic impact on the employment relations framework.

The legislative events also chart the ability of trade unions to influence employment relations regulation through political action in two structurally different contexts—*collective laissez-faireism* to a *liberal market* economy. The first environment is at a juncture of strong union-party attachment (pre-1979) with high levels of trade union density and collective bargaining coverage. Collective laissez-faireism was enabled by an interventionist state, which constructed supportive institutions and associated bodies (Kahn-Freund, 1965). The framework was characterised by an inclusive approach to trade unions in the management of the economy by the state and the principal political parties, despite significant differences between the latter (Howell, 2000). In contrast, the liberal market economy is an environment characterised by weaker union-party attachment. It is reflective of decollectivist, deregulatory and privatisation policies adopted by successive Conservative Governments (1979–97). The institutional deconstruction facilitated low levels of trade union density and collective bargaining coverage through a series of interventionist measures by the state. The liberal market is generally characterised by a marginalised role for trade unions in the economy at variance with the empowerment of employer prerogative.

There is an extensive body of literature on trade unions, which focuses on industrial revitalisation strategies—see Heery et al. (2003), Boxall (2008) and Heery and Simms (2008). In addition, there is a significant body of literature on the Labour Party and trade union links through the political science approach. This includes influential works by Harrison (1960), A. Taylor (1987), Minkin (1992, 2014) and Hayter (2005). Nevertheless, there has been inadequate examination of the strategic choices of trade union leaders and the process of strategising by British trade unions in order to influence employment relations through political action in a liberal market. The relatively recent work of Daniels and McIlroy (2009) and Coulter (2014) has partially addressed this gap, with a particular emphasis on the first and second terms of New Labour (1997–2005). May (1975) originally identified the variance in coverage between the influence of business leaders and trade union leaders. Accordingly, the book focuses on the 'locus of leadership' in trade unions, which has been identified as general secretary leadership (Boxall and Haynes, 1997: 570). The findings and observations derive from 'key informants', principally trade union leaders, Labour Government minsters and advisors (Eisenhardt, 1989: 541). The book also addresses the limited detail on the content and importance of informal processes utilised by trade union leaders for political action purposes as opposed to the employment relations arena (Findlay et al., 2009).

Bibliography

Boxall, P. (2008). Trade union strategy: Varieties of capitalism and industrial relations. In: P. Blyton, N. Bacon, J. Fiorito and E. Heery, eds., *The SAGE handbook of industrial relations*. London: SAGE Publications.

Boxall, P. and Haynes, P. (1997). Strategy and effectiveness in a liberal environment. *British Journal of Industrial Relations*, 35(4), pp. 567–591.

Coulter, S. (2014). *New Labour policy, industrial relations and the trade unions*. Houndmills: Palgrave Macmillan.

Daniels, G. and McIlroy, J. (eds.) (2009). *Trade unions in a neoliberal world: British trade unions under New Labour*. London: Routledge.

Eisenhardt, K.M. (1989). Building theories from case study research. *Academy of Management Review*, 14(4), pp. 532–550.

Findlay, P., McKinlay, A., Marks, A. and Thompson, P. (2009). Collective bargaining and new works regimes: Too important to be left to bosses. *Industrial Relations Journal*, 40(3), pp. 235–251.

Harrison, M. (1960). *Trade unions and the Labour Party since 1945*. Museum Street, London: George Allen and Unwin Limited.

Hayter, D. (2005). *Fightback: Labour's traditional rights in the 1970's and 1980's*. Oxford Road, Manchester: Manchester University Press.

Heery, E., Kelly, J. and Waddington, J. (2003). Union revitalization in Britain. *European Journal of Industrial Relations*, 9(1), pp. 79–97.

Heery, E. and Simms, M. (2008). Constraints on union organising in the United Kingdom. *Industrial Relations Journal*, 39(1), pp. 24–42.

Howell, C. (June 2000). Constructing British industrial relations. *British Journal of Politics and International Relations*, 2(2), pp. 205–236.

Kahn-Freund, O. (1965). *Labour relations and the law: A comparative study*. Boston, MA: Little.

Ludlam, S. and Taylor, A. (December 2003). The political representation of the labour interest in Britain. *British Journal of Industrial Relations*, 41(4), pp. 727–749.

May, T.C. (1975). *Trade unions and pressure group politics*. Saxon House: D.C. Heath Ltd.

Minkin, L. (1992). *Contentious alliance: Trade unions and the Labour Party*. Edinburgh: Edinburgh University Press Limited.

Minkin, L. (2014). *The Blair supremacy: A study in the politics of the Labour Party's management*. Manchester: Manchester University Press.

Taylor, A. (1987). *The trade unions and the Labour Party*. Burrell Row, Beckenham, Kent: Room Helm Ltd. (Provident House).

Webb, S. and Webb, B. (1913). *Industrial democracy*. Printed by the Authors for the Trade Unionists of the United Kingdom. London: Longmans Green and Co.

Webb, S. and Webb, B. (1920). *The history of trade unionism*. Rev. ed. London: Longmans Green and Co.

1 Trade Union Strategy, Influence and Power in Contemporary Britain

An Introduction

Introduction

The book is guided by Hamann and Kelly's (2004) four factors of influence, which are identified as shaping trade union decision-making as a theoretical framework.[1] The book terms these factors as follows: (1) economic and political institutions; (2) union ideology; (3) employer, political party or state strategies; and (4) strategic choices of union leaders. By employing these factors, the book will combine broad structural, ideational and agency explanations that help us to understand and explain trade union decision-making. Accordingly, the chapter will begin by introducing Varieties of Capitalism theory in order to assess the structural and institutional change in advanced capitalist economies. This will provide a wider context to the political and economic institutional reconfiguration in contemporary Britain. As a direct consequence of the economic and legislative change post-1979, the chapter will outline the function of political action through the Labour Party as a channel for influencing the employment relations arena. The centrality of trade union strategy, agency, structure and ideology as factors in this process will be outlined.

Varieties of Capitalism

Economic and political institutions directly shape trade unions, employers and political parties both subtly and overtly. These institutions can increase or constrain the opportunities for trade unions seeking to attain positive outcomes in the employment relations arena. The structural constraints on trade unions have facilitated an intense academic debate to explain the causal factors resulting in cross-country convergence and divergence. The Varieties of Capitalism (VoC) approach gives credence to divergence between nation states. The main emphasis in the comparative work lies in contrasting Anglo-Saxon states (e.g. United States and Britain) with continental European and Asian models (Hall and Soskice, 2001). The approach has grouped capitalist systems, especially those of the Organisation for Economic Co-operation and Development (OECD), into several categories: Liberal Market Economies (LMEs), Coordinated Market Economies and Mediterranean Economies. Underlying each model are sets of institutional arrangements involving the state, employers and trade unions.

Hamann and Kelly (2008), Hyman and Gumbrell-McCormick (2010) and Appelbaum and Schmitt (2013) through the application of various time series data present findings that correspond with the VoC approach. Hamann and Kelly (2008) present statistics that show trade union density decline has been steeper in LMEs for the 1980–2000 period compared with fourteen non-LMEs assessed (median percentage point declines were 20.7 and 9, respectively). The differences within the non-LME group were 'striking', as the four Scandinavian economies (Norway, Sweden, Denmark and Finland) stand out as density rose in one of them and fell only slightly in the other three (−0.5 per cent average across all four countries over a twenty-year period). Over the 1980–2000 period, the gap between these Scandinavian economies and the other countries widened, leading to the conclusion that "there is no evidence of convergence" (Hamann and Kelly, 2008: 137). In a longer time-series presented by Appelbaum and Schmitt (2013), only one country showed a slight increase in trade union density pre-global recession (2007), which was Finland (1980, 69.4 per cent to 2007, 70.3 per cent).

Visser (1992) also drew attention to the comparable stability of trade union density in Scandinavia and Belgium compared with other advanced capitalist countries. The explanation for the difference was principally attributed to the role performed by trade unions in the provision of unemployment benefit—the 'Ghent system'. All four 'Ghent' countries along with Norway remained the most stable countries analysed. According to the logic of the Ghent framework, trade unions can be institutionally insulated from economic pressures, but they are simultaneously vulnerable to changes in policy by the state. The assertion is corroborated by the sharp drop in trade union density statistics in Sweden from 76 per cent in 2005 to 69.3 per cent in 2010. The centre-right Swedish Government elected in 2006 made changes to unemployment insurance as the membership fees of most unemployment funds increased meaning a corresponding increase in the 'total union fee' (Kjellberg, 2011).

In LMEs, markets are ascribed as performing the role of managing relations between economic actors and capital is allocated primarily through stock markets. This is designed to ensure high levels of labour flexibility and capital mobility, which can facilitate sharp economic adjustments. Liberal markets are generally characterised by relatively low wages and low-skills levels in conjunction with weaker trade unions and less employment protection. These manifestations stem from the underlying structural conditions, principally greater degrees of deregulation, decentralisation and decollectivisation (Howell, 2004). In contrast, employers in coordinated market economies have an interest in strong trade unionism because they "form an essential part of productive strategies focusing on high-skill, high-quality export manufacturing goods" (King and Wood, 1999: 387). The statistics in Table 1.1 illustrate the

Table 1.1 Trade Union Bargaining and Density 1980 and 2007

Type	Country	Union Density (1980)	Union Density (2007)	1980–2007 % change	Coverage (1980)	Coverage (2007)	1980–2007 % change
CME	Austria	56.7	29.9	-47.3%	95	98	3.2%
CME	Belgium	51.3	54.7	6.6%	96	96	0.0%
CME	Germany	34.9	19.9	-43.0%	85	61.7	-27.4%
CME	France	18.3	7.5	-59.0%	77.4	98	26.6%
CME	Italy	49.6	34	-31.5%	80	80	0.0%
CME	Netherlands	34.8	19.3	-44.5%	76.7	79	3.0%
CME	Switzerland	27.5	18.5	-32.7%	50	44.8	-10.4%
Avg		**39.0**	**26.3**	**-32.7%**	**80.0**	**79.6**	**-0.5%**
LME	Australia	49.6	18.5	-62.7%	84.3	54.7	-35.1%
LME	Britain	51.7	27.3	-47.2%	69	34.6	-49.9%
LME	Canada	34	29.4	-13.5%	37.1	29.4	-20.8%
LME	Ireland	57.1	31	-45.7%	63.5	40.5	-36.2%
LME	Japan	31.1	18.3	-41.2%	31.1	17.8	-42.8%
LME	New Zealand	69.1	21.3	-69.2%	70	17.8	-74.6%
LME	United States	22.1	11.6	-47.5%	25	12.7	-49.2%
Avg		**45.0**	**22.5**	**-50.0%**	**54.3**	**29.6**	**-45.4%**
EDE	Greece	38.9	24.1	-38.0%	85	83	-2.4%
EDE	Spain	13.5	15.5	14.8%	76	76.4	0.5%
EDE	Portugal	54.8	20.8	-62.0%	70	84.9	21.3%
Avg		**35.7**	**20.1**	**-43.7%**	**77**	**81.4**	**5.8%**
NME	Denmark	78.6	67.9	-13.6%	82	81	-1.2%
NME	Finland	69.4	70.5	1.6%	70	87.7	25.3%
NME	Norway	58.3	53	-9.1%	70	70	0.0%
NME	Sweden	78	71	-9.0%	88	91	3.4%
Avg		**71.1**	**65.6**	**-7.7%**	**77.5**	**82.4**	**6.4%**

Note: The average calculations are based on horizontal figures rather than vertical averages.

Source: Visser (October 2015). The figures are as close to 1980 and 2007 as possible; in some instances, the year extends to several (+/–) for either density or collective bargaining depending on the available data. The data for collective bargaining coverage in Ireland (1980) is sourced from Appelbaum and Schmitt (2013) and for trade union density in Australia and the United States (2007), it is sourced from ILOStat (2018).

specific set of economic and political dynamics in operation in LMEs, which have contributed to sharp decreases in trade union density and collective bargaining coverage. The table follows the same categorisation of advanced industrialised economies as Appelbaum and Schmitt (2013) except referring to Sweden, Norway, Denmark and Finland as Nordic Market Economies (NMEs) not Social-Democratic. In addition to LMEs, the other categorisations are as follows: CMEs (continental market economies) and EDEs (ex-dictatorship economies). Gallie (2009: 381) stated that Britain is the 'clearest' European example of a liberal market economy as density (–47.2 per cent) and bargaining coverage (–49.9 per cent) fell sharply over a twenty-seven-year period.[2]

Deconstruction and Reconstruction

The notion of path dependence (Pierson, 1997) relates to a trajectory that becomes difficult to reverse. Incentives are created for actors to find solutions, which modify existing institutions rather than wholesale abolition or replacement. Accordingly, institutions will often persist for long periods and influence actors' strategies in the short term to a greater degree (Ebbinghaus and Visser, 2000). It is entirely consistent, therefore, for specific political systems and bi/tripartite architecture to be retained in order to manage economic transformation. The process is principally organised and managed by government through social-pact processes as experienced in Italy, Ireland and Spain (Hyman, 2001). Howell and Kolins Givan (2011) highlighted that countries which use or reform existing institutions will also exhibit greater degrees of stability.

Pizzorno (1978) described a *social-pact* process as one of 'political exchange', whereupon the state offers greater economic involvement and increased legal rights to trade unions in return for commitments particularly on wage moderation. The level of political exchange is determined by the extent of corporatist mechanisms. A. Taylor (1989: 97), in a succinct description of the *corporatist approach*, stated that it was a framework whereby "economic interest groups (recognised as authoritative and representative by government) participate in the policy process". Trade union participation through such an approach is characterised by three dimensions: (1) trade unions represent members within the process, (2) trade unions accordingly bargain with government on policy and (3) trade unions participate in the implementation of policy.

In Britain, collective bargaining agreements and corporatist structures had 'shallow roots' because they were "not anchored in legal or constitutional foundations as in many other parts of Western Europe" (Kelly, 2013: 181). Trade unions, rather than enjoying enshrined legal rights, historically had campaigned for the restoration of legal immunities. Economic transformation was structurally easier and made speedier by the absence of strong market coordinating mechanisms (Howell, 2004;

Coulter, 2014). A majoritarian political system also limited the need for consensus through social-pacts as experienced across the continent of Europe.[3] A structural factor facilitating economic transformation was the trend towards firm level bargaining through productivity agreements by multinational companies in the post-1945 era. These agreements were designed to provide firms with controllable and predictive wage costs in order to remove working practices considered inflexible by employers. Productivity agreements altered employment relations relationships from an externally constructed framework outside the firm, namely via national unions, national employers and the state, to internalised relations at the firm level (Gospel, 1992). The firm-centric structural shifts, supported in certain quarters by powerful trade unions in response to wage restraint measures during the 1950s and 1960s, would have profound consequences for a future Labour Government attempting to control inflation and minimise industrial action between 1974 and 1979. The tensions stemmed from attempts to centralise and control wages in tandem with decentralisation to the firm (Undy et al., 1981).

Due to these economic and political structural vulnerabilities, trade unions were brutally exposed in the post-1979 period as part of the Conservative Party's response in government to the 'Winter of Discontent' (1978–79) strike wave. The neoliberal reform project of the Margaret Thatcher–led Conservative Government was directed towards decentralisation, decollectivism and the individualisation of employment relations (see Box A). In Britain, the introduction of neoliberal policies did not entertain any notion of consensual institutional deconstruction and reconstruction with trade unions (Wilkinson, 2007). It would herald a new settlement leading to the exclusion and marginalisation of trade unions. The Conservative Government brought forward the Employment Act of 1980, which contained measures to restrict the closed shop, limit industrial action picketing and reduce dismissal costs.[4] This would also include the repeal of Schedule 11 in the Employment Protection Act (1975), which had guaranteed workers a statutory route to collective recognition when confronted by a hostile employer. Successive measures further restricted trade unions' organisational abilities and immunities.[5]

Neoliberal reform included the abolition of the wage and trades boards through the Trade Union Reform and Employment Rights Act (1993). This removed the remaining minimum wage protection for around 2.5 million low-paid workers. The Trade Boards Act (1909) had sanctioned tripartite machinery (i.e. government, employers and trade unions), which would characterise employment relations for decades. The Boards established a bottom-floor of minimum wages and conditions and facilitated collective bargaining. These agreements were legally enforceable in the industries where they were established. In those industries where the presence of trade unionism was strong enough, the government facilitated parallel structures in order to encourage stability in industry and the wider economy.

Box A What Is Neoliberalism?

Neoliberalism is a macro-economic strategy involving trade and financial liberalisation, fiscal discipline and the promotion of deflationary tactics. The approach necessitates structural reforms and an enabling institutional architecture particularly in the sphere of employment relations.

The dynamics identified include deindustrialisation, decollectivisation, decentralisation to the firm, economic deregulation including trade liberalisation (the European Union), flexible labour markets, individualisation of employment relations and privatisation.

Conservative Governments pursued an aggressive policy of privatisation in public industries and corporations, which would have significant implications for all trade unions. The list of major privatised industries included gas, electricity, water, nuclear energy, steel, telecommunications, coal and railways. In total, the number of people working in the public sector fell by 2.2 million from 7.45 million in 1979 to 5.23 million in 1995. The vast majority of the decline (1.7 million) resulted from privatisation, as the workforce of the nationalised industries and public corporations fell by 83 per cent (Howell, 1998: 295). The impact of the liberal market reforms was devastating for trade unions in Britain. Collective trade union membership fell from 13.2 million (1979) to 7.8 million in 1998, which brought density in the workforce to 29.9 per cent down from a peak of 50.7 per cent (1979).

New Labour: Continuation of Neoliberalism or Breaking With the Past?

The New Labour Government elected in 1997 complemented rather than conflicted with the Thatcherite reforms.[6] Labour stated it would neither repeal the fundamental tenets of the Conservative employment relations framework nor return privatised industries to public ownership. New Labour's political and economic reforms, despite being influenced by neoliberal dynamics, were distinct in comparison with the Conservative Governments (1979–97), as the book will evidence. The findings will challenge economically structurally determinist arguments regarding the inability of trade unions to meaningfully shape the employment relations framework.

The new approach was advanced through the notion of *social partnership*, which was informed by European approaches to employment relations (Ackers, 2002). Social partnership was based on the premise that firms are most successful when employers, managers and employees work together, which should be supported by the state. At the heart of the 'Third Way' narrative was a focus on supply-side initiatives such as skills, training and flexible labour markets (Wood, 2000). Social partnership would feature a more inclusive approach by the state and sections of the business community towards trade unions after the long period of exclusion under the Conservatives. Ackers and Payne (1998: 546) adroitly characterised the social partnership approach as consisting of two core elements: (1) it shifted the debate through 'rhetoric of rights and reconstruction' and (2) it appealed beyond union members who were now a minority of the working population to encompass all workers.

In contrast, Ewing (2005) critiqued social partnership as an approach that allocated a subordinate role for trade unions in the economy premised on the need to cooperate with employers. Nonetheless, social partnership represented a "key break in public policy" (Heery, 2005: 3). The approach facilitated the involvement of the trade union movement through the TUC in the development of employment relations policy "to an extent unknown for twenty years" Brown (2000: 315). In this context, Metcalf (2005: 27) stated that social partnership signified a shift from 'hostile forces' to a more enabling environment for trade unions. The inclusivity of the approach theoretically widened the opportunity for trade unions to gain legislative outcomes due to the "favourable industrial relations terrain" (Ackers and Payne, 1998: 544). The extent of this favourable terrain and the ability of trade unions to meaningfully shape it will be debated in the book.

Baccaro and Howell (2011) persuasively characterise the Labour Governments' (1997–2010) employment relations regime as being shaped by two twin themes: social partnership and individual rights within a decollectivised trajectory. Accordingly, a more appropriate descriptor of the regulatory approach by the Labour Government over its three terms in government has been termed *regulated individualism* by the book. The descriptor captures the emphasis on statutory individual rights rather than trade union and collective rights; yet correctly recognises the break from the "atomism, individualism and exclusive concern with profitability allegedly characterizing Thatcherism" (Howell, 2004: 13). Legislation and institutions such as the Low Pay Commission (LPC), which would be established to guide the government on the national minimum wage, would underpin a series of positive individual legal rights with collective implications.

Labour Party: A Channel for Trade Union Political Action

Due to the dual-drag of low trade union density and collective bargaining coverage, the opportunity for trade unions to redress perceived imbalances of employment relations power has been progressively constrained. For that reason, an evaluation of political action by trade unions through the Labour Party as a channel for influencing the employment relations regime is of critical importance. The book primarily focuses on the largest affiliated Labour Party trade unions and evidences how these trade unions sought to utilise institutional power and influence through political action. It is important to acknowledge other strategies worthy of analysis associated with political action such as social movement unionism epitomised in the United States. This particular form of political action is becoming an increasing feature of the activities of trade unions in the post–global crash era (i.e. 2007). Social movement unionism is an attempt by trade unions to seek viable 'escape-routes' in response to the continued diminution of power. An illustration is trade union alliances with anti-austerity organisations. However, Heery et al. (2003: 92) contend that before the financial crash, such ties between trade unions and social movements "exerted a limited influence on union recovery".

During the 1970s as the key juncture of analysis in the book, there were five principal institutional avenues available to trade unions in order to influence Labour Party policy-making to varying degrees: (1) the Parliamentary Labour Party (PLP), (2) the Labour Party Annual Conference, (3) the National Executive Committee (NEC) of the Labour Party, (4) the Liaison Committee and (5) Constituency Labour Parties (CLPs) (May, 1975). The cumulative effect of these levers demonstrated "the constraining influence of the informal ethos of formal party practices" (Drucker, 1991: 246). In essence, these levers provided trade unions with access to various formal, intermediary and informal processes that could constrain the desires of the parliamentary leadership, particularly when the Labour Party was in government. Of these various mechanisms, the Liaison Committee was described as the 'most vital decision-making body' in the labour movement (R. Taylor, 1976: 403). The Liaison Committee was an intermediary mechanism designed to build greater mutual understanding and help offset the tensions between the PLP and trade unions following the experiences of the 1964–70 Labour Government (Paynter, 1970; Heffer, 1972; R. Taylor, 1991).

The liaison body is a fascinating example of a political exchange process with contemporary implications. Specifically, employment relations policy-making was developed through an intermediary mechanism and implemented during Labour's tenure in government in a social-pact process. The Social Contract (1974–79) was viewed as seminal because it represented a 'decisive break' with the past adherence to collective laissez-faireism (R. Taylor, 1976: 406). The process symbolised a shift towards greater state involvement in the management of employment relations in concert with trade unions. The observation is complemented by A. Taylor (1987: 28) who characterised the approach as a shift away from 'negative-defensive unionism' towards 'positive initiative unionism'. The

Liaison Committee would decline in importance, particularly after the Labour Party's 1983 general election defeat, until it effectively ceased to operate by 1990. The change was accentuated by the aspiration of the TUC to influence Conservative Government policy based on its corporatist philosophy (A. Taylor, 1987; Minkin, 1992). Simultaneously, the TUC sought to withdraw from its close engagement with the Labour Party due to the internal wrangling which beset the party during the 1980s, as Chapter 3 on Employment Relations Reform under New Labour will discuss.

The strategic shifts by the TUC were mirrored by a strong body of opinion in the PLP who had historically supported greater policy-making power being transferred to the parliamentary leadership. There were consistent efforts by factions in the Labour Party, in particular, Members of Parliament (MPs), who wanted to reduce the power of trade unions in the party's structures. The efforts focused on widening the franchise on issues such as parliamentary selections and leadership contests.[7] The discourse gained greater traction after the election of Neil Kinnock as Labour Party leader in 1983. This process was emboldened by the neoliberal dynamics unleashed by Conservative Governments, which progressively constrained the influence of trade unions in the wider economy post-1979.

A major dilemma for those trade unions affiliated to the Labour Party in the 1980s was framed around trade unions having to reduce their individual and collective institutional leverage in the Labour Party due to its perceived negative impact on the party's electoral prospects. The failure to do so according to this narrative would continue to harm Labour's electoral appeal. Undy (2002: 638) stated 'mainstream' union leaders in response to the perceived strength of this discourse were persuaded by contextual arguments to reduce the institutional role of trade unions in the Labour Party's structures to varying degrees. The National Graphical Association (NGA), for example, was described as having agreed to internal policy reforms on the basis that it was electorally advantageous, thus "industrial pragmatism superseded political purity" (Gennard and Hayward, 2008: 201). The pro-leadership stance adopted by individual trade unions affiliated to the Labour Party for electoral reasons was not universally accepted as other trade unions resisted policy changes based on ideology and desire to retain institutional leverage (Basset, 1991; Minkin, 1992).

The Policy Review Group (PRG) process of the Labour Party launched in 1987 was considered an essential component of the reform strategy to widen Labour's electoral appeal. The process shifted power away from the party's Annual Conference, hence away from trade unions. The continuation of internal party reform during the 1990s under the successive leaderships of John Smith and, in particular, Tony Blair, resulted in power being progressively shifted towards the parliamentary leadership. The collective trade union vote at party conference was reduced to 50 per cent in 1995 from 70 per cent in 1992 and from 90 per cent beforehand (Minkin, 1992; Freeden, 1999; Bodah et al., 2003). At the 1993 Labour Party Annual Conference, the voting procedures were also reformed to introduce the principle of 'One Member One Vote', extending more institutional power away from trade unions. Trade unions and CLPs were required to ballot members individually with results allocated proportionately. The weighting of votes in the party's electoral college was also changed to give each section (PLP, CLPs and trade unions) a third of the share of votes. The weighting of votes for the election of Labour Party Leader and Deputy Leader as established at the 1981 special party conference had been previously set on the following terms: PLP was given 30 per cent of the vote, the CLPs 30 per cent and the affiliated trade unions allocated 40 per cent.

The Labour Party NEC reinforced the pro-leadership stance by voting to support further restructuring of the policy-making process (Hayter, 2005). The reform process prior to Labour's general election victory in 1997 would culminate in the publication of 'Labour into Power: a Framework for Partnership' (1997). The new National Policy Forum (NPF) policy-making process left the affiliated trade unions with 17 per cent of the voting power in the forum (i.e. thirty seats out of one hundred and seventy-five in 1997). The number of seats also filled by the trade unions fell from seventeen out of thirty to twelve out of thirty-three on the NEC in 1998.[8] Wickham-Jones (2014: 52) stated that due to successive rounds of Labour Party internal reform, trade unions "enjoy little formal influence over some of the institutions of the Labour party". In this context, trade unions could endeavour to facilitate the development of policy through new processes inside the Labour Party to challenge these institutional constraints. This potentially opened up alternative processes for trade union strategising in order to exert power and influence on the employment relations framework during Labour's tenure in government from 1997 to 2010, as the book will evidence. Moreover, the contemporary validity of Wickham-Jones' point in light of Jeremy Corbyn's assent to the Labour leadership in 2015 is an issue the book will return to.

Trade Union Leadership, Strategy and Structure

Morgan and Smircich (1980: 498) cogently argued that when one 'relaxes' the ontological assumption that the world is a 'concrete structure', then social agents can create strategy.[9] Hansen and Kupper (2009: 2), in the strategy-as-practice approach, add that "strategy rather implicates a dynamic component: it is an activity that can be better described as a process of strategising". Therefore, environmental variability may attract the 'most attention' according to Child (1972: 3), but it neither determines trade union behaviour nor sufficiently explains the 'deeper dynamics' in operation (Frege and Kelly, 2003: 12). The proposition remains valid despite the opportunities for success being significantly more constrained in a liberal market economy.

Trade union structures are a pivotal factor in the development and enactment of trade union strategies. Structures are ascribed as comprising horizontal and hierarchical organisation features (centralised or decentralised union organisation, unitary or multiple-peak federations), in concert with relationships among trade unions. Factored into these structural processes are national union leaderships and their corresponding relations with other union officials and union representatives at the workplace. Trade union institutional structures are not uniform across advanced industrialised nations, and significant structural differences exist. This, in turn, frames the opportunities for strategising and strategic action (Hyman, 2007). German and Scandinavian trade union leaders in market economies 'rely more on collective decision-making' due to greater degrees of centralisation and coordination. German unions, through this structure, are 'better placed' than Spanish or Italian counterparts to engage employers in new bargaining initiatives due to the 'denser networks' of local trade union representatives (Frege and Kelly, 2003: 14).

The German trade union network derived from the legally mandated works councils and the Vertrauensleute system.[10] The historical implications of the system meant less reliance upon political action by trade unions due to the institutional focus on works councils. Moreover, trade unions do not have formal institutional access through the German Social Democratic Party, in contrast with British counterparts (Hamann and Kelly, 2004). The American and British union confederations alternatively are described as being 'relatively weak' in comparison with their national affiliates. Accordingly, the opportunity for trade union leaders to act in greater coordination in Britain has been limited by what Frege and Kelly (2003: 14) describe as an 'individualist leadership structure' akin to a Chief Executive Officer in a major company. Moreover, Rallings (1983: 71) complemented this observation by drawing attention to the centrality of agency by describing trade union members as being 'content' to "allow responsibility for the 'political' direction of their union to rest in the hands of the elected and/or bureaucratic leadership". These institutional factors emphasise the reasons for evaluating trade union leadership in Britain, as it performs a more discretionary institutional role than European counterparts.

Structural reorganisation is identified as part of an endeavour to exercise greater political and industrial leverage in response to economic transformation. Evans et al. (1992: 580) argued that due to the combination of falling trade union membership and finances in conjunction with employer and state opposition, this "intensified merger activity as a means to concentrate scarce resources and members and enhance at minimal cost their presence in political and industrial spheres". Trade union mergers and internal reorganisation are ascribed as having a positive impact on the following basis: (1) strengthened union organisation through economies of scale; (2) increased labour market and/or political power and eliminating inter-union division and (3) increased power resources that could boost membership levels. The intent of structural reorganisation on this basis can be substantiated in the following statistics. In 1933, there were two hundred and eight trade unions affiliated to the national trade union bureaucratic centre (i.e. the TUC) compared with one hundred and fifty in 1970. The number of affiliates then decreased to sixty-eight in 1994 and finally to forty-nine in 2018. Between 1978 and 1994, there were one hundred and forty-three mergers involving TUC unions (Undy, 1999). The process is further highlighted by public and private sector unions merging in the post-1979 period partly as a response to decollectivism, deregulation and the privatisation policies initiated under successive Conservative Governments.[11]

The British merger pattern follows trends in other classic LMEs in response to structural changes. Moody (2009: 680–683) identified mergers in the United States as a partial response to economic restructuring in order to address contractions in trade union density, overall membership and collective bargaining levels. The five 'conglomerate unions' in the United States (Service Employees Union, the Food and Commercial Workers, the Communications Workers, Teamsters and the Steelworkers) in 2005 were responsible for the proportion of mergers rising from 13 per cent in the 1970s to 80 per cent in the 2000s.[12] In a pan-European study by Waddington (2006), the contention that there is a general merger trend across advanced industrialised countries by trade unions as a strategic response to a more hostile structural environment is supported.

These recent studies lend credence to Clegg's (1976) seminal analysis in 'Trade Unionism under Collective Bargaining', which claimed the level of collective bargaining was the primary explanatory factor in trade union structural development. During the period of collective bargaining expansion, there was a series of trade union mergers facilitated by the Whitley Committee proposals. The process, through five reports, concluded in 1926 with a number of measures proposed which were designed to promote economic stability. In 1917, three tiers of machinery were recommended: (1) Joint Industrial Councils at national level, (2) joint district councils and (3) works committees. In total, seventy-four joint councils were established between 1918 and 1921. The emergent industrial framework was in sync with the expansion of trade union membership, which rose to 7.93 million members in 1919 as trade union density hit 43.1 per cent in the same year. By the end of 1920, it was estimated that trade and wage boards covered 3 million workers, or over 15 per cent of the employed population (Milner, 1994).

There were similar merger spikes also identified by Clegg (1976) and Waddington (1988) during the nationalisation of key industries and the expansion of the public sector post-1945 in Britain. The Labour Government (1945–51) further expanded the collective bargaining framework through national agreements and statutory machinery. The Wages Council Act (1945) established minimum wages for the first time in sectors such as retailing and hairdressing to complement the Catering Wages Act of 1943 and the Agricultural Wages Regulation Act of 1947. The Trade Boards became known as Wages Councils from 1945, with around one in four of all workers at this point being covered by statutory regulation (Fraser, 1999). In contrast, the 1960s and 1970s merger wave coincided with the structural changes in the economy epitomised by the shift towards productivity bargaining (Howell, 2005).

Boxall and Haynes (1997: 570) contend that one must endeavour to capture trade unions strategising and the factors of influence upon this process through the 'locus of leadership'. The process is more difficult to identify in a trade union in contrast with businesses because the former manifests as voluntary and democratic associations of workers. The book identifies the 'locus' of power in the relationship between the largest trade unions and the Labour Party—and between trade unions themselves—as general secretary leadership. As will be demonstrated, this form of leadership has profound implications for the strategic choices adopted by trade unions. The strategic choices of union leaders are informed by economic and political institutional factors, union ideology and inherited traditions as well as personalities. These factors are not fixed but variable.

May (1975: 38) perceptively identified the 'unwarranted assumptions' regarding trade union leadership being "a fixed rather than a potentially changeable element". The element can be identified by shifts in political action and activity by trade union leaders. The Labour Party parliamentary leadership was described as having control of policy-making up until the mid-1950s, but as a result of trade union leadership changes, contestation over policy areas such as defence and nuclear weapons began to emerge (Harrison, 1960; McKenzie, 1966; Flanders, 1968). Trade union leadership was instrumental in the creation of the Liaison Committee in 1971 and central to the operation and breakdown of the Social Contract, as Chapter 2 will illustrate.

Furthermore, trade union leadership directly influenced the political posture of individual unions in relation to the internal reform of the Labour Party in the period of political opposition on issues such as the European Union, employment relations and defence between 1979 and 1997 (Minkin, 1992). There are also notable contemporary insights into the centrality of internal union election results in the post-2000 period, which ushered in a new set of trade union leaders. The new trade union leadership began to adopt adversarial positions both individually and collectively towards the Labour Government, as will be discussed in Chapter 6 on the Warwick Agreement. The importance of the strategic choices by trade union leaders was accentuated because despite the broad ideological convergence on the need to utilise legislation through political action, it simultaneously became more difficult for trade unions to achieve employment relations outcomes via the state.

The Blair leadership developed an 'arms-length' approach towards trade unions, which resulted in 'mounting frustration' (Waddington, 2003: 354). In particular, the frustrations focused on the minimalist interpretations of the employment relations framework established by the Labour Government and policies associated with the reform of public services (Grant and Lockwood, 1999; Smith and Morton, 2001; Ludlam and Taylor, 2003; Charlwood, 2004). Moreover, due to the process of union-party detachment fostered by the liberal market economy, the opportunities for creating mechanisms such as the Liaison Committee were limited as Labour entered government in 1997. Certain options for trade union action were perceived as being closed-off and not viable, partly due to the experiences of the 1974–79 Labour Government. This made trade union leadership strategies even more critical to organisational survival and growth. However, the notion of trade union strategising and operationalised strategies as distinct from 'business-style strategic planning processes' is still regarded to be in its 'infancy' (Boxall and Haynes, 1997: 567). The aforementioned is a deficit the book will address through the legislative events.

Conclusion

Hamann and Kelly (2004: 112) assert that the strategic choices made by trade union leaders "largely reflect the channels of influence they perceive as available to them (the opportunity structure)". The specific 'opportunity structure' in Britain is based on one trade union confederation and a more discretionary institutional role for individual trade union leadership decision-making. It is also framed by the political configuration (i.e. one major centre-left party) and a majoritarian electoral system, which permits financial donations by trade unions to the Labour Party. Accordingly, the structure has shaped the form of trade union political action, degree of trade union coordination and the development of informal processes. The opportunities open to British trade unions contrasts significantly with trade unions in continental European nation states where there are greater degrees of party political autonomy and affiliation. This is partly due to stronger corporatist institutions, historical political and religious cleavages, and formal political neutrality that prohibit trade unions from funding parties on the continent such as in Germany (Hamann and Kelly, 2004, 2008; Hyman and Gumbrell-McCormick, 2010).

In a world of increasing decentralisation, decollectivisation and the individualisation of employment relations, the book seeks to contribute to understanding the reasons for the successes achieved by trade unions in the employment relations arena through political action. The book has selected legislative events which chart the transition from two structurally different contexts characterised by dramatically differing degrees of trade union strength. The lessons and observations in the following chapters are designed to nurture a climate of hope on the basis that trade union influence and power can be positively exercised through effective strategies. It is a lesson of increasing importance as political action is progressively utilised as a substitute for collective bargaining in contemporary Britain.

Notes

1. Hamann and Kelly (2004) called these four factors (1) economic and political institutions, (2) choices of political and government leaders, (3) union identity and (4) union leadership.
2. The trade union statistics in terms of membership, collective bargaining and density apply to the whole of the United Kingdom (i.e. inclusive of Northern Ireland) throughout the book. However, for purposes of consistency, the book will use Britain.
3. For further reading on European social-pacts see Frege and Kelly (2003) and Hamann and Kelly (2004).
4. The closed shop is a form of agreement under which an employer agrees to employ trade union members only and thereafter employees must remain members of the union in order to remain in employment.
5. This also included the Employment Act (1982, 1988, 1989, 1990), the Trade Union Act (1984), Public Order Act (1986) and Trade Union and Labour Relations (Consolidation) Act (1992).
6. For further reading see Wilkinson, (2007); Smith and Morton (2009); McIlroy and Daniels (2009); Baccaro and Howell (2011); Kelly (2013).
7. For further reading on historical attempts and opinions on widening the franchise in the Labour Party see Yates (1960); Heffer (1975); Seyd (1978); The Political Quarterly (1995); Hayter (2005).
8. For further reading on Labour Party internal reform see Minkin (1992); Alderman and Carter (1994); McIlroy (1998); Kelly (2001); Ludlam and Taylor (2003); Hamann and Kelly (2004); Hayter (2005); Laffin and Shaw (2007).
9. Ontological assumptions concern the nature of the world and human beings in social contexts.
10. The system of Vertrauensleute has typically evolved into an organisational infrastructure for works councils, to the extent that the "latter became more representative and was adopted by the unions as their chosen instrument for workplace interest representation" (Streeck, 1995: 336).
11. The three largest public sector unions, National Union of Public Employees (NUPE), National and Local Government Officers' Association (NALGO), and the Confederation of Health Service Employees (COHSE), merged into UNISON in 1993. Unite the Union was also formed on 1 May 2007 by the merger of AMICUS and the Transport and General Workers' Union, predominantly both private sector unions.
12. See Boxall and Haynes (1997) for analysis of trade unions in New Zealand.

Bibliography

Ackers, P. (2002). Reframing employment relations: The case for neo-pluralism. *Industrial Relations Journal*, 33(1), pp. 2–19.

Ackers, P. and Payne, J. (1998). British trade unions and social partnership: Rhetoric, reality and strategy. *The International Journal of Human Resource Management*, 9(3), pp. 529–550.

Alderman, K. and Carter, N. (1994). The Labour Party and the trade unions: Loosening the ties. *Parliamentary Affairs*, 47(3), pp. 321–337.

Appelbaum, E. and Schmitt, J. (2013). Chapter 7: Employment relations and economic performance. In: C. Frege and J. Kelly, eds., *Comparative employment relations in the global economy*. London: Routledge Publications.

Baccaro, L. and Howell, C. (2011). A common neoliberal trajectory: The transformation of industrial relations in advanced capitalism. *Politics and Society*, 39(4), pp. 521–563.

Basset, P. (1991). Chapter 16: Unions and labour in the 1980's and 1990's. In: B. Pimlott and C. Cook, eds., *Trade unions in British politics: The first 250 years*. 2nd ed. Harlow: Longman House.

Bodah, M., Ludlam, S. and Coates, D. (2003). The development of an Anglo-American model of trade union and political party relations. *Labour Studies Journal*, 28(2), pp. 45–66.

Boxall, P. and Haynes, P. (1997). Strategy and effectiveness in a liberal environment. *British Journal of Industrial Relations*, 35(4), pp. 567–591.

Brown, W. (2000). Putting partnership into practice in Britain. *British Journal of Industrial Relations*, 38(2), pp. 299–316.

Charlwood, A. (June 2004). The new generation of trade union leaders and prospects for union revitalisation. *British Journal of Industrial Relations*, 42(2), pp. 379–397.

Child, J. (1972). Organisational structure, environment and performance: The role of strategic choice. *Sociology*, 6(3), pp. 1–22.

Clegg, H. (1976). *Trade unionism under collective bargaining*. Oxford: Basil Blackwell.

Coulter, S. (2014). *New Labour policy, industrial relations and the trade unions*. Houndmills: Palgrave Macmillan.

Drucker, H.M. (1991). Chapter 12: The influence of the trade unions on the ethos of the Labour Party. In: B. Pimlott and C. Cook, eds., *Trade unions in British politics: The first 250 years*. 2nd ed. Harlow: Longman House.

Ebbinghaus, B. and Visser, J. (2000). *Trade unions in Western Europe since 1945*. London: Macmillan Reference.

Evans, S., Ewing, K. and Nolan, P. (September 1992). Industrial relations and the British economy in the 1990's: Mrs Thatcher's legacy. *Journal of Management Studies*, 29(5), pp. 570–589.

Ewing, D.K. (March 2005). The function of trade unions. *Industrial Law Journal*, 34(1), pp. 1–22.

Flanders, A. (1968). Collective bargaining: A theoretical analysis. *British Journal of Industrial Relations*, 6(1), pp. 1–26.

Fraser, W.H. (1999). *A history of British trade unionism 1700–1998*. Basingstoke: Macmillan.

Freeden, M. (1999). The ideology of New Labour. *The Political Quarterly*, 70(1), pp. 42–51.

Frege, C. and Kelly, J. (2003). Union revitalization strategies in comparative perspective. *European Journal of Industrial Relations*, 9(1), pp. 7–24.

Gallie, D. (2009). Institutional regimes and employee influence at work: A European comparison. *Cambridge Journal of Regions. Economy and Society*, 2(3), pp. 379–393.

Gennard, J. and Hayward, G. (2008). *A history of the graphical, paper and media union*. Beecles: CPI William Clowes.

Gospel, H. (1992). *Markets, firms and the management of labour in modern Britain* (Cambridge studies in management). New York: Cambridge University Press.

Grant, D. and Lockwood, G. (1999). Trade unions, political funds ballots and party political funding. *Policy Studies*, 20(2), pp. 77–94.

Hall, P. and Soskice, D. (2001). *Varieties of capitalism: The institutional foundations of comparative advantage*. Oxford: Oxford University Press.

Hamann, K. and Kelly, J. (2004). Unions as political actors: A recipe for revitalization? In: C. Frege and J. Kelly, eds., *Varieties of unionism: Strategies for union revitalization in a globalizing economy*. Oxford: Oxford University Press.

Hamann, K. and Kelly, J. (2008). Varieties of capitalism and industrial relations. In: P. Blyton, N. Bacon, J. Fiorito and E. Heery, eds., *The SAGE handbook of industrial relations*. London: SAGE Publications.

Hansen, N.K. and Kupper, W. (2009). Power strategies and power sources of management: The micro-politics of strategising. Paper for presentation at the *25th EGOS colloquium 2009 in Barcelona*, 2–4 July.

Harrison, M. (1960). *Trade unions and the Labour Party since 1945*. Museum Street, London: George Allen and Unwin Limited.

Hayter, D. (2005). *Fightback: Labour's traditional rights in the 1970's and 1980's*. Manchester: Manchester University Press.

Heery, E. (2005). *Trade unionism under New Labour*. The Shirley Lerner Memorial Lecture 2005. Manchester Industrial Relations Society.

Heery, E., Kelly, J. and Waddington, J. (2003). Union revitalization in Britain. European *Journal of Industrial Relations*, 9(1), pp. 79–97.

Heffer, E.S. (1972). Labour's future. *The Political Quarterly*, 43(4), pp. 380–388.

Heffer, E.S. (October 1975). Two Labour Parties or one? *The Political Quarterly*, 46(4), pp. 385–394.

Howell, C. (1998). Restructuring British public sector industrial relations: State policies and trade union responses. *Policy Studies Journal*, 26(2), pp. 293–309.

Howell, C. (March 2004). Is there a third way for industrial relations? *British Journal of Industrial Relations*, 42(1), pp. 1–22.

Howell, C. (2005). *Trade unions and the state: The construction of industrial relations institutions in Britain, 1890–2000*. Princeton: Princeton University Press.

Howell, C. and Kolins Givan, R. (June 2011). Rethinking institutions and institutional change in European industrial relations. *British Journal of Industrial Relations*, 49(2), pp. 231–255.

Hyman, R. (2001). Trade union research and cross-national comparison. *European Journal of Industrial Relations*, 7(2), pp. 203–232.

Hyman, R. (2007). How can unions strategically act? *European Review of Labour and Research*, 13(2), pp. 193–210.

Hyman, R. and Gumbrell-McCormick, R. (2010). Trade unions, politics and parties: Is a new configuration possible? *European Review of Labour and Research*, 16(3), pp. 315–331.

ILOStat (2018). *Collective bargaining and trade union destiny statistics.* Available at: http://laborsta.ilo.org [Accessed 31 July 2018].

Kelly, J. (2013). The United Kingdom. In: C. Frege and J. Kelly, eds., *Comparative employment relations in the global economy.* London: Routledge Publications.

Kelly, R. (2001). Farewell conference, Hello Forum: Making of labour and Tory conference. *The Political Quarterly*, 72(3), pp. 329–334.

King, D. and Wood, S. (1999). The political economy of neoliberalism: Britain and the United States in the 1980's. In: H. Kitschelt, P. Lange, G. Marks and J.D. Stephens, eds., *Continuity and change in contemporary capitalism.* Cambridge: Cambridge University Press.

Kjellberg, A. (2011). The decline in Swedish union density since 2007. *Nordic Journal of Working Life Studies*, 1(1), pp. 67–93.

Laffin, M. and Shaw, E. (2007). British devolution and the Labour Party: How a national party adapts to devolution. *British Journal of Politics and International Relations*, 9(1), pp. 55–72.

Ludlam, S. and Taylor, A. (December 2003). The political representation of the labour interest in Britain. *British Journal of Industrial Relations*, 41(4), pp. 727–749.

May, T.C. (1975). *Trade unions and pressure group politics.* Saxon House: D.C. Heath Ltd.

McIlroy, J. (December 1998). The enduring alliance? Trade unions and the making of New Labour 1994–7. *British Journal of Industrial Relations*, 36(4), pp. 537–564.

McIlroy, J. and Daniels, G. (2009). An anatomy of British trade unionism since 1997. In: G. Daniels and J. McIlroy, eds., *Trade unions in a neoliberal world: British trade unions under New Labour.* London: Routledge.

McKenzie, R.T. (Summer 1966). Book section. *Parliamentary Affairs*, 19(3), pp. 373–384.

Metcalf, D. (2005). *British unions: Resurgence or perdition?* London: The Work Foundation.

Milner, S. (December 1994). *Charting the coverage of collective pay setting institutions: 1895–1990.* Discussion Paper no. 215. Centre for Economic Performance.

Minkin, L. (1992). *Contentious alliance: Trade unions and the Labour Party.* Edinburgh: Edinburgh University Press Limited.

Moody, K. (2009). The direction of union mergers in the United States: The rise of conglomerate unionism. *British Journal of Industrial Relations*, 47(4), pp. 676–700.

Morgan, G. and Smircich, L. (1980). The case for qualitative research. *The Academy of Management Review*, 5(4), pp. 491–500.

Paynter, W. (October 1970). Trade unions and government. *The Political Quarterly*, 41(4), pp. 444–454.

Pierson, P. (1997). Path dependence, increasing returns, and the study of politics. Paper presented at the *Seminar on the state and capitalism since 1800*, Center for European Studies. Harvard University.

Pizzorno, A. (1978). Political exchange and collective identity in industrial conflict. In: C. Crouch and A. Pizzorno, eds., *The resurgence of class conflict in Western Europe*. Vol. 1. London: Macmillan.

The Political Quarterly (1995). Commentary. *The Political Quarterly*, 66(3), pp. 121–125.

Rallings, C. (June 1983). White-collar workers, unionisation and political behaviour. *Industrial Relations Journal*, 14(2), pp. 60–73.

Seyd, P. (October 1978). Labour Party reform. *The Political Quarterly*, 49(1), pp. 38–43.

Smith, P. and Morton, G. (2001). New Labour's reform of Britain's employment law: The devil is not only in the detail but in the values and policy too. *British Journal of Industrial Relations*, 39(1), pp. 119–138.

Smith, P. and Morton, G. (2009). Employment legislation: New Labour's neo-liberal legal project to subordinate trade unions. In: G. Daniels and J. McIlroy, eds., *Trade unions in a neoliberal world: British trade unions under New Labour*. London: Routledge.

Streeck, W. (1995). Chapter 11: Works councils in Western Europe: From consultation to participation. In: J. Rogers and W. Streeck, eds., *Works councils: Consultation, representation, and cooperation in industrial relations*. Chicago: University of Chicago Press.

Taylor, A. (1987). *The trade unions and the Labour Party*. Burrell Row, Beckenham, Kent: Room Helm Ltd. (Provident House).

Taylor, A. (1989). *Trade unions and politics: A comparative introduction*. Houndmills, Hampshire: Macmillan Education Ltd., p. 290.

Taylor, M. and Cruddas, J. (1998). *New Labour, new links*. London: Unions 21.

Taylor, R. (October 1976). The uneasy alliance—labour and the unions. *The Political Quarterly*, 47(4), pp. 373–496.

Taylor, R. (1991). Chapter 9: The trade union 'problem' in the age of consensus 1960–1979. In B. Pimlott and C. Cook, eds., *Trade unions in British politics: The first 250 years*. 2nd ed. Harlow: Longman House.

Undy, R. (1999). New Labour's 'industrial relations settlement': The third way? *British Journal of Industrial Relations*, 37(2), pp. 315–336.

Undy, R. (2002). New Labour and New Unionism, 1997–2001: But is it the same old story? *Employee Relations*, 24(6), pp. 638–655.

Undy, R., Ellis, V., McCarthy, W.E.J. and Halmos, A.H. (1981). *Change in the trade unions: The development of United Kingdom unions since 1960*. London: Hutchison.

Visser, J. (1992). The strength of labour movements in advanced capitalist democracies: Social and organizational variations. In: M. Regini, ed., *The future of labour movements*. London: SAGE Publications, pp. 17–52.

Visser, J. (October 2015). *ICTWSS database*. version 5.0. Amsterdam: Amsterdam Institute for Advanced Labour Studies AIAS. Open access database available at: www.uva-aias.net/nl/data/ictwss [Accessed 31 Dec. 2016].

Waddington, J. (1988). Trade union mergers: A study of trade union structural dynamics. *British Journal of Industrial Relations*, 26(3), pp. 409–430.

Waddington, J. (2003). Heightening tension in relations between trade unions and the Labour Government in 2002. *British Journal of Industrial Relations*, 41(2), pp. 335–358.

Waddington, J. (2006). The trade union merger process in Europe: Defensive adjustment or strategic reform? *Industrial Relations Journal*, 37(6), pp. 630–651.

Wickham-Jones, M. (2014). Introducing OMOV: The Labour Party—Trade union review group and the 1994 leadership contest. *British Journal of Industrial Relations*, 52(1), pp. 33–56.

Wilkinson, F. (2007). Neo-liberalism and New Labour policy: Economic performance, historical comparisons and future prospects. *Cambridge Journal of Economics*, 31(6), pp. 817–843.

Wood, S. (2000). From voluntarism to partnership: A third way overview of the public policy debate in British industrial relations. In: H. Collins, P. Davies and R. Rideout, eds., *Legal regulation of the employment relation*. Amsterdam: Kluwer Law International.

Yates, I. (July 1960). Power in the Labour Party. *The Political Quarterly*, 31(3), pp. 300–311.

2 The Social Contract (1974–79)

Introduction

The state of relations between trade unions and Labour Government (1964–70) is vital to evaluate in order to provide context to the Social Contract. The chapter will outline the Donovan Commission (1968) and 'In Place of Strife: a policy for industrial relations' (1969). The trade union strategic response to the Conservative Government's (1970–74) employment relations policies, principally the Industrial Relations Act (1971), is vital to analyse. A key part of the strategic response included the creation of the Liaison Committee in 1971 as a mechanism for coordinating the repeal of the IRA (1971). The Liaison Committee has been described as 'fathering' the Social Contract (1974–79), which was a political exchange process partly designed to curb inflation through a voluntary incomes policy in partnership with the TUC (May, 1975: 126). The process would collapse through strategic miscalculations by both the trade unions and the Labour Government, which would result in the Winter of Discontent (1978–79).

Donovan Commission and In Place of Strife

The trade union movement was thrown into turmoil by a House of Lords judgement in the 'Rookes and Barnard' case (1964). The case threw into question the exact status of trade union legal immunities, as it was judged that industrial action by the Draughtsmen's and Allied Technicians' Association to maintain a closed shop, which previous court decisions appeared to have allowed, was, in fact, illegal. A union official could be liable for the tort of conspiracy for inducing some other person to break a contract of employment. The TUC Congress Report (1965: 58–9) highlighted that the trade union body believed the judgement made it "possible to regard merely the giving of a strike notice in itself as constituting a threat to break a contract of employment". The TUC attained from the Labour Government a restoration of legal protection through the Trades Disputes Act (1965), but the legislation presented an opportunity for the government to address the growing incidence of industrial action.[1]

The Labour Prime Minister, Harold Wilson, persuaded the TUC to agree to a full independent inquiry into trade unions through the Royal Commission on Trade Unions and Employers' Associations chaired by Lord Donovan (1965–68). The Donovan Commission, as it would become widely known, recommended that the 'voluntarist' system of employment relations should be retained but made an argument that there should be a better regulated system with clearer written agreements, better procedures and structures. The report identified that alongside formal procedures for industrial bargaining at a national level, there also existed a second tier of informal structures and practices at the workplace level. The increasing prevalence of the informal was symptomatic of economic structural dynamics which accelerated workplace bargaining—a dynamic intensified by government incomes policies. The result of the two-tier system was a growing gap between nationally agreed pay rates and actual earnings, which heightened the potential for conflict between the formal and informal systems unless the latter was incorporated into the former (Howell, 2005).

The issue of industrial stoppages per se did not overly concern the Donovan Commission, but the form of the stoppages did. Studies appeared to confirm that the strikes were overwhelmingly unofficial and unconstitutional, breaching both disputes procedures and the decision-making procedures of trade unions. Out of more than 2,000 disputes each year between 1964 and 1966, fewer than a hundred had official sanction (United Kingdom Royal Commission, 1968; Fraser, 1999). As such, one of the key recommendations was to facilitate an employment relations architecture which incorporated the shop-stewards movement grounded in the workplace and the informal system. There were in 1968 approximately 175,000 shop-stewards according to an extensive survey made for the Donovan Commission. Jack Jones, as the newly elected leader of the country's largest trade union in 1968, the Transport and General Workers' Union (TGWU), observed that the Donovan recommendations were "more favourable to my way of thinking than I had dared hope" (Jones, 1986: 198). The favourable assessment was predicated on the endorsement of the primacy of free collective bargaining, recognition of the growing role of shop-stewards in the workplace, the rejection of compulsory industrial ballots and legal sanctions. This was despite a recommendation to introduce 'cooling-off' periods on industrial action.

The Labour Government's White Paper 'In Place of Strife' (January 1969) proceeded to endorse a greater transfer of power to the relevant government minister than the Donovan Commission recommended. In relation to official strikes, the government minister would have the ability to reserve power to order a ballot of the respective union members wherever it was determined that a strike might pose 'a serious threat to the economy'. To address the rise of unofficial strikes, the government could intervene in the form of ordered conciliation pauses of up to twenty-eight days whenever it was deemed that the strike might have 'serious' consequences. The White Paper repeated the central theme in the report that the rise of unofficial strikes required the reform of trade union structures and behaviour. The Labour Government offered a number of incentives for the trade unions to agree to the proposals. This consisted of reforms relating to dismissals, proposals to subsidise union education services and union amalgamations and elections supervised by the Commission on Industrial Relations for the choice of a national union. However, it was the incursions into the free collective bargaining framework through proposed penal sanctions which provoked a furious reaction. At the 1969 Biennial Delegate Conference of the TGWU, the retiring General Secretary Frank Cousins warned the Labour Government that the union "would resist attempts by any Government to limit the freedom of the Union to act on behalf of its members" (Richter, 1973: 235). Under growing internal pressure from grassroots union members, shop-stewards and union leaderships, a special conference of union executives coordinated through the TUC met in June 1969 to approve a 'Programme for Action'. Trade union–sponsored MPs reflected the TUC's position as the minutes of the Trade Union Group (TUG) in parliament illustrate on 17 January 1969. At a meeting requested by the relevant government minister, Barbara Castle, she was informed of the following:

> The members would not accept that the Government were entitled to insert penal clauses in the White Paper.

Victor Feather, TUC General Secretary in 1969, appeared before the TUG on 18 February 1969, re-emphasising the TUC's opposition to 'penal legislation'. In several appearances by the Prime Minister before the TUG on 'In Place of Strife', the minutes of the 17 June 1969 meeting specifically reported the following:

> The Prime Minister informed the members that they would be introducing a Bill which would contain penal clauses as it was essential for such kind of clauses to be in an act unless the trade union movement would accept greater responsibility. The majority of the members were opposed to his suggestion.

The role of informal processes during this episode are also illuminated by Jack Jones whereby the TGWU leader highlighted a private meeting in May 1969 with fellow trade union leaders Hugh Scanlon of the Amalgamated Union of Engineering Workers (AUEW) and Victor Feather of the TUC. The individuals were the three most powerful leaders in the trade union movement. In discussion with the Prime Minister and Barbara Castle, Jones recalled:

Barbara {Castle} was rather shrewish, trying to put Hughie {Scanlon} and me in our place. We were told once again that 'the public is looking for action on unofficial strikers. Action must be taken by the Government; you've had your chance, boys'! The nearest thing to a conciliatory tone was adopted when they explained their attitude to 'criminal sanctions', as we called them. 'No', said Barbara, 'people will not go to prison, fines could be imposed but they would be collected as civil debts'.

Jones (1986: 204–205)

The response to 'In Place of Strife' was an inevitable reflex by the trade union movement, as its direct interests and freedoms were being potentially curtailed by the law. The Labour Government withdrew the proposals in light of the strong resistance by trade unions in particular through the TUC as the respective channel and the TUG as the mechanism for policy influence. Fatchett (1987: 57), in an insightful contribution, judged that "the usual processes of accommodation broke down, often into open hostility. As substantial sections of the Party in general, and the Parliamentary Party, in particular, lent their weight to the trade unions' case, the Government found itself isolated". The state with the Labour Party at its helm had moved from an enabling to a constraining disposition from a trade union perspective. In the aftermath of the White Paper, key sections of the trade union leadership initiated a series of strategic steps in an effort to bind the political and industrial spheres of the labour movement. The strategy would become even more pressing, as the Conservative Party would win the general election in 1970.[2]

The Industrial Relations Act (1971)

The Conservative Government produced a consultative document in October 1970 containing eight central pillars, which it had 'no intention of removing' and were 'non-negotiable' (May, 1975: 102). The prospective legislation offered trade unions a statutory recognition procedure and restricted union legal immunities during strikes. Inter-union and secondary disputes were also not covered by immunity. A new National Industrial Relations Court would adjudicate on trade union behaviour declaring which actions were considered 'unfair' (Ibid). The government through emergency powers would also deal with industrial strikes if they were damaging to the economy by imposing a sixty-day 'cooling-off' period and a strike ballot. The latent ambition of the proposals was to reduce the incidence of strikes via injunctions, cooling-off periods, emergency powers, no strike agreements, restrictions on legal immunities and an unfair dismissal procedure designed to prevent disputes occurring in the first instance.

The objective of opposing the government's proposals led to enhanced cooperation and coordination between the Labour leadership and the

TUC. On 10 November 1970, the minutes of the TUG in parliament state: "After Mrs Castle had outlined this vicious document it was agreed that we should oppose any Bill that was based on the issues contained therein". In December 1970, the Labour Party would affirm its total opposition to the Conservatives' proposals and urged the PLP, NEC of the party and TUC to develop "a workable accord between a future Labour Government and their members that can be put to the electorate" (A. Taylor, 1987: 7). The progress of the Bill could not be prevented, as it passed its first and second readings by December. In response, the TUC and the Labour Party agreed to create a liaison body to coordinate opposition and prepare for the repeal of the legislation.

A major rank and file resistance from trade union members emerged in opposition to the proposals, principally from the country's two largest unions (AUEW and TGWU). Jack Jones and Hugh Scanlon attempted to persuade the TUC to back a one-day strike in February 1971, but this was outvoted. The AUEW organised two one-day strikes against the Bill on 1 and 18 March, with both strikes receiving substantial membership support. The TGWU regarded both as non-cooperation days, although it did back the second strike in the engineering and shipbuilding industries. The TUC General Council, at variance with its two biggest affiliates, formulated a strategy of advising unions not to register under the government's proposals, which they were required to do to be certified trade unions. The formula received the approval of a Special Congress in March 1971, but the debate made it clear that the formula was perceived as weak in the eyes of some larger unions, principally the TGWU and AUEW, and too strong in the view of others, including NALGO. The inherent difficulties arising from trade union heterogeneity were evident as there was "considerable difficulty in formulating an agreed programme of action" (May, 1975: 110–111). The IRA (1971) passed its final stage on 24 March 1971.

The net result of the TUC strategy was that by the time of the 1972 Annual Congress, only thirty-two unions with a total of half a million members were suspended from the TUC for registering. The final act of expulsion involved trade unions representing some 353,000 out of the body's 10 million affiliated membership in 1973.[3] Howell (2005: 113) stated the legislation "appeared to be a stunning confirmation of the Donovan Commission's justification for why using penal sanctions to modify the behaviour of industrial relations policy would not work". The legislation was considered a failure, with an estimated 3.3 million working days lost in opposition to it (Undy et al., 1981; Kessler and Bayliss, 1995; Fraser, 1999). The IRA (1971) was even broadly ignored by large employers, as the government enforced the cooling-off period clause only once in relation to a railway ballot in 1972. The Conservative Government failed to use the mechanism in the miners' dispute in late 1973 into 1974 as the Prime Minister, Edward Heath, announced a three-day week to save fuel, which resulted in power cuts.

In this context, the Conservative Party would fight the general election in February 1974 on the infamous platform of 'Who Governs Britain?' The electorate answered, if somewhat ambiguously, by returning Labour to government with a minority status—301 seats (37.2 per cent of the vote) to the Conservatives' 297 seats (37.9 per cent of the vote). The proceeding Labour Governments from February 1974 until May 1979 would witness the most fascinating period of relations between both wings of the labour movement encapsulated in the Social Contract.[4] May (1975: 40) stated: "It is important to note that the main thrust of union activity in policy making within the Labour Party after 1970 took place in the Liaison Committee and not through the customary machinery of the NEC and its sub-committees". Marsh (1992: 42) reiterated the primacy of the Liaison Committee stressing that "during the 1972–6 period, the most important channel was probably the least well known; the Trade Union-Labour Party Liaison Committee". As such, Marsh noted that it was 'surprising' that there has been no major study of the Liaison Committee despite the crucial role it performed in the development of Labour Government policy between 1974 and 1979. The remainder of the chapter will contribute to addressing this deficit through an evaluation of the repeal of IRA (1971) and the formation of the Social Contract.

The Social Contract in Formation

The National Council of Labour (NCL) in the inter-war period had been described as the 'most authoritative' policy formulating mechanism in the labour movement despite its lack of constitutional party authority (Bodah et al., 2003: 49). Nonetheless, Minkin (1974: 20) highlighted that the NCL had become 'moribund' during the Labour Government (1964–70), as it met only four times between 1966 and the 1970 general election. In this context, Jack Jones (1986: 237–238) highlighted the difficulties of trying to attain policy agreement through the NCL as he recalled the following in relation to the Labour Party Annual Conference in 1970:

> During the conference I talked to everyone I could about the need for a joint body which would bring Parliamentary leaders as well as the NEC together with the TUC, in regular sessions. I said to Harold Wilson: 'Surely to God, we can knock out essentials on which we can all agree, the bedrock minimum which will get the support of the public. And then let's campaign for it'. I made clear that we would all have to sacrifice some of our old ideas to get agreement.

Jones repeated the need at a Fabian Society meeting during the Labour Party Annual Conference in 1971 to develop a process of greater 'liaison' which could 'work out a clear programme' for government. Jones would highlight his personal efforts to persuade Labour to improve upon the Conservative Government's position of an increase in the pension by £1 a week in the autumn of 1971 as the catalyst for a new strategic approach. Moreover, Jones identified the influence of 'intellectuals' in the Labour Party as a contributory factor to the weakening of the links between the industrial and political wings during the previous Labour Government (1964–70) which had to be addressed, he noted:

> Well there was a tendency on the part of many in the Labour Party, the Labour Party professionals, some of them were MP's who joined the party without any trade union connections, without any responsibility to the trade unions. So, I fought very strongly to try and establish some unity, to strengthen it and to help it to grow. It was vital that there should be closer links. So, there was no question on my part and I used my endeavours to make sure the unions played a part in the Labour Party and that individual unionists were persuaded.
>
> (Extract from Jack Jones, Interview 1)

Jones added that the liaison process required fellow key trade union leader—Hugh Scanlon of the AUEW—being convinced to support an alternative strategy:

> Hugh Scanlon was a bit lukewarm and of course Scanlon had come from the Communist Party but eventually I persuaded him to help support the Labour Party but it was general support it had not come up from individual membership.
>
> (Ibid)

The necessity of mending relationships after 1970 was not "simply an institutional matter" (Minkin, 1992: 122); rather, it focused on new processes designed to induce more favourable policy outcomes. The 'structural manifestation' of the new strategic approach was the Liaison Committee (Marsh, 1992: 49). Lord Lea, who would become the forum's joint secretary on behalf of the TUC, said:

> On the origins of the TUC-Labour Party Liaison Committee, I think that the formula I had originally agreed with Len Murray was something along the line of what actually emerged. I put this to Jim Callaghan after a meeting at Transport House of the Labour Party Home Policy Committee he said: 'Well, you know the Labour Party is the National Executive Committee'.[5] I said 'Jim you know as well as I do our people are not interested in talking to the National Executive Committee. It's their number two's that are on the National Executive Committee, it's the Shadow Cabinet, it's the leaders of the Labour

Party'. He said, 'David you do know' . . . this is Jim Callaghan talking to me. . . 'you do know that you're treading on a thousand principles here of the Labour Party?' I said, 'Well I may be but I'm not treading on the realities which is what I am talking about is the catastrophic breakdown between members of the shadow cabinet or cabinet through the National Executive'. He said 'alright'. So, we agreed this formula, which was TUC, NEC, and PLP more or less.

(Extract from Lord Lea, Interview 2)

Importantly, to reinforce Lord Lea's point in the relation to 'number twos', the Liaison Committee provided a forum for direct engagement between the principal trade union and Labour Party leaders. The former did not sit on the Labour Party NEC but on the TUC General Council. Irrespective of the exact origins, leading trade unionists corroborated the need to initiate a response through a new process. The Liaison Committee would incorporate the TUC rather than Labour Party affiliated unions exclusively. The involvement of non-Labour Party affiliated unions such as NALGO was perceived as necessary to the success of any pact. According to Minkin (1978: 473), the Liaison Committee was a 'new bridge'. Lord Monks, then a TUC researcher, identified the benefits of the inclusive approach as being the determining factor over the composition of the Liaison Committee:

Yes, well in Jones, he could use the TUC as a vehicle for bringing along non Labour Party affiliated people. Secondly, it solved the issue, as the TUC General Secretary was involved, who was going to be the Secretariat. You didn't have to agree it with the Right of the General Council—the GMWU led Group—it was up to the TUC.[6] Jones was confident that in this set-up he could play a leading role.

(Extract from Lord Monks, Interview 3)

Lord Whitty, an employee of the TUC's Economic Department during this period, complemented the previous analysis. Whitty agreed that an inclusive process, which positioned the TUC as the primary trade union channel, was more desirable and optimised the chances for policy outcomes to be attained:

The relatively new TGWU General Secretary, Jack Jones, felt that we needed a better mechanism. His view, and it was also the view of other trade union leaders, was that the relationship should be between the TUC and the party, and a Labour Government when it was elected. That was seen as the policy-making nexus rather than via the party's internal mechanisms.

(Extract from Lord Whitty, Interview 4)

The Liaison Committee was composed of six representatives from the PLP, the NEC and the TUC. Secretarial support came from the TUC and the Labour Party jointly as the chair rotated amongst the three parties concerned.[7] The liaison strategy consisted of three elements: (1) voluntary reform based on the Donovan Commission report, (2) an independent element in resolving conflict and (3) the extension of industrial democracy. The decision not to cooperate with the IRA (1971) shifted the emphasis on to the Liaison Committee. At the Liaison Committee's first meeting on 21 February 1972, it was agreed to formulate a repeal Bill. The proposals would be introduced in the first session of parliament upon Labour's return to power. Further meetings of the Liaison Committee, however, would illustrate that the immediate repeal of the legislation would not be as straightforward as first imagined. Nonetheless, the TUC was accredited as having acted as an 'organised bloc' by Thomson (1979: 47) as the broad details of legislation to replace the IRA (1971) and an extension of worker rights was agreed to by July 1972 through the 'Statement on Industrial Relations'.

A series of meetings of the Liaison Committee took place late September 1972 in conjunction with the circulation of 'Labour's Programme for Britain'. The document was primarily designed to address the key economic post-war problem of delivering inflation-free growth along with proposals on public spending, achieving a positive balance of payments and raising personal consumption levels.[8] The Labour leadership asserted these objectives could be attained only through economic growth and the planned redistribution of resources. This would require "interim measures to regulate the purchasing power of consumers" (Labour Party, 1972 cited in A. Taylor, 1987: 17). The TUC responded to the document by suggesting the party contact the affiliated unions to the TUC in order to publicise its content. The reasoning for the approach is attributed to the "reluctance on the part of the TUC to be seen to be closely tied to the Labour Party and avoid making a commitment on wage restraint" (A. Taylor, 1987: 23–24).

The TUC also had a growing representation of non-Labour Party affiliated unions who were the primary victims of governmental pay restraint in the public sector. This was illustrated by NALGO, which was the fourth largest union in the country with nearly 400,000 members in 1970.[9] Jack Jones warned the Labour leadership of the dangers in pushing for an incomes policy without a more comprehensive strategy, contending that as would produce splits in the trade union movement (Jones, 1986: 279). Hostility to statutory price controls was palpable at the TUC Congress of 1973. David Basnett, who became General Secretary of the GMWU, moved Composite 7 (anti-inflation policy) at the Congress, which rejected any notion of a statutory pay policy. Basnett, in control of the third largest trade union, endorsed the Liaison Committee's work but premised support on the maintenance of free collective bargaining as the only workable solution to consensual economic management. Jack Jones seconded the composite, urging delegates to support closer cooperation through the Liaison Committee. Lord Whitty adds that the role of the GMWU 'solidified' the role of the TUC in the Liaison Committee. This was primarily due to the union's new leadership seeking closer relationships with other key unions—principally the TGWU. Whitty said the following:

> His {Basnett's} view of things was that the TGWU and GMWU needed to talk on particular policies and particular politics and they had to be close so that there was greater centre politics in the TUC. He and others, including Geoffrey Drain the leader of NALGO, which was a non-affiliated union, wanted to ensure that the TUC was not polarised between Left and Right and that there was a quite solid centre.
>
> (Extract from Lord Whitty, Interview 4)

The deliberations at the TUC Congress in 1973 highlighted two fundamental problems at the outset. First, the process was strongest at the top and how far a spirit of cooperation trickled down to the membership was highly debatable. Second, the reality of the any social-pact was theoretical and aspirational. It could be judged only against Labour entering government. If, and when, outcomes were then matched against statements when Labour was in government, this could undermine the entire process. Despite the validity of the prior points, it is also important to state that the purpose of the Liaison Committee from the perspective of leading trade union actors was also to rebuild relationships, create dialogue and foster a positive political exchange climate wherein objectives could be optimised. The purpose and significance of the Liaison Committee's purpose during the years of the Conservative Government (1970–74) cannot be underestimated, as Geoffrey Goodman states:

> It was a very serious attempt to try and establish an understanding between the Labour Party and trade unions. Not only a Labour Government but in opposition and through it came the birth of the Social Contract too. It was a recognition by the trade unions that they too had been lacking in the past in this vision and the need to develop a better understanding with the political side of the movement . . . it was a very important development.
>
> (Extract from Geoffrey Goodman, Interview 5)

The discussions surrounding the Liaison Committee statements principally the 'Statement on Industrial Relations' (1972) and the 'Economic Policy and the Cost of Living' (1973) illustrated that the TUC and, in particular, Jack Jones, was "an assertive force in shaping the broad understanding on policy and procedure which became known as the Social Contract" (Minkin, 1992: 118). Additionally, A. Taylor (1987: 27) stated that the liaison process offered "the prospect of a significant shift away from negative-defensive unionism to positive initiative unionism even if the price asked was high". The Social Contract was insufficiently developed as a programme to be presented at the general election of February 1974. Speaking on television, in advance of the election, Labour Leader Harold Wilson claimed the party had a 'great social contract' with the TUC. On the same day, illustrative of the problems that would confront the Social Contract, Hugh Scanlon of the AUEW outlined the nervousness regarding any suggestion of an agreed incomes policy, he said: 'we {the TUC} are not agreed on any specific policy as of now' (A. Taylor, 1987: 29–30). However, the importance placed on repealing the IRA (1971) through a Labour general election victory is illustrated by the affiliated trade unions giving over £3 million to Labour for its 1974 election campaign compared with £1.6m in the 1970 election.[10]

The Social Contract in Operation

To promote coordination, the monthly Liaison Committee meetings took place on the Monday before the Labour Party NEC and TUC General Council meetings. The Liaison Committee met on 22 April 1974 to approve a process for the coordination of a 'Social Contract'.[11] Lord Lea, in relation to the formulation of the process, stated the following:

> Another of my half-baked ideas was in the form of the Social Contract. I don't claim exclusive authorship of this as a formal concept but I think I used it before anybody else. . . . It was a wages and prices and pensions policy and child benefit and unfair dismissals policy, development policy and so what do you call all that lot?
>
> (Extract from Lord Lea, Interview 2)

The 'Collective Bargaining and The Social Contract' (1974: 4) document sharpened the contours of the programme as the TUC affirmed that the Liaison Committee process was engendering "a strong feeling of mutual confidence which alone would make it possible to reach the wide-ranging agreement which is necessary to control inflation and achieve sustained growth in the standard of living". The TUC circulated a repeal Bill to the IRA (1971) within days of Labour taking office. However, the Employment Minister, Michael Foot, relayed that repeal could not take place in one stage. Lord Monks described the initial stages in the formation of what would be called the Trade Union and Labour Relations Bill:

> There was a lot of serious effort, and indeed by the time the election came in February 1974 we had, courtesy of Bill Wedderburn and

some other guy, we had a Bill that was the basis of the Trade Union Labour Relations Bill. When members of the General Council first saw it, it was pretty thick with 29 or 30 clauses I think; they thought this isn't a one clause Bill which repeals and replaces the Industrial Relations Act but we had been advised that you couldn't actually do that. The Industrial Relations Act had itself repealed previous laws; it had not been an amended Bill itself.

(Extract from Lord Monks, Interview 3)

The Trade Union and Labour Relations Act (1974) restored some of the immunities that had resulted in legal action being taken against trade unions for inducing breaches of contract and protected employers from actions on unfair dismissals for dismissing non-union members of a closed shop (Kessler and Bayliss, 1995). TULRA (1974) represented the culmination of years of preparatory work in conjunction with out-right opposition to the IRA (1971). The 'Collective Bargaining and The Social Contract' (1974: 6) document emphasised to all TUC-affiliated unions that the TUC General Council looked to trade unions to take into account the 'constructive policies' of the Labour Government (see Box B). The TUC checklist of the Labour Government's achievements during its first eight months in office was described as having "amounted to a virtual item implementation of the February 1973 Liaison Committee statement on economic policy" (R. Taylor, 1980: 132).

Box B **Trade Union List of Labour's Achievements (1974)**

- National Union of Mineworkers (NUM) and Coal Board settlement putting an end to three-day week.
- £10 weekly pension increase for single person and £16 weekly increase for married couples.
- Tax changes to help 'less well-off' through increased allowances and higher incomes tax rates.
- Closing of tax loopholes; introduction of a 'wealth tax' and a 'gift-tax'.
- An extra £500M for food subsidies.
- Freezing of house rents and allocation of £350M to local authorities to expand housing programme.
- Keeping mortgage rates low through £500M loan to building societies.
- The repeal of IRA (1971) in the Trade Union Labour Relations Act (1974).
- The abolition of the Pay Board and its associated powers.
- Intention to establish an Advice and Conciliation Service and Employment Protection Bill to extend legal rights of workers and unions.
- The Health and Safety at Work Act (1974) which codified existing legislation and made enforcement more effective through extending protection to 8 million workers.

The TUC also noted that there would be 'restricted scope' for real income increases and advocated income protection through 'threshold agreements' in industrial sectors to compensate for price rises. Accordingly, the 'Collective Bargaining and the Social Contract' (1974: 9) document stated that it would be "important in the current situation to ensure a smooth transition from statutory controls to voluntary collective bargaining". To achieve these objectives, the TUC advised that its affiliates apply a twelve-month rule between major pay increases. In return, trade unions expected a continuation of favourable Labour policies. R. Taylor (1976: 405) claimed the growing prominence of the Liaison Committee was partly based on the Labour Government's attempts to 'ignore' the party's NEC due to its left-wing majority. The government correspondingly turned to the Liaison Committee for 'guidance and discussion'. Jack Jones (1986: 281) supported this assessment, affirming that Labour Government minsters 'preferred to deal' with the Liaison Committee. Lord Monks reinforced these points by identifying the 'stabilising' role the trade unionists were performing in the Liaison Committee:

> The Prime Minister found it quite useful because the trade unions were a kind of civilising block, even though they were Right and Left they were fairly cohesive, they were respectful of government without being subservient to it but they were not trying to score political points that the Left on the NEC were trying to do. So, it was a stabilising body, but the meetings were extremely entertaining.
>
> (Extract from Lord Monks, Interview 3)

In a sign of the emerging economic problems, trade union leaders urged the Chancellor, Denis Healey, to support public spending by £975 million in the Spring Budget of 1975. The Chancellor moved in the opposite direction with cuts totalling £1 billion. The TUC in 'The Development of the Social Contract' (July 1975: 5) rebuked the 'inadequate discussion' associated with the budgetary process. The lack of consultation is recorded at the Liaison Committee meeting on 23 June 1975. The meeting discussed the forthcoming TUC document, which focused on the need for a price target, pay target and a reduction in unemployment levels. Jack Jones and Len Murray of the TUC were present from the trade unions as the Prime Minister commented that the Liaison Committee was not the forum for detailed policy deliberations. Rather, the body was a public opinion 'influencer' due to its role at the 'centre of the Labour movement' (A. Taylor, 1987: 55). Harold Wilson's remarks were at variance with the central policy-making role the Liaison Committee had developed post-1971. It was indicative of the Labour leadership's future intentions to constrain incomes and prices in light of the deteriorating economic environment, which was described as "the deepest recession in the western world since the Second World War" (The Development of the Social Contract, July 1975: 5). There had been six quarters out of nine from the third quarter of 1973 until the same quarter in 1975 in economic contraction (*The Guardian*, 25 October 2013). Rising oil prices and catch-up wage settlements due to the legacy of incomes and prices policies all contributed to an escalating inflationary situation. In this context, the TUC was described as having to 'swallow some unpalatable truths' regarding the state of the British economy (R. Taylor, 1980: 135).

Nonetheless, 'The Development of the Social Contract' (July 1975) highlighted that the employment relations programme was being successively enacted from the perspective of trade unions. The Employment Protection Act (1975) restored trade union immunities and abolished the Commission on Industrial Relations, the National Industrial Relations Court and the Registrar of Trade Unions and Employers' Associations. The legislation allowed for a trade union to refer a recognition dispute to the new Advisory, Conciliation and Arbitration Service (ACAS) (see Box C). Protection against unfair dismissal was extended, as companies were required to provide maternity pay for women and to preserve their jobs during maternity leave. Longer notices of redundancy were also enshrined in statute, as was the ability of trade union officials to carry out their duties.[12] The Trade Union Amendment Act (1976) followed, which tightened the loopholes with respect to the closed shop restricting non-union membership to religious beliefs. Progress was also made on an Industry Bill and proposals relating to industrial democracy. The completion of this latter stage of the trade union programme it was envisaged would "reinforce the standing and function of trade unions and trade unionism at every level of economic activity" (The Development of the Social Contract, 1975: 5).

Box C ACAS Functions

- To provide facilities for conciliation, mediation and arbitration.
- To publish codes of practice.
- To make recommendations on applications for trade union recognition under statutory guidelines.
- To provide a free advisory service on industrial relations and personnel issues.

On the incomes policies component, the majority of the TUC General Council (nineteen to thirteen) endorsed a self-regulated Phase One pay policy. The agreement contained a £6 per week rise for everybody except those earning over £8,500 a year who received nothing beyond increments for the coming year until 1 August 1976. The policy was approved by 6,945,000 votes to 3,375,000 at the TUC Congress. The objective of Phase One was to reduce inflation from the level of 25 per cent in May 1975 to a figure of 10 per cent in the following year. The Labour Government agreed to accept the TUC approach, but the Remuneration, Charges and Grants Act (July 1975) was passed, which gave ministers the powers to act should voluntary restraint fail. The TUC in 'The Development of the Social Contract' (1975: 9) re-emphasised the position that there was "no viable alternative to a continuation of voluntary collective bargaining". The TUC would guide and police the policy, which was not significantly breached by any union despite special cases in the 'region' of 30 per cent. The aforementioned cases related to local authority manual workers and NHS ancillaries in order to bring minimum rates into line with the TUC's low pay target of £30 for a normal full-time week.

The TUC outlined in 'The Social Contract (1976–77)' (June 1976: 3) document that the Labour Government had "for its part continued its broad programme of legislative advance". In turn, the trade union movement 'without exception' had adhered to the £6 pay policy. The document lauded TULRA (1974) and the Employment Protection Act (1975), alongside a series of measures contained within the wider Social Contract. The measures included the Social Security Pension Act (1975), Sex Discrimination Act (1975), Community Land Act (1975), Race Relations Act (1976) and the Housing Act (1974), which introduced significant state funding for housing associations and the introduction of the Capital Transfer Tax (1975).[13] In addition, the TUC welcomed Chancellor Denis Healey's spring budget decisions not to put up the price of school meals by 5 pence at a cost of £35 million. A further £15 million for training and job creation by the Manpower Services Commission along with a commitment to put 100,000 people into jobs or training through selective measures were also commended by the TUC.

Despite these significant achievements, the Social Contract would increasingly be defined by its most contentious element: an incomes policy. The TUC and Labour Government agreed to target a reduction in the rate of inflation in 1977 to a figure 'well below 10 per cent', with the government aiming at a further 'halving' of the inflation rate by December 1977. An agreement was reached between the TUC and government ministers on a new 5 per cent pay policy on total earnings for all hours worked from August 1976 to August 1977. This contained a £4 upper cash maximum increase as the ceiling and £2.50 minimum a week as the floor. The twelve-month rule would once again apply in Phase Two. The trade unions, faced with the real prospect of the demise of the Labour Government during the unfolding economic crisis, endorsed the second year of a tighter pay policy by a vote of twenty to one (9,262,000–531,000 votes) at the TUC Special Congress in June 1976. The agreement came despite the TUC acknowledging 'problems' were arising from the effects of the previous £6 flat-rate supplement on pay differentials and the value of overtime, shift and payment-by-results increments (The Social Contract 1976–77, June 1976: 5–7).

In the deteriorating economic context, the new Prime Minister, Jim Callaghan, and Chancellor Healey told senior trade union leaders on 14 July 1976 that the government would have to take measures to cut back its Public Sector Borrowing Requirement (PSBR).[14] The move was part of government efforts to restore overseas confidence in the British economy. The Chancellor agreed to set up a joint government and TUC working party to review the problem of sterling balances, but he did not accede to TUC pressures on policy priorities. Ultimately, the Labour Government sought an International Monetary Fund (IMF) loan with the terms announced by Healey on 15 December 1976. This would involve public expenditure cuts of £1 billion in 1977–78 and £1.5 billion in 1978–79. In return, the government received a loan of £2.3 billion. The regional employment premium was abolished, food subsidies were brought to an end and the government's holdings in British Petroleum were reduced to 51 per cent from 68 per cent (Hoopes, June 1994).

The TUC lent support to the government despite opposing the cuts. The qualified support was on the basis that the policies being enacted under the Social Contract were sustained "against the background of a desire to maintain a Labour Government in office" (R. Taylor, 1980: 138). However, the emergent signs of the Social Contract's forthcoming disintegration came during the September 1976 TUC Congress. A motion moved by USDAW and seconded by the TGWU supported a return to free collective bargaining during 1977. The aforementioned unions involved two of the biggest affiliates to the Labour Party and TUC (see Table 2.1). The signals were clear from the trade union movement, among even the most loyal of trade union leaders, that a system of pay restraint, albeit on a voluntary basis, was becoming infeasible beyond the summer of 1977.

Table 2.1 Affiliated Labour Party Trade Unions 1974—Top Six

Trade Unions Affiliated to the Labour Party in 1974	*Affiliated Members*
TGWU	1,000,000
AUEW	870,000
GMWU	650,000
Electrical, Electronic, Telecommunications and Plumbing Union (EETPU)	350,000
Union of Shop, Distributive and Allied Workers (USDAW)	292,568
Association of Scientific, Technical and Managerial Staffs (ASTMS)	151,000

Source: Statistics provided by House of Commons Library derived from Labour Party Conference Report 1974 and Annual Report of the Certification Officer 1976.

The TUC and its affiliated unions in public maintained the spirit of cooperation but Jack Jones (1986: 305) articulated the growing concerns:

> But I was in no doubt that our agreement with the Government was wearing thin. I told both Jim Callaghan and Denis Healey: 'We will have to get back to normal collective bargaining. The most you can expect from us is an attempt to organise an orderly return with emphasis on some priorities'. Denis acted as if he didn't believe it.

Lord Monks commented on the severity of the economic situation and the emergent tensions developing inside the labour movement:

> The economy, the inflation rate went to 26 per cent in 1976, I think, and a fairly disastrous period. Then the Liaison Committee agreed to firm up the Social Contract and essentially tried to limit wages to inflation. There were no legal restrictions as nobody would accept that and this is where relations got tough with Mikardo and people who said, 'no you have got to have free collective bargaining in a capitalist system' and so on.[15]
>
> (Extract from Lord Monks, Interview 3)

Inflation reached a high of 26.9 per cent in August 1975 before coming down to 14.3 per cent in September 1976. During the economic turbulence, Jack Jones addressed the TUG on 30 November 1976 to discuss "the present economic situation, the Government and its relations with the Trade Unions. The need to increase production and to maintain a Labour Government". Hugh Scanlon reinforced this sentiment on 18 January 1977 at the TUG, as he made "special mention of the terrific pressures the trade unions had experienced by keeping, to the limits, the conditions of the Social Contract". In a significant setback for the Labour Government and Jack Jones, TGWU union delegates voted for a return to 'unfettered collective bargaining' by August 1 at the union's Biennial Delegate Conference in July 1977. The conference decision was influenced by the increasing prominence of workplace bargaining, ideological support for free collective bargaining and the overall inflationary position having significantly improved. As a result, the active membership of largest trade union in the country became officially opposed to the state's incomes policy strategy. The 1977 TUC Congress in the aftermath of the TGWU conference decision also backed a return to free collective bargaining.

The Labour Government pushed forward with a pay guideline target in order to bring the rate of inflation down into single percentage figures. The government adopted a position that sought to ensure that national earnings would amount to no more than 10 per cent in the period from August 1977 to August 1978. In this context, the Social Contract was increasingly defined as a pay policy rather than 'a wider social platform' (Jones, July 1977). However, the TUC General Council strategy during 1977 was described as being one of 'acquiescence' (Dorfman, 1983: 129–131). The TUC opposed a third year of wage restraint but reluctantly accepted its implementation. The 'acquiescence' was partly induced by the rising levels of unemployment, which increased from 641,000 in October 1974 to 1.518 million by October 1977.

The Liaison Committee published a broad policy statement on 27 July 1977 with few specifics—'The Next Three Years and Into the Eighties'. The main thrust of the document emphasised: "Our task to ensure that the sacrifices of recent years have not been in vain" (TUC Report, 1977 cited in R. Taylor, 1980: 141). The 'twelve-month rule' in Phase Three was respected by the TUC as it evolved a 'nod and wink' understanding with the government (Minkin, 1992: 125). Despite the TUC's opposition to another wage limit, the body did not seek to mobilise the trade union movement against government policy. The point is crystallised by a firefighters' strike, which was discussed at the TUC General Council meeting in December 1977. In a close vote (21 to 19), the meeting voted against the TUC giving support to the Fire Brigades Union (FBU) campaign for a 30 per cent pay rise (TUC Report, 1978: 288).

The average increase in earnings from August 1977 to August 1978 came out around 14–15 per cent (see Table 2.2). Albeit more than the government desired, in the economic realities of the day, it was a result

Table 2.2 Nominal Wage Growth and RPI Inflation 1975–78

	Average Weekly Earnings Growth %	Retail Price Index %
Q1 1975	32.94	20.3
Q2 1975	31.11	24.3
Q3 1975	28.28	26.6
Q4 1975	23.58	25.3
Q1 1976	20.35	22.5
Q2 1976	19.49	16.0
Q3 1976	14.17	13.7
Q4 1976	13.74	14.9
Q1 1977	11.03	16.5
Q2 1977	9.93	17.4
Q3 1977	8.28	16.6
Q4 1977	8.72	13.1
Q1 1978	11.26	9.5
Q2 1978	12.90	7.7
Q3 1978	15.29	7.9
Q4 1978	14.81	8.1

Source: Dataset provided by Taylor et al. (31 January 2014).

more favourable than most observers perceived to be possible as trade union membership in the late 1970s approached its peak. The pay measures to control inflation were also achieved in line with a fall in average living standards from 1975 to 1978 as Table 2.3 illustrates. Shepherd (2013: 83–84) further highlights that Alan Fisher, General Secretary of NUPE, claimed the average weekly earnings of male ancillary workers in the NHS had dropped to 76 per cent of the national average for all male industrial workers from 84 per cent over the 1975 to 1978 period.

The brewing tensions between the industrial and political wings of the labour movement were in full public display by the summer of 1978. The precarious balancing act was ended by the Labour Cabinet's decision to set an overall pay increase figure for Phase Four no more than 5 per cent. The policy was contained in the government's paper titled 'Winning the Battle Against Inflation' (July 1978). The government's pay target flew in the face of the industrial and political realities. The Transport Minister at the juncture, William Rodgers, acknowledged the figure was 'unrealistically low' (Rodgers, 1984: 173). Inflation had come down from 26.9 per cent in August 1975 to a low of 7.4 per cent by June 1978, which was 'about the average for industrial countries and lower' (Winning the Battle Against Inflation, July 1978: Section 5). In this context, Lord Lea states:

> I remember on one occasion I met the Treasury official who wanted to discuss pay policy, I remember him saying five per cent and I said 'just like that? No discussion?' What am I supposed to say? Goodbye?' You know it was quite difficult as it were to do the 1978 conversation because we—that's Jones and Scanlon and everybody—had told Denis Healey that pay restraint and deals like that were not a permanent way of life.
>
> (Extract from Lord Lea, Interview 2)

The tension was palpable in the TUG scheduled list of meetings from 2 May 1978 until 3 May 1979 just prior to the general election. Of the eleven scheduled meetings, ten were cancelled due to 'low attendance', individuals unable to be present or key votes in parliament. Divisions

Table 2.3 Real Wage Growths From 1974 to 1978

	1974	1975	1976	1977	1978
Quarter 1	−1.06	12.64	−2.15	−5.47	1.76
Quarter 2	−0.52	6.81	3.49	−7.47	5.20
Quarter 3	3.73	1.68	0.47	−8.32	7.39
Quarter 4	7.99	−1.72	−1.16	−4.38	6.71

Source: Dataset provided by Taylor et al. (31 January 2014).

within the trade union movement, however, boosted the Labour Government's 5 per cent pay gamble as the Iron and Steel Trades Confederation, GMWU, Union of Post Office Workers, NALGO and the National Union of Railwaymen (NUR) were in favour of accepting the pay policy. In contrast, the NUM, NUPE and TGWU opposed. The Labour Government hoped trade unions could be persuaded to accept one more year of guidance on the premise of economic recovery but sympathetic union leaderships were angered by the government's refusal to concede a 35-hour week as part of the bargain due to lobbying by the Confederation of British Industry (CBI) (A. Taylor, 1987). At the TUC Congress of September 1978, various trade union leaders were determined to make it clear that the government's 5 per cent pay policy was politically and industrially infeasible. The tensions were exacerbated before the end of the Congress where to the "obvious surprise and indignation of most union leaders" the Prime Minister indicated his intention to stay on for another parliamentary session deferring an anticipated general election (R. Taylor, 1980: 144). William Rodgers (1984: 173) stated the decision came as an 'immense surprise' to fellow Cabinet ministers. Lord Lea expands upon the informal 'understandings' surrounding this episode:

> I remember a dinner with Jim Callaghan in June of 1978 which had just a few of us there it included Moss Evans, who had replaced Jack [Jones], Scanlon and so on and there was an understanding that they would produce their five per cent White Paper in July and there would be an election in October. Jim never said 'well that's it then, we agree'. But, there was an understanding in our view.
>
> (Extract from Lord Lea, Interview 2)

Lord Lea added:

> So, for all the four-letter words that get thrown at us of course it was something that Jim bless him miscalculated because he was the most pro-trade union Prime Minister ever, but it was a tragedy and I can't understand what got into him. We thought we would have won in the October (1978).
>
> (Ibid)

A number of motions were moved at the Labour Party Annual Conference in October 1978 championing a return to free collective bargaining (Dorfman, 1983). Moss Evans, the new General Secretary of the TGWU, argued that whereas the labour movement was 'united' behind curtailing inflation, he 'disputed' that it was the 'only battle to be won'. The TGWU position was supported by the GMWU. Alan Fisher, General Secretary of NUPE, also rejected the government's contention that the pay policy had benefited the low paid, stating, "100 per cent of nothing is bugger all". In a forewarning of the imminent public sector unrest, Fisher added NUPE would 'willingly' break the 5 per cent policy (Labour Party Conference Report 1978 cited in A. Taylor, 1987: 102–103). The decisive composite motion moved by Liverpool Wavertree CLP on 2 October 1978 stated the following:

> Conference demands that the government immediately cease intervening in wage negotiations and recognise the right of trade unions to negotiate freely on behalf of their members. Conference further declares that it will only support the planning of wages when prices, profits and investment are planned within the framework of a socialist planned economy.[16]

R. Taylor (1980: 144–145) declared that the major trade unions had 'amazingly' decided to "throw their considerable weight behind this shrill resolution". However, the frustrations of the trade union movement were widely publicised and privately intimated to Labour Government ministers by trade union leaders. Denis Healey (1989: 398) acknowledged that trade union officials had warned him that it was "simply impossible to operate a national incomes policy for another year" but the Cabinet had been "blind to these warnings". In conjunction with the retirement of Hugh Scanlon of the AUEW and Jack Jones of the TGWU, the Social Contract simultaneously unravelled. Geoffrey Goodman re-emphasised the importance of the strategic choices of trade union leaders as being critical to the sustenance of the Social Contract but noted the defeat of Jack Jones was a decisive moment. In essence, it fired the gun on the transition to formally and publicly oppose voluntary wage restraint:

> I have no doubt at all when Jack Jones lost that vote, it was a crucial watershed. Ok it was predictable at the time as there was tremendous unrest on the shop floor. A lot of trade union opposition came from the leadership as well, people like Moss Evans who succeeded Jack, was opposed to the Contract. It was a period of immense upheaval and change.
>
> (Extract from Geoffrey Goodman, Interview 5)

In tandem with the deteriorating economic situation, the role of the Liaison Committee declined "probably accelerated by the retirement of the leaders of the two largest unions" (Marsh, 1992: 41). In this context, Dorfman (1983: 71–73) described the TUC General Council as missing its "two great leaders of the previous decade". In contrast, the new leaders of the country's largest unions, Terry Duffy (AUEW) and Moss Evans (TGWU), were described as "hardly being on speaking terms" (Ibid). The consequences of this left a vacuum at the heart of the trade union leadership at precisely the juncture when it needed its greatest cohesion.

A series of factors ultimately contributed to the Social Contract's demise. This included trade union leadership, union ideology and the deteriorating economic situation in conjunction with the government possessing a marginal majority. Progress on the outstanding element of industrial democracy as part of the Social Contract was limited by these factors and minimal parliamentary time. The TUC would have favoured imminent legislation or a White Paper rather than have the intervening stages of the Bullock Committee, which produced a divided report in January 1977 (Thomson, 1979; R. Taylor, 1980; Whiteley, 1981). The majority report came down in favour of equal representation for trade union and shareholders on the boards of Britain's top 735 companies, with over 2,000 workers on their payrolls. The Bullock Committee majority also favoured co-opted directors from outside the company which would be mutually agreed upon by the rest of the board and constitute no more than a third of the entire board. This was called the 2X + Y formula, which would have given Britain a potentially more radical system of worker representation in private industry than Scandinavia.

Due to the outright opposition by employers and other political parties along with divisions in the TUC among the largest trade unions, the Labour Government's White Paper finally emerged on 23 May 1978 (see Table 2.4). This was fifteen months after the publication of the majority report (Kessler and Bayliss, 1995; Howell, 2005). In its evidence to the Bullock Committee in 1976, the EETPU argued it was impossible to separate boardroom consultation from negotiating with an employer citing the creation of 'irreconcilable split loyalties' among worker directors themselves. The GMWU also voiced concerns regarding a law which would require all employers to negotiate on strategic issues like corporate planning, closures and mergers as well as mass redundancies. In contrast, the AUEW appeared to reject worker representation on the boards of

Table 2.4 Largest TUC-Affiliated Unions 1977 and 1979

TUC-Affiliated Unions	1977		1979
TGWU	1,929,834	TGWU	2,072,818
AUEW	1,412,076	AUEW	1,199,465
GMWU	916,438	GMWU	964,836
NALGO	683,011	NALGO	729,405
NUPE	650,530	NUPE	712,392
EETPU	420,000	ASTMS	471,000
Top 6 % of Total	52.2%		50.7%
Total Unions	115		112
Total Membership	11,515,920		12,128,078

Source: Membership Statistics as reported in TUC Annual Report of 1977 and 1979.

private companies advocating "the unrestricted extension of collective bargaining" (R. Taylor, 1980: 167). The divisions between trade unions highlighted for Towers (1999: 91) that when trade unions are at their strongest

> they are often suspicious of supportive legislation or find it unnecessary, as in the opposition of the TUC and its affiliates to the Bullock Committee's proposals supporting workers on the board which they saw as diluting the 'single channel' representation form of collective bargaining.

There were degrees of progress made on the industrial democracy front. 'The Regeneration of British Industry' White Paper (August 1974) proposed the creation of a state holding company and a National Enterprise Board (NEB). Proposals were brought forward to introduce planning agreements through jointly worked-out plans for the future of a company between management and unions. The White Paper stated that the government envisaged a 'major development' in the industrial democracy agenda, with the NEB playing "its part in ensuring that enterprises under its control provide for the full involvement of employees in decision-making at all levels". Accordingly, the TUC welcomed the Industry Bill (November 1975), which proposed to fund the NEB with an initial £700 million. The funding was designed to foster the creation of voluntary planning agreements and the sharing of information regarding a company's investment plans in the manufacturing industry. However, the government refused to make the disclosure of company information mandatory. As such, the Industry Act (1975) was "far less radical and far-reaching than the TUC had wished for" (R. Taylor, 1980: 159). The 'biggest failure' was over planning agreements where it was envisaged that all strategic decisions of larger companies should be a matter of joint control. With the exception of a planning agreement with Chrysler, which 'quickly proved worthless' due to its deal with Peugeot-Citroen in 1978, no private sector agreements emerged (Ibid). Coates and Topham (1980: 43) described this aspect of the legislation as a "dead letter from the date of its inception". In contrast, relative progress would be made through the Aircraft and Shipbuilding Industries Act 1977, which nationalised large parts of the aerospace and shipbuilding industries illustrated by the creation of British Aerospace and British Shipbuilders.

The Winter of Discontent (1978–79)

In November 1978, the incomes component of the Social Contract formally ended in a meeting described by Dorfman (1983: 70) as a 'watershed in the long history of incomes policies'. At the TUC General Council meeting, the vote to commit the TUC to a 5 per cent policy was defeated on the casting vote of the Chairman, Tom Jackson, on a 14–14 tie (TUC Report, 1979: 272). The vote followed the Ford motor plant strike which acted as the catalyst for the industrial unrest in the winter of 1978–79. On 24 August 1978, the Ford unions submitted a claim for a £20 per week increase and a 35-hour week—25 per cent overall increase—but the company offered 5 per cent. On 22 September, 15,000 took direct action, and on the 26th, the AUEW recognised the strike and the TGWU followed. Ford management broke the stalemate by offering talks out-side the 5 per cent guideline as the unions recommended acceptance of a 16.5 per cent offer after certain disciplinary clauses were removed on 20 November. Work at Ford resumed on 24 November after a nine-week strike, but the government announced on 28 November that sanctions would be imposed on Ford, along with 220 other companies, for breach of the pay policy (A. Taylor, 1987; Minkin, 1992). The announcement produced protests from the CBI, as the employer body said that it would challenge the legality of sanctions. The Conservatives put down a motion in the House of Commons to revoke the sanctions, which on 13 Decem-ber passed by 285–283 votes. Prime Minister Callaghan responded by putting down a motion of confidence for the next day, which although the government won by ten votes (300–290), it accepted that sanctions would not be invoked. The vote politically deprived the government of any means of enforcing the 5 per cent policy.

A symbolically important strike took place involving a two-day stop-page on the 21st and 22nd of December at the BBC, which was 'hastily resolved' by the government (Hay, 2015: 192). The Cabinet Papers dated 15 February 1979 confirm a 16.5 per cent pay award by the Central Arbitration Committee (CAC)—three times above the government's own pay target (Cabinet Memoranda 1979. CP (79) 11, 15 February 1979). The award was despite the minutes of the Ministerial Committee on Economic Strategy, Sub-Committee on Pay Negotiations (EY(P)) reiter-ating to the Cabinet on 4 December 1978 that the government should "firmly stand by the policy and guidelines" in the White Paper 'Winning the Battle Against Inflation' (Cabinet Memoranda 1978. CP (78) 125, 4 December 1978).

A series of strikes took place during the winter in various sectors involving bakers, journalists, water workers and civil servants.[17] It was the manifestations of the industrial action in the transport and public sec-tors, in particular, which would come to shape the image of trade unions. In particular, this focused on gravediggers and waste collectors in the early months of 1979 (Shepherd, 2013; Lyddon, 2015). In January 1979, 20,000 railwaymen held four one-day strikes exacerbated by industrial action by petrol tanker drivers who settled for 20 per cent and by haulage drivers who agreed to a 15–21 per cent deal (A. Taylor, 2001; Hay, 2010; Shepherd, 2013). On 22 January, a one-day national strike in the public sector took place, with an estimated 1,300,000 local authority, ancillary

NHS and university manual workers engaged in the action with up to 200,000 indirect workers also participating (Lyddon, 2015).

Local authority workers were subsequently offered a 9 per cent general pay rise in conjunction with a pay comparability study (i.e. Clegg Comparability Commission). The government agreed to fulfil the commission's decisions in stages (i.e. 1 August 1979 and 1 April 1980) in an effort to end the dispute. The St Valentine's Day Concordat, as it was known, planned for a reduction in the annual rate of inflation to 5 per cent by 1982. The proposals were contained in the joint government and TUC statement 'The Economy, the Government and Trade Union Responsibilities'. Minkin (1992: 410) interestingly noted that the discussions surrounding the document excluded the Liaison Committee. Trade union leaders refused to accept that the document should form the basis for future wage bargaining in annual pay rounds, although it was agreed to hold annual assessments each spring (R. Taylor, 1980, 1991; Dorfman, 1983).

The pay offer was accepted by the TGWU, GMWU and COHSE in early March. NUPE agreed to the deal for its local authority membership but industrial action in the NHS ended only on 27 March, on the eve of the government losing a vote of no confidence in the House of Commons.[18] The agreement was on the basis that the extra £1 per week advanced to other public sector workers was increased to £2.50 for nurses alongside the 9 per cent (A. Taylor, 1987; Hay, 2010; Martin López, 2014; Lyddon, 2015). Tragically, the terms agreed to in the public sector were comparable to those discussed at a private meeting held between officials of the GMWU prior to Christmas Eve in 1978 with the Prime Minister. The informal discussion was designed to avert the forthcoming national day of industrial action. Lord Whitty, then head of the GMWU's research department, expands upon the discussions at the meeting:

> By the end of December breakdown seemed inevitable. Derek Gladwin, Regional Secretary of GMWU Southern Region, had been the both local government officer leading the earlier conflict with the Heath Government and a significant fixer for the Right in the party. He had a good personal relationship with Jim Callaghan—he had been his election campaign road manager in 1974. He also had contacts with his former researcher David Lipsey by then in the Political Office at Number Ten. He was anxious to avoid conflict if we could. Derek asked me to draft a possible framework for an agreement, which achieved a good settlement for the members but also saved face for the government. I drafted an outline agreement—a one-sider with about four or five paragraphs as I recall. Derek and I then showed it to David Basnett who agreed it with minor changes. He then spoke to the other three General Secretaries {Alan Fisher—NUPE, Moss Evans—TGWU and Albert Spanswick—COHSE} who agreed the

outline terms. They did not put it to their negotiators let alone their membership or their representatives.

My view was that the NUPE members would not accept—and the GMWU and other unions were doubtful. I delivered it to Number Ten a day or two before Christmas. David Basnett spoke to Jim Callaghan about it but I understand he was told it would open the floodgates on the Incomes Policy. At that point the start of industrial action was set for January 22—a month ahead. There could have been negotiations. Instead after two months of disruptive and politically damaging strikes at the end of March we agreed a deal that was very similar to the one we had proposed—an immediate 9 per cent upfront settlement plus the Clegg Commission. My view at the time, and forty years later, was that it was a serious political misjudgement by the Callaghan administration. Agreement on those lines could have prevented the Winter of Discontent or it could have split the unions—either way the government would have regained control of events. At the very least they should have tried.

(Authorised notes by Lord Whitty on 16 March 2018)

Lord Monks elaborates on the divergent positions between public sector unions during the pay negotiations:

But the terrible thing in the 79 Winter of Discontent was that the GMWU at that moment had decided that never again, as NUPE was getting so big at their expense, never again would they settle first and be accused of selling out. Supposedly, NUPE General Secretary Alan Fisher who was not particularly left-wing was ready to sign the deal but was over turned by Rodney Bickerstaffe and a guy called Bernard Dix both were two young officers. This prolonged it by another month, with piles of rubbish, the unburied etc.

(Extract from Lord Monks, Interview 3)

Evaluation and Reflections

It is critical to emphasise that the economic crisis epitomised by the IMF loan in 1976 occurred against a background of successive incomes policies by previous Labour and Conservative governments. It was at a juncture when trade union membership and union density approached its peak (see Table 2.5). Trade unions with high industrial density could attain higher wage demands through industrial power in the private and public sectors above any governmental target. This is exactly what occurred when the Conservative Government brought forward in 1962 a wages and salaries target within a 2.5 per cent figure in industries such as electricity and transport (Hutt, 1975; Fraser, 1999). The 'pay norm' figure was changed to 3.5 per cent as the 1964 general election approached

Table 2.5 Key Statistics 1970–79

Year	Union Membership	Union Density (%)	Unemployment (%)	Aggregate Number of Days Lost
1970	11,179	44.8	2.7	10,980
1971	11,128	45.2	3.5	13,551
1972	11,350	46.1	3.8	23,909
1973	11,444	45.4	2.7	7,197
1974	11,044	46.4	2.6	14,750
1975	11,656	43.7	4.2	6,012
1976	12,133	46.5	5.7	3,284
1977	12,719	48.3	6.2	10,142
1978	13,054	50.2	6.1	9,405
1979	13,212	50.7	5.7	29,474

Source: (1) Trade union membership and aggregate number of days lost (*The Guardian*, 8 April 2013); (2) union density (Visser, 2015) and (3) unemployment (Denman and McDonald, January 1996).

(Kessler and Bayliss, 1995). In this context, a general policy of wage restraint could not be enforced by unions at the workplace level. The latter point is crystallised by the largest trade union in the country—the TGWU—railing against the incomes policies of the 1960s. In fact, workplace productivity bargaining was lauded by Jack Jones during this period as a 'secret weapon' designed to get around Labour's 'early warning' incomes policies contained in the Prices and Incomes Act (1966) (Richter, 1973: 235).[19] The effects of economic decentralisation meant trade unions centrally would be unable to control wage demands at the workplace level. This spectacularly came to fruition within the TGWU in 1977 despite Jack Jones' unstinting support for the Social Contract. Howell (2000: 227) expands upon these points:

> Decentralisation made it impossible for union leaders to deliver wage restraint, while near-continuous incomes policies overwhelmed efforts to create stable bargaining structures inside the firm. In seeking to use the industrial relations system to manage macroeconomic crisis, the British state doomed its reform project.

Undy et al. (1981) and Marsh (1992) state that irrespective of the strength of the union-party link and the personal relationships, which existed between trade union and Labour Government leaders, it could not override the effects of economic decentralisation. Pizzorno (1978) outlined that the success of a political exchange process is reliant upon the extent of market coordination mechanisms. In contrast with continental European states, the Social Contract unravelled due to absent and weak economic coordination mechanisms in Britain. The demise, for many, would become associated with the structural weaknesses of trade unionism and the inability of union leaderships to restrain the workplace demands of their respective memberships (Dorfman, 1983: 60–61). As Hay (2009: 547) contends, the Winter of Discontent, if anything, is a 'story of union weakness' rather than one of strength. Critics of the social-pact process accordingly argued that it was "built on flimsy, contradictory foundations" (R. Taylor, 1976: 398). However, the industrial unrest is in danger of completely overshadowing the significant outcomes and lessons which can be drawn from the Social Contract and the Liaison Committee process by which it was 'fathered'. It is critical to re-emphasise that the purpose of the Liaison Committee was two-fold: (1) to create a climate of mutuality involving Labour Party affiliated unions and non-party affiliated unions through the TUC as the channel of influence with the Labour (Shadow) Cabinet, and (2) through the liaison process the opportunities for favourable employment relations outcomes could be optimised. The key protagonist from the perspective of trade unions, Jack Jones of the TGWU, expands upon these points in response to whether the Liaison Committee facilitated progress:

> I believe it did. From the basic point, that if anything strengthens the link between the party and the unions can only be a good thing. We got to know more about each other. The Labour Party people who were prominent who joined the party without being a member or having any connection with a trade union thought of us as something different. However, I always believed that the two were vital associates of each other.
>
> (Extract from Jack Jones, Interview 1)

A sense of shared objectives existed during the 1970–78 period. The fruits of the process are evidenced by TULRA (1974), the Health and Safety at Work Act (1974), Employment Protection Act (1975), Industry Act (1975) and the Aircraft and Shipbuilding Industries Act (1977). The industrial struggles of 1978–79 and subsequent election defeat of Labour according to Coates (1980: 260) "should not distract our attention from the remarkable degree of working class industrial restraint that ministers managed to orchestrate prior (to the Winter of Discontent)". In fact, the 'orchestration' was achieved primarily by the strategic choices of trade union leaders to support and sustain the Social Contract from its inception until Phase Four of the incomes policy in November 1978. These efforts are substantiated by the 1977–78 wages round not exceeding the 10 per cent target by the TGWU, outside "one or two justifiable exceptions", despite Jack Jones' conference defeat (Jones, 1986: 323).

The tangible successes of the Liaison Committee process should be considered through a more positive reflective lens. First, the Labour Government was prevented from falling with its minimal majority at an earlier juncture through the unfolding economic turbulence. The voluntary wage restraint exercised by trade unions was an essential component in this strategy. Second, the legislative outcomes would not have been as favourable without a less formalised process in the form of the Liaison Committee. Lord Monks supports these previous assertions in a critical appraisal of the Social Contract stating that "the process worked but so did the outcomes" (Extract from Lord Monks, Interview 3). Thomson (1979: 41) suggested the Social Contract represented "probably the high watermark of the exercise of power by any union movement anywhere in the Western World". Geoffrey Goodman also claimed the trade union coordination was "on a level that you have probably never had before" (Extract from Geoffrey Goodman, Interview 5). These observations are substantiated despite an acknowledgement of the damaging effects of the industrial strife following the collapse of Phase Four of the incomes policy.

The inevitability of the Social Contract's demise as a process can be critiqued on several fronts. The social-pact was initiated at a period of severe economic instability epitomised by the 1976 IMF loan and associated public expenditure cuts, periodic high inflation and rising unemployment. The tensions in the employment relations environment were exacerbated from the perspective of trade union leaders by the unrealistic wage guideline set in 1978. The government's own 5 per cent target was itself smashed towards the end of year in the public sector (i.e. BBC) and private sector (i.e. Ford) prior to the widespread public and transport sector unrest. Denis Healey (1989: 462) reflected on the 5 per cent pay target, remarking:

> We in the Cabinet should have realised that our five per cent norm would be provocative as well as unattainable. If we had been content with a formula like 'single figures', we would have had lower settlements, have avoided the Winter of Discontent, and probably won the election too.

The Labour Government's incomes policy approach was also backed up by the threat of legislation, which was an anathema to trade unions. A contributory factor well-rehearsed in the literature surrounding the Social Contract's collapse was the failure to hold an anticipated general election in the autumn of 1978. Hay (2015: 196) argues that it would have been 'astonishing' had Callaghan chosen an election, which it was "far from clear that he would have won". The Prime Minister deferred in an attempt to further consolidate economic progress made on curtailing inflation through the 5 per cent pay target and gambled on trade unionists being more worried about an imminent Conservative Government, rather than another round of pay restraint. The previous point on Callaghan's calculations may be valid. However, leading trade unionists intimated to the Prime Minister that an early election was needed in order to contain the brewing industrial unrest at the grassroots level. Rodgers (1984: 173) also called the failure to hold an autumn election a 'grievous error' as the Labour Party was only 1 per cent (42 per cent) behind the Conservatives (43 per cent) in the opinion polls in November 1978. At the end of January 1979, the gap had widened to nineteen points (55 per cent to 36 per cent) (Ipsos Mori, 2009). These points should not be misinterpreted as an assertion that Labour was in any sense assured victory in 1978. Rather, it is designed to present an alternative historical lens which judges that an autumn election based on 'understandings' between leading trade unionists and the Prime Minister was the optimum opportunity for Labour's success.

The significant achievements of the wider Social Contract until the present day have been drowned out by the negative narrative fashioned during and after the winter of 1978–79. Lyddon (2015: 207), for example, highlights an estimated 16 million days were lost due to the national strikes in the engineering sector from 6 August to 2 October in 1979 during the Conservative Government's tenure. In contrast, it is the 7.6 million working days estimated to have been lost from January to April 1979 associated with the Winter of Discontent, which would come to shape public perceptions. Specifically, the narrative nurtured by the political-right focused on the apparent inability of Labour to work with the trade unions in the interests of the country, which hitherto had been viewed as a unique selling point of the party in comparison with the Conservatives (A. Taylor, 2001; Hay, 2010, 2015; Lyddon, 2015; Shepherd, 2015).

There are a number of factors which all indicate the incomes policy reached its culmination. It most certainly had on the basis of a 5 per cent pay round. The factors include trade union ideological support for free collective bargaining, economic decentralisation and weak market coordination mechanisms in conjunction with real terms incomes reductions and an overall improving inflationary position. The leadership changes in the largest two trade unions during 1978 (i.e. TGWU and AUEW) at the Social Contract's most critical juncture contributed to the disintegration. Yet, in one of the labour movement's greatest 'what ifs', the evidence lends weight to the argument that the subsequent unravelling could have been minimised and contained, which is a point government ministers at the time acknowledge (Rodgers, 1979; Healey, 1989). The scale of the industrial unrest could have been minimised if the Prime Minister, in particular, had made different strategic choices. The strategy should have involved a realistic pay target for 1978–79 (i.e. 'single figures' as outlined by Healey), an autumn 1978 general election and, due to the failure to hold one, efforts to speedily agree a public sector pay deal (e.g. BBC settlement) along the terms presented to the Prime Minister in December 1978. The latter proposal was broadly similar to the deal finally agreed to in March 1979. If different strategic choices had been adopted, this could have reinforced the perceptions that the Labour Party remained best positioned to successfully negotiate and work better with trade unions in the interests of the country.

The industrial unrest provided powerful ideological ammunition for the Conservative Party regarding the dangers allegedly associated with trade unions being a special interest group 'out of control'. It was a narrative which found degrees of sympathy from certain quarters in the centre-left of British politics including the Labour Party (R. Taylor, 1980; A. Taylor, 1987; Minkin, 1992; Undy, 2002). Lord Monks added that the stigma associated with the winter period 'ended large trade union influence' on government:

> So, it's something we have never lived down, and if David Lea was here he would say 'ah no no, it was very successful we brought inflation down etc etc' but what happened in 1978–9, particularly 1979, swamped the recollections of many in the public mind. It became a disaster.
>
> (Extract from Lord Monks, Interview 3)

The trade union movement would be roundly blamed for the loss of Labour at the 1979 general election. In the debris of the winter, a new employment relations model was fashioned which would severely curtail trade union economic and political power until the present day.

Notes

1. From 1955 to 1965 (27,561 stoppages took place) in contrast with 17,911 stoppages from 1945 to 1954. This represented 41,833,000 aggregate number of working days lost in stoppages compared with 20,963,000 over the same period. British Labour Statistics, Historical Abstract, 1886–1968, Table 197.
2. The Conservative Party attained 330 seats, taking a share of 46.4 per cent in contrast with the Labour Party, with a share of 43.1 per cent and 288 seats.
3. This included the Electrical Trades Union and several other unions of significant size such as the National Union of Seamen (43,000), the Bakers' Union (50,000), National Union of Bank Employees (103,000) and COHSE (113,000).
4. The Labour Government called a new election in October 1974, gaining 319 seats to the Conservatives' 277, with 39.3 per cent of the electorate in contrast with the latter's 35.8 per cent. A majority of three.
5. Len Murray, Assistant General Secretary of TUC (1969–73) and General Secretary (1973–84). Jim Callaghan MP, Chancellor of Exchequer, 1964–67, Foreign Secretary 1974–76 and thereafter Prime Minister, 1976–79.
6. National Union of General and Municipal Workers (NUGMW) from 1924 to 1974 and from 1974 to 1982 the union was called the General and Municipal Workers' Union (GMWU). For the purposes of consistency in this chapter, the union will be referred to as the GMWU.

7. At the outset, the Liaison Committee consisted of the following individuals: PLP (H. Wilson, J. Callaghan, D. Healey, D. Houghton, R. Mellish and R. Prentice); the NEC (A.W. Benn MP, B. Castle MP, J. Chalmers (Boilermakers), A. Kitson (Scottish Motormen), I. Mikardo MP and Sir Harry Nicholas (General Secretary of the Labour Party); and the TUC (G. Smith TUC Chairman, Amalgamated Society of Woodworkers), Lord Cooper (vice-chairman and GMWU), Sir Sidney Greene (NUR), Jack Jones (TGWU), H. Scanlon (AUEW) and Vic Feather.

8. The balance of payments of a country is the measurement of all economic transactions between a country and the rest of the world in a particular period (over a quarter of a year or over a year).

9. NALGO was also the fourth largest trade union affiliated to the TUC in 1974 with 518,117 members. TUC Annual Report (1974).

10. According to a report by the Registrar of Friendly Societies, a total of 7,120,000 trade unionists in Britain paid the political levy in 1974 (cited in R. Taylor, 1976: 400).

11. Castle Diaries (1980: 85). Barbara Castle states it was at this meeting the term social contract was agreed in preference to social compact.

12. The Employment Protection Act (1975) stated that an employer proposing to dismiss one or more employees who recognised a trade union "shall consult representatives of that trade union with regards to the proposed redundancy with consultations beginning at the earliest opportunity". This was on the following basis: (1) if the employer is proposing to dismiss 100 or more employees within a period of ninety days or fewer, consultations must begin at least ninety days before the first redundancy would take effect and (b) if the employer is proposing to dismiss ten or more employees within a period of thirty days or fewer, consultations must begin at least sixty days before the first redundancy would take effect. The right to claim unfair dismissal was introduced by the Industrial Relations Act 1971, with the qualifying period of two years being reduced to one year in 1974 and to six months in 1975 by the Trade Union and Labour Relations Act 1974. The only workers able to claim unfair dismissal were those who worked twenty-one hours or more a week, but the Employment Protection Act 1975 reduced this to sixteen hours a week and allowed part-time workers who worked between eight and sixteen hours a week to claim the right after five years' service.

13. Part III of the Finance Act 1975 introduced a new tax on all gratuitous transfers of capital, both by way of lifetime gift and on death. The 1972 Housing Finance Act reduced the council housing subsidy and replaced controlled rents with 'fair' rents—in effect, a rent increase. The 1975 Housing Rent and Subsidies Act reversed the policy of 'fair' rents and empowered local authorities to set rent levels.

14. Labour Leader and Prime Minister, Harold Wilson, resigned on 16 March 1976, taking effect as of 5 April 1976.

15. Ian Mikardo MP. On 27 March 1974, Mikardo was elected chairman of the Parliamentary Labour Party.

16. The Wavertree resolution was passed by 4,017,000 votes to 1,924,000, despite an appeal from Employment Minister Michael Foot for a remittance of the motion. The motion is cited in R. Taylor (1980: 144).

17. For more extensive reading on the various industrial disputes see R. Taylor (1980); A. Taylor (1987); Martin López (2014); Lyddon (2015); Seifert (2015); Shepherd (2015).
18. The vote of no confidence on 28 March was lost by the Labour Government by one vote (311 to 310). The result forced a general election which was subsequently won by the Conservatives on 3 May. The Conservatives won a majority of forty-three seats.
19. The Act permitted the government to monitor rising levels of wages at around 8 per cent per annum which could result in giving orders for a wages standstill.

Bibliography

Bodah, M., Ludlam, S. and Coates, D. (2003). The development of an Anglo-American model of trade union and political party relations. *Labour Studies Journal*, 28(2), pp. 45–66.
British Labour Statistics (1971). *Historical abstract, 1886–1968: The Department of Employment*. London: Her Majesty's Stationary Office.
Castle, B. (1980). *The Castle Diaries*. London: Weidenfeld and Nicolson.
Coates, D. (1980). *Labour in power: A study of the Labour Government, 1974–1979*. London: Longman.
Coates, K. and Topham, T. (1980). *Trade unions in Britain*. Nottingham: Spokesman.
Denman, J. and McDonald, P. (January 1996). Unemployment statistics from 1881 to the present day. *Labour Market Trends*, 104(1), pp. 5–18.
Dorfman, G.A. (1983). *British trade unionism against the Trades Union Congress*. London: Macmillan.
Fatchett, D. (1987). *Trade unions and politics in the 1980's*. Kent: Croom Helm Ltd.
Fraser, W.H. (1999). *A history of British trade unionism 1700–1998*. Basingstoke: Macmillan.
The Guardian Online (8 April 2013). How Britain changes under Margaret Thatcher. Available at: www.theguardian.com/politics/datablog/2013/apr/08/britain-changed-margaret-thatcher-charts#data [Accessed 18 Nov. 2016].
The Guardian Online (25 October 2013). UK GDP since 1955. Available at: www.theguardian.com/news/datablog/2009/nov/25/gdp-uk-1948-growth-economy#data [Accessed 18 Nov. 2016].
Hay, C. (2009). The winter of discontent thirty years on. *The Political Quarterly*, 80(4), pp. 545–552.
Hay, C. (2010). Chronicles of a death foretold: The winter of discontent and construction of the crisis of British Keynesianism. *Parliamentary Affairs*, 63(3), pp. 446–470.
Hay, C. (2015). Review essays symposium: The winter of discontent. The trade unions and the 'winter of discontent': A case of myth-taken identity? *Historical Studies in Industrial Relations*, (36), pp. 181–203.
Healey, D. (1989). *The time of my life*. London: Michael Joseph Limited.
Hoopes, H.B. (June 1994). *The privatization of UK oil assets 1977–87: Rational policy-making, international changes and domestic constraints*. Available at: http://etheses.lse.ac.uk/1332/1/U062840.pdf [Accessed 14 April 2016].

House of Commons Library. Trade unions affiliated to the Labour Party in 1974. *Statistics derived from Labour Party conference report 1974 and annual report of the certification officer 1976.*

Howell, C. (June 2000). Constructing British industrial relations. *British Journal of Politics and International Relations*, 2(2), pp. 205–236.

Howell, C. (2005). *Trade Unions and the state: The construction of industrial relations institutions in Britain, 1890–2000.* Princeton: Princeton UP.

Hutt, A. (1975). *British trade unionism: A short history.* Southampton: Camelot Press.

Ipsos Mori (24 December 2009). *Looking back: 1979—Labour doomed.* Available at: www.ipsos.com/ipsos-mori/en-uk/looking-back-1979-labour-doomed [Accessed 20 April 2015].

Jones, J. (July 1977). *Interview at TGWU conference—Jack Jones on collective bargaining.* British Universities Film and Video Council. Available at: http://bufvc.ac.uk/tvandradio/lbc/index.php/segment/0007100435002 [Accessed 18 April 2016].

Jones, J. (1986). *Union man: Autobiography.* London: Collins.

Kessler, S. and Bayliss, F. (1995). *Contemporary British industrial relations.* 2nd ed. Hampshire: Macmillan Press.

Lyddon, D. (September 2015). Striking facts about the 'winter of discontent'. *Historical Studies in Industrial Relations*, (36), pp. 205–218.

Marsh, D. (1992). *The new politics of British trade unionism: Union power and the Thatcher legacy.* Houndmills, Hampshire: Macmillan Press.

Martin López, T. (2014). *The winter of discontent: Myth, memory and history.* Liverpool: Liverpool University Press.

May, T.C. (1975). *Trade unions and pressure group politics.* Saxon House: D.C. Heath Ltd.

Minkin, L. (1974). The British Labour Party and the trade unions: Crisis and compact. *Industrial and Labour Relations Review*, 28(1), pp. 1–37.

Minkin, L. (1978). The party connection: Divergence and convergence in the British Labour Movement. *Government and Opposition*, 13(4), pp. 458–484.

Minkin, L. (1992). *Contentious alliance: Trade unions and the Labour Party.* Edinburgh: Edinburgh University Press Limited.

Pizzorno, A. (1978). Political exchange and collective identity in industrial conflict. In: C. Crouch and A. Pizzorno, eds., *The resurgence of class conflict in Western Europe.* Vol. 1. London: Macmillan.

Richter, I. (1973). *Political purpose in trade unions (1973).* London: George Allen and Unwin.

Rodgers, W. (October 1979). Labour's predicament: Decline or recovery? *The Political Quarterly*, 50(4), pp. 420–434.

Rodgers, W. (April 1984). Government under stress: Britain's winter of discontent. *The Political Quarterly*, 55(2), pp. 171–179.

Royal Commission on Trade Unions and Employers' Associations, 1965–1968, report (June 1968). Cmnd 3623. London: Her Majesty's Stationary Office.

Seifert, R. (2015). Public-sector strikes in the 'winter of discontent'. *Historical Studies in Industrial*, 36, pp. 219–226.

Shepherd, J. (2013). *Crisis? What crisis? The Callaghan government and the British 'winter of discontent'.* Manchester: Manchester University Press.

Taylor, A. (1987). *The trade unions and the Labour Party.* Burrell Row, Beckenham, Kent: Room Helm Ltd. (Provident House). *TUC congress report* (1965). London: TUC.

Taylor, A. (1989). *Trade unions and politics: A comparative introduction.* Houndmills, Hampshire: Macmillan Education Ltd.

Taylor, A. (2001). The 'Stepping Stones' programme: Conservative party thinking on trade unions, 1975–9. *Historical Studies in Industrial Relations*, (11), pp. 109–133.

Taylor, C., Jowett, A. and Hardie, M. (31 January 2014). *The Office of National Statistics: An examination of falling real wages, 2010–2013.* Data available at: http://webarchive.nationalarchives.gov.uk/20160106021125/www.ons.gov. uk/ons/rel/elmr/an-examination-of-falling-real-wages/2010-to-2013/index. html [Accessed 28 Dec. 2016].

Taylor, R. (October 1976). The uneasy alliance—Labour and the unions. *The Political Quarterly*, 47(4), pp. 373–496.

Taylor, R. (1980). *The fifth estate: Britain's trade unions in the modern world.* Rev. ed. London: Pan Books Ltd.

Taylor, R. (1991). Chapter 9: The trade union 'problem' in the age of consensus 1960–1979. In: B. Pimlott and C. Cook, eds., *Trade unions in British politics: The first 250 years.* 2nd ed. Burntmill, Harlow: Longman House.

Thomson, A.W.J. (October 1979). Trade unions and the corporate state in Britain. *Industrial and Labor Relations Review*, 33(1), pp. 36–54.

Towers, B. (1999). Editorial: ' . . . the most lightly regulated labour market. . .' The UK's third statutory recognition procedure. *Industrial Relations Journal*, 30(2), pp. 81–95.

Trade Union Group of Labour Members of Parliament. Minutes of Meeting dated: 17 January 1969, 18 February 1969, 17 June 1969, 10 November 1970, 23 June 1976, 30 November 1976, and 18 January 1977.

TUC (1965). *TUC congress report.* London: TUC.

TUC (1974a). *Collective bargaining and the social contract (1974).* London: TUC.

TUC (1974b). *TUC annual report of 1974.* London: TUC.

TUC (1975). *The development of the social contract (1975).* London: TUC.

TUC (June 1976). *The social contract 1976–77: Report to special Trades Union Congress June 1976.* London: TUC.

TUC (1977). *TUC annual report of 1977.* London: TUC.

TUC (1978). *TUC annual report of 1978.* London: TUC.

TUC (1979). *TUC annual report of 1979.* London: TUC.

TUC and UK Government (February 1979). *The economy, the government and the trade union responsibilities.* Joint Statement by the TUC and the Government. London: Her Majesty's Stationary Office.

Undy, R. (2002). New Labour and New Unionism, 1997–2001: But is it the same old story? *Employee Relations*, 24(6), pp. 638–655.

Undy, R., Ellis, V., McCarthy, W.E.J. and Halmos, A.H. (1981). *Change in the trade unions: The development of United Kingdom unions since 1960.* London: Hutchison.

United Kingdom Government (1969). *In place of strife: A policy for industrial relations (January 1969).* Cmnd 3888. London: Her Majesty's Stationary Office.

United Kingdom Government (August 1974). *The Regeneration of British industry*. White Paper, Cmnd, 5710. London: Her Majesty's Stationary Office.

United Kingdom Government (1978). Cabinet Memoranda 1978. CAB 129/204, 12 October to 15 December. CP (78) 125, 4 December 1978. Memorandum by the Chancellor of the Exchequer. Pay: Action following the talks with the Trades Union Congress (4 December 1978). Available at: www.nation alarchives.gov.uk/cabinetpapers/cabinet-gov/cab129-post-war-memoranda. htm#Cabinet%20Memoranda%201979 [Accessed 31 Oct. 2017].

United Kingdom Government (July 1978). *Winning the battle against inflation*. Presented to Parliament by the Chancellor of the Exchequer by Command of Her Majesty. London: Her Majesty's Stationary Office.

United Kingdom Government (1979). Cabinet Memoranda 1979. CAB 129/205, 8 January 1979–28 March 1979. CP (79) 11, 15 February 1979. British Broadcasting Corporation Royal Charter. Available at: www.nationalarchives.gov.uk/ cabinetpapers/cabinet-gov/cab129-post-war-memoranda.htm#Cabinet%20 Memoranda%201979 [Accessed 31 Oct. 2017].

Visser, J. (October 2015). *ICTWSS database*. version 5.0. Amsterdam: Amsterdam Institute for Advanced Labour Studies AIAS. Open access database available at: www.uva-aias.net/nl/data/ictwss [Accessed 31 Dec. 2016].

Whiteley, P. (April 1981). Who are the labour activists? *The Political Quarterly*, 52(2), pp. 160–170.

Whitty, L. (16 March 2018). Authorised written notes via email communication.

3 Employment Relations Reform Under New Labour

Context, Continuity and Change

Introduction

The chapter is a critical prelude to the National Minimum Wage (1998) and the Employment Relations Act (1999). The chapter will examine the economic, industrial and political shifts that detrimentally affected the ability of trade unions to influence the employment relations framework before Labour would enter government again in 1997. Political dynamics including internal Labour Party factionalism during the 1980s and institutional configuration (i.e. majoritarian system) enabled greater opportunities for the state in partnership with employers to deconstruct and reconfigure employment relations frameworks. The chapter will outline the accommodation by trade unions with the Labour Party's reform programme as means to offsetting the Conservative Governments' (1979–97) liberal market reforms with reference to the literature and from the perspectives of actors. In the context of formal mechanisms such as the Labour Party Annual Conference and the Liaison Committee receding in importance, informal processes became more prevalent. The function and outcomes associated with informal processes are examined in the transition of successive Labour leaders culminating in Tony Blair. The chapter further discusses the role of the Trade Union and Labour Party Liaison Organisation (TULO) and its antecedents, which coordinated trade union electoral support for the Labour Party among trade unionists.

Conservative Liberal Market Reform

The Conservative Party election victory in 1979 marked a Rubicon moment in the industrial landscape. It would herald the dramatic weakening of trade unions through structural changes in the economy and employment relations arena by the time Labour came to power in 1997.[1] In an important contribution, Undy (2002: 638) stated that 1979 represented a 'watershed' moment that would lead to "a radical reappraisal of the relationship between the political and industrial wings of the labour movement". As discussed in the Introduction, the liberal market reform project initiated by Prime Minister Margaret Thatcher's Conservative

Government was principally directed towards decentralisation, decollectivism, the individualisation of employment relations and privatisation. The state's approach was illustrated by a low-wage, low-skill and flexible labour market. Unemployment would also significantly rise and remain higher throughout the Conservative Party's tenure in government as the post-war policy consensus on full employment was abandoned. Unemployment averaged 9.8 per cent under the Conservatives from 1980 to 1994, compared with an average of 5.6 per cent during the tenure of the previous Labour Government (1974–79) (Denman and McDonald, 1996).

The Conservative Governments pursued an aggressive policy of privatisation in public industries and corporations, which would have significant implications for all trade unions. The industries incorporated within the privatisation strategy included gas, electricity, water, nuclear energy, steel, telecommunications, coal and railways. The number of people working in the public sector fell by 2.2 million from 7.45 million in 1979 to 5.23 million in 1995, with the vast majority of the decline (1.7 million) due to privatisation of the nationalised industries and public corporations. The delivery of public services was also decentralised to local authorities. Education and health services could opt out of local government control, and compulsory tendering was introduced for services such as catering, cleaning and estates maintenance. The decentralisation of public services in the 1980s illustrated through Pay Review Bodies mirrored that of the private sector to the firm level during the 1970s. Howell (1998: 297) stated that the cumulative effect of the Conservative Governments' exclusionary measures "served to create a demonstration effect to employers of the acceptability of doing without trade unions".

The second central policy agenda aimed to reduce trade union power through a series of legislative measures. The start of the legislative transformation can be identified in the Employment Act of 1980. The legislation contained measures to restrict the closed shop, limit picketing and reduce dismissal costs for employers. The latter component was an essential part of empowering employer prerogative and framing the previous Labour Government's employment protection as 'burdens' on business, which were argued to act as a deterrent to employment. The 1982 Employment Act soon followed which "moved further in the anti-union direction" by restricting the definition of lawful union industrial action and introduced further limitations to the closed shop whereby 80 per cent support was required in a ballot to legalise a closed shop (Rueda, 2006: 391). The power of trade unions was further curtailed through the 1984 Trade Union Act, which required trade union political fund ballots every ten years and secret ballots before industrial action. A key element of intent in the aforementioned legislation was to damage the Labour Party's reliance on trade union financial donations, as approximately three-quarters of the party's income came from trade unions in 1984 (Brown, 1991).

Industrial action to maintain a post-entry closed shop was also made illegal and further restrictions including the right of trade unions to discipline members for crossing a picket line during a lawful strike were abolished in the 1988 Employment Act. The Conservative Government also used the 1989 Employment Act to reduce the administrative costs of dismissals by making it unnecessary for employers to provide a reason for dismissals unless the employee had been continuously employed for two years when it had previously been six months.[2] The legislative measures implemented in tandem with liberalising employment relations reforms dramatically changed the character and form of trade unions and the wider economy by 1997.

Political Action: New Mechanisms

In the lead-up to the general election of 1979, an important development by Labour Party–affiliated trade unions was the creation of Trade Unions for a Labour Victory (TULV) in 1978. The development was initiated by a number of senior trade union leaders, in particular, the General Secretary of the GMB, Dave Basnett, who led the third largest trade union in the country (Golding, 2003).[3] The newly created mechanism was partly attributed to a 'bad conscience' over the Winter of Discontent but "more substantially union leaders were concerned at the growing separation of the unions and the party which could not be remedied by the Liaison Committee" (A. Taylor, 1987: 124). TULV coordinated trade union support through the mobilisation of resources in marginal seats and advanced the case for Labour specifically among trade unionists (Marsh, 1992).

The organisational efforts of trade unions to support the Labour Party at elections are not the primary purpose of the book, but it is essential to outline the trajectory of trade union–initiated mechanisms inside the Labour Party's structures. This is central to understanding how trade union mechanisms inside the structures of the Labour Party have evolved and transformed in response to a neoliberal environment. A brief constitution was endorsed in September 1980 following the 1979 general election defeat, as thirty-seven unions affiliated constituting 90 per cent of the affiliated membership. Minkin (1992) alluded to the potential of TULV performing a counterweight to the TUC due to its role inside the structures of the Labour Party. Minkin's assertion was prescient as it pointed towards the potential of TULV—and its successors—to develop a bureaucratic and policy-making machinery to displace the role of the TUC in negotiations with the Labour leadership.

The Conservative Government returned to a tactic exemplified by the Trade Disputes and Trade Unions 1927 Act, which established the opting-in for the payment of the political levy. It was a move designed to suppress the strength of the Labour Party. Harrison (1960) highlighted that through the simple reversal of making trade union members opt out of political funds, which was re-established in the Trade Disputes and Trade Unions Act 1946, the number of trade union members officially contributing to political funds increased by 3,800,000 between 1945 and 1947. The Trade Union Act (1984), as previously refereed to, required all trade unions to hold a secret ballot before calling industrial action and mandated all trade unions to ballot their members on whether they wished to maintain a political fund. The legislation required the validation of the political fund every ten years and changed the definition of 'political objects'. Specifically, a new clause required a political fund for trade unions to campaign for or against a political party or candidate (Minkin, 1992: 563). Public sector unions, in particular, believed their ability to campaign against government policy, which was also 'de facto' party political policy, could be constrained without a political fund (Leopold, 1997: 24).

Trade union leaders met in November 1983 to discuss how political fund ballot campaigns might be conducted. This was in the context of uncertainty and nervousness regarding the level of support for trade union political funds and the Labour Party.[4] Accordingly, trade unions responded to the economic and legislative attacks through the creation of the Trade Union Coordinating Committee (TUCC) in October 1984. Grant and Lockwood (1999: 79) asserted that such was "the importance attached to the outcome of the ballots that, rather than leaving it to individual unions to run their campaigns separately, unions organised a centrally coordinated campaign that was administered by a small team of experts". The central strategy of the TUCC was one based upon "playing down the Labour link" (Marsh, 1992: 155). The position is emphasised by a notice sent to the TUG on 12 December 1984, which emphasised that the political fund campaign was "first and foremost a Trades Union campaign".[5]

Twenty-one unions produced 'yes' votes of over 80 per cent and six even managed a 'yes' vote of over 90 per cent. The average 'yes' vote was 84 per cent with a range of 59–93 per cent. The political fund results indicated substantial support "for the continuation of trade union political funds with turnout varying markedly between postal and workplace ballots" (Leopold, 1997: 25).[6] Brown (1991: 278) also noted that "contrary to all predictions", the first round of ballots revealed a high level of support for trade union political funds, with fifty-three unions voting yes.[7] The overwhelming success of the political fund ballots halted the Conservative Government's strategy. However, as R. Taylor (1987) stressed, the success was substantially attributable to the trade union movement campaigning on the principle of whether trade unions should possess a general political fund. This was a different proposition from a specific affirmation of links between trade unions and the Labour Party. In recognition of this latter point, another new mechanism was formed in

February 1986—Trade Unions for Labour (TUFL). The body, like its pre-decessor TULV, would perform no role in policy-making, with its explicit aim to improve the links between the trade unions and the Labour Party to help achieve a general election victory (Basset, 1991).

Ideological Disunity, Space and Convergence: Opposition Years

The Left-Right political factionalism inside the Labour Party during the 1980s and 1990s is beyond the remit of the book. There are a number of notable contributions on this facet such as A. Taylor (1987), Minkin (1992), Undy (2002), Golding (2003) and Hayter (2005). Nonetheless, it is important to outline the broad contours of this period in order to provide context to the diminishing degrees of institutional leverage trade unions would possess inside the party's structures by the time Labour came to power in 1997. In the aftermath of 1979, Labour MPs elected Michael Foot leader in November 1980 following James Callaghan's res-ignation. The election of Foot and the subsequent policy direction of the party was a catalyst for the factionalism inside the Labour Party.[8] The policies encompassed within 'The New Hope for Britain' general election manifesto in 1983 would be infamously given the epitaph of the "longest suicide note in history". The manifesto called for unilateral nuclear dis-armament, withdrawal from the European Economic Community, aboli-tion of the House of Lords, and the return to public ownership of recently privatised industries including British Telecom and British Aerospace.

Neil Kinnock replaced Michael Foot in the aftermath of Labour's defeat in 1983 through the first use of the new electoral college to choose the party leader, where the trade unions wielded 40 per cent of the votes.[9] During Kinnock's tenure, the NEC of the Labour Party would become a key battleground for the leadership's attempts to control institutional power in the party. Symbolic of the internal factionalism, left-wing Mili-tant members would be expelled in 1984/5 (Hayter, 2005). A process of policy and institutional space was simultaneously initiated by the TUC in this context due to the growing ideological splits inside the Labour Party during the 1980s (Minkin, 1992). The shift was also a strategic response to the Conservatives' public expenditure cuts and signified attempts by the TUC to create a dialogue with the government on the basis of its corporatist philosophy.

A. Taylor (1989: 52–53) highlighted that the TUC "periodically asserted its independence" due to many trade unions and their mem-berships not being Labour Party affiliates. As such, the TUC had to "attempt to influence all governments". The extent of the TUC distanc-ing itself from the Labour Party is illustrated by Lord Monks' address to the TUG on 13 April 1994 as TUC General Secretary. The notes of the meeting confirm the following: "He {John Monks} made the point

Table 3.1 Largest TUC-Affiliated Unions 1983 and 1987

TUC-Affiliated Unions	1983	1987
TGWU	1,632,952	1,377,944
AUEW	1,001,000	857,559
GMB	940,312	814,084
NALGO	784,297	750,430
NUPE	702,152	657,633
USDAW	417,241	381,984
Top 6 % of Total	52.1%	52.4%
Total Unions	102	87
Total Membership	10,510,157	9,243,297

Source: Membership Statistics as reported in TUC Annual Report of 1983 and 1987.

that the TUC was now looking outwards towards other political parties apart from the Labour Party albeit aware that this was attracting some predictable criticism". A new trade union strategy emerged led by the TUC, which shifted the focus onto legal rights for individual workers, mirroring the decentralisation of employment relations. Howell (2005: 117) aptly characterised the strategic reorientation as an acceptance by trade unions to the "greater juridification of labour law". The strategic shift was also informed by the fluctuating balance of power inside the trade union movement away from the industrial craft and general unions who historically supported free collective bargaining (Howell, 1998). The statistics in Table 3.1 illuminate the growing representation of non-Labour Party affiliated unions, the feminisation of the labour market and growth of public sector unions. For example, the non-Labour Party–affiliated NALGO was the fourth largest union in the country, with 750,430 members in 1987 and 67 per cent of NUPE's membership were female in the same year.[10] A correlated factor to the strategic reorientation was the growing incidence of trade union mergers. This is illustrated by the creation of UNISON in 1993 which was the product of a merger between COHSE (201,993 members), NALGO (759,735 members) and NUPE (551,165 members). The union became Britain's largest trade union with an initial total membership of 1,512,893. The number of affiliated TUC unions also totalled eighty-seven in 1987, in contrast with one hundred and sixty in 1968. The merger pattern illustrates that structural reorganisation has been central to political action shifts and reflective of an endeavour to exercise greater political and industrial leverage during periods of intense economic transformation.

Progressive Centralisation

The Labour Party's 1986 policy document 'People at Work' prior to the 1987 election defeat highlighted the party's official commitment to "repeal the legislation enacted since 1979" (Labour Party, 1986: 45). However, several key employment relations issues emerged of significant importance at this juncture. The issues principally coalesced around the Labour leadership's accommodation with substantial elements of the Conservatives' employment relations legislation. Simultaneously, the party also endorsed a statutory minimum wage despite initial opposition from two of the four largest affiliates—the TGWU and AUEW (Minkin, 1992). The largest trade unions had historically opposed the regulation of market affairs by the state based on an ideological belief in a free collective bargaining, as the following chapter will discuss. The strategic reappraisal by the Labour leadership was emboldened by the dramatic drop in the TUC affiliated membership from 12,128,078 members (1979) to 9,243,297 (1987) members in the space of eight years.[11] Undy (2002: 638) stated that both Kinnock and John Smith, who succeeded the former, would, in fact, be 'reliant' upon trade union support to implement reform on policy items such as defence, Europe and employment relations. McIlroy (1998: 552), in the following contribution, noted the impact of economic and political structural change, which induced trade union support for internal Labour Party reform:

> Desperate in the face of decline, union leaders perceived a Labour Government as necessary, if insufficient, for union recovery. To deal with their predicament, they moved in the same direction as Labour—though difference remained. Accommodation to reform was selected as the best response to a hostile environment.

Accordingly, the 1987 Labour Party Annual Conference approved a new policy-making process following the election defeat, which would strengthen the centralisation of power in the Labour leadership. Marsh (1992: 158) emphasised that the 'impetus' behind the creation of the new process came from within the trade union movement. Tom Sawyer, Deputy General Secretary of NUPE, in September 1987 presented a paper to the Home Policy Committee of the Labour Party NEC titled 'An Approach to Policy Making'. The paper provided the foundations for the Policy Review Process (PRP).[12] The impact of the new policy-making would be profound. Bodah et al. (2003: 55–56) contend that it would set in motion "the theoretical framework for the birth of New Labour in the early 1990's". John Edmonds, former General Secretary of the GMB, considered the new process as an essential shift away from Labour Party Annual Conference:

> The Policy Review group process and with the economic issues being led by John Smith and Gordon Brown, I thought, was extraordinarily important. Before that we had Phillip Gould. The forming of economic policy, therefore, I thought was of great importance because

this idea where you put policy together a few weeks before an election, writing a manifesto and going out to campaign on it is a very stupid way of doing things.

(Extract from John Edmonds, Interview 6)

In the PRP report in 1989 titled 'Meet the Challenge—Make the Change', which was followed by 'Looking to the Future' in 1990, the Labour Party critically committed to retaining the Conservatives' pre-strike ballots and ruled out the restoration of the closed shop. A set of 'positive rights' were advanced which included a legal right to trade union recognition through a new Industrial Court if sufficient support existed in the workplace. The concept would be an important signal for the future trajectory of the Labour Government's approach to employment relations.[13] By 1991, four PRP reports formed the basis of the 1992 general election manifesto. According to Hayter (2005: 192), the new process "completely repositioned the party's stance on the market and working with industry, high taxation and uncontrolled public expenditure, trade union responsibilities and—vitally—defence". The policy shifts were illustrative of the decisive ideological break by the Labour leadership from the collective laissez-faireism of the past (Marsh, 1992; Howell, 1998).

Formal to Informal Processes

The Liaison Committee and other historically important institutional mechanisms such as the Labour Party NEC and Labour Party Annual Conference receded in importance post-1987. Power became increasingly centralised in the hands of successive Labour leaders. In an era of growing union-party detachment, informal processes were pivotal to ideological reorientation as they progressively replaced the influence of formal party mechanisms. Symptomatic of this transition, the TUG is also cited as experiencing significant periods of inactivity according to the minutes. A TUG note dated 7–8 February 1990 stated: "The Parliamentary Labour Party Trade Union Group, which comprises all sponsored Labour MP's, has been re-established following a period of inactivity". Lord Whitty provides an important explanatory reason for the demise of the Liaison Committee following his appointment as Labour Party General Secretary in 1985. The Liaison Committee reports ceased to feature in the TUC Annual Reports (1989). In doing so, Whitty draws attention to the internal Labour Party divisions as being a central reason:

> By this time, the Liaison Committee had almost dropped out of sight.
> The TUC stopped being enthusiastic about it largely because at the
> time the party was taking very Left positions and the TUC didn't

want to take them. The TUC were part of the body politic not the revolutionary Left. So, that focus for policy-making had almost gone by 1987. It was in existence strictly speaking but it very rarely met and did so only for a couple of years thereafter.

(Extract from Lord Whitty, Interview 4)

Minkin (1992: 142) highlights the shift from formal to informal processes, citing the Liaison Committee meetings being progressively replaced by 'regular private meetings' of leading members of the Shadow Cabinet, the Labour Party and representatives from the TUC General Council. Trade union leadership changes at two of the four largest trade unions in the country aided the process as John Edmonds replaced Dave Basnett at the GMB in 1986, and Ron Todd replaced Moss Evans at the TGWU (R. Taylor, 1987). The informal arrangements were referred to as the 'Contact Group'. The new approach would involve trade union leaders choosing to increase their involvement in the Labour Party, principally in support of the Labour leadership (Basset, 1991). Lord Monks emphasised that the Contact Group process was established in an era where the institutions and mechanisms of the party were undermining the Labour leaderships' policy preferences. An alternative vehicle was, therefore, created to nurture common ground. Lord Monks said:

Let me just say the Contact Group was a device that was set up to get rid of the NEC when the NEC was not under Kinnock's control. The second thing was that there was a feeling that the process—and everyone remembered the Winter of Discontent and the thing had failed—no Labour Government, no Labour person once Kinnock got a bit of confidence was going to let the TUC be seen running the government or even be accused of that as that was castrating the leader of the Labour Party.

(Extract from Lord Monks, Interview 3)

Lord Morris, former General Secretary of the TGWU, reinforced the informal nature of the Contact Group in the following contribution. In doing so, Morris illustrates the transition in processes from formal to informal:

The Contact Group was never a regular event like every second Wednesday it was informal when I decided to ask for a discussion when we had big issues such as the minimum wage for example. . . . I think the title defines, it was 'contact'. Nothing was ever cast in stone, it didn't make policy, and it was always a two-way flow of opinions and ideas.

(Extract from Lord Morris, Interview 7)

John Edmonds illuminated the procedural differences between the Liaison Committee and the Contact Group processes, contributing the following remarks:

> The Liaison Committee was very much of its time, much more formal, much more tied to particular mechanistic ways in reaching a decision. The Contact Group was much more informal and productive. It focused less on communiqué and much more on an element of trust. It was a different sort of animal.
>
> (Extract from John Edmonds, Interview 6)

As the extracts illustrate, a close informal working relationship between the general secretaries of the largest trade unions, the TUC and the Labour leadership evolved. The Contact Group discussions became more structured where discussions, understandings and accommodations could be arrived at, which were then transmitted into the PRP. A manifestation of the informal arrangements was a 'common agreement' on public ownership, whereby in successive TUC and Labour Party Annual Conferences (1987, 1988, 1989) it was affirmed that a future Labour Government would not be committed to renationalisation (Minkin, 1992: 469). Furthermore, Lord Monks in relation to the closed shop emphasised the importance of informal processes in facilitating employment relations policy change in December 1989. The support for reform on this particular aspect of employment law by a number of the largest trade unions drew them into conflict with trade unions often of smaller numerical size. Lord Monks stated:

> When Blair had become the Employment spokesperson he was giving some pro-social Europe speech and this was in the years just after Jacques Delors had been to the TUC. In 1988, the TUC was pro-Europe; the Labour Party shifted its position in 1989. Blair was saying we need the same social rights as European workers and Michael Howard who was then his counter-part said 'hold on wait a minute, the European Social Chapter says everyone has got the right to be or not to be a union member. How do you square that with your commitment to reintroduce the closed shop which had been abolished'?[14] Blair flannelled and the Tories called a debate on the whole issue of the closed shop in ten days' time to really skewer Blair. Now what he did was he went round, two or three times, key union leaders and I steered him round who he needed to talk to . . . after that he said we are not going to restore the closed shop we are going to go for the Social European agenda.
>
> With the exception of the GPMU [Graphical, Paper and Media Union], which was then the [National Graphical Association], he got the support of Bill Morris, John Edmonds and so on—and it was all

done informally. . . . Now none of that was done with the Contact Group, it was all done informally with the encouragement of Kinnock and Charles Clarke, who was a very important fellow at the time, and when it became clear that a choice had to be made between the social Europe agenda and the closed shop I remember Bill Morris saying quizzically 'how many black people got in through the closed shop in the print industry? Or the docks?'

(Extract from Lord Monks, Interview 3)

Former General Secretary of the NGA union, Tony Dubbins, highlighted the organisational differences by trade unions as he recounted the same episode:

We had the involvement of a number of academics including John Gennard and Paul O'Higgins. This was after Blair had made the announcement, without consulting us, who had more members working under a closed shop than the rest of the movement put together at that time. Mostly, a pre-entry closed shop. We got Blair up to see us the day after he made the announcement and we had quite an exchange. We went to see Kinnock afterwards with those industrial relations professors and they were saying there was nothing contradictory about the imposition of restoring the closed shop and at the same time introducing the Social Chapter. They weren't contradictory. But of course, the damage was already done by the approaches Blair had already made to a number of trade union general secretaries.

(Extract from Tony Dubbins, Interview 8)

The closed shop policy shift illustrated the coordination problems and ideological differences in the labour movement. The strategic choices of leaders in the largest trade unions were increasingly framed through a wider economic lens during the Conservative era. The closed shop episode would also illustrate the 'diminished' power of trade unions within the Labour Party to the extent that it was now the Labour leadership and not the trade unions who would 'determine' the party's employment relations policy (Ludlam and Taylor, 2003: 729).

John Smith was elected Labour Leader following the resignation of Neil Kinnock after the 1992 general election loss.[15] The internal voting procedures in the party were modified, as the principle of 'One Member One Vote' was approved at the 1993 Labour Party Annual Conference. The decision reduced the institutional power of trade unions in future leadership contests.[16] The continuation of internal reform would culminate in the collective trade union vote at Labour Party Annual Conference being reduced to 50 per cent in 1995 (Freeden, 1999; Bodah et al., 2003). In the context of institutional and leadership change, John Edmonds alluded to the significant procedural and relational changes, which emerged during the transition of leaders following the death of John Smith after his brief tenure as leader (18 July 1992–12 May 1994):

> Of course, with John Smith we managed to get an agreement on a schedule of legal changes, which he was committed to—he was a God awful difficult person to convince of anything—but the great thing was if you managed it, he stuck there. He put us through hoops on union recognition even on the minimum wage although he was much softer on his support for that in the sense of it was much easier to convince him on this. On those specific issues, that was the centre-piece for the discussions in the Contact Group.
>
> (Extract from John Edmonds, Interview 6)

Lord Monks also drew attention to the shifts in informal processes, which arose following the election of Tony Blair as party leader in 1994, in contrast with John Smith's approach to managing relations with trade union leaders:[17]

> Smith was a bit different, I think Smith was a bit more—I think in a way he believed in the Liaison Committee type of joint approach. He was confident enough not to be told the unions were running the country. . . . The coup de grâce was the election of Tony Blair. His approach—I'm running it. I'm saying what's happening.
>
> (Extract from Lord Monks, Interview 3)

The extracts support Basset's (1991: 309) assertion in relation to the informal processes that are built up and exist between leading figures in the trade unions and the Labour leadership, which were "tradition-ally, though privately, the most effective method by which either side brings its demands and wishes to bear on the other". However, the personal relationship dynamic would undergo significant shifts dur-ing Tony Blair's leadership. The Blair approach diluted the inclusive role of informal processes under the Kinnock and Smith tenures, which put in motion the progressive marginalisation of trade union leaders. In conjunction with the absence of powerful formal mechanisms, these dynamics restricted the ability of trade unions to constrain the leader-ship of the Labour Party in opposition—and crucially in government. Successive internal party institutional reforms in tandem with Labour's accommodation with the general thrust of the Conservatives' employ-ment relations reforms significantly reduced trade union leverage inside the Labour Party and the wider macro-economy. In this context, trade unions increasingly emphasised the need for political action and the specific need for political funds in order to possess the ability to launch campaigns irrespective of the political party at the helm of government in a liberal market.

1993–97 Political Fund Ballots

The TUCC was re-established in 1992 in preparation for the second round of political fund ballots in tandem with the Trade Union and Labour Relations (Consolidation) Act 1992.[18] Further changes to the 1988 Employment Act, as amended by the Trade Union Reform and Employment Rights Act 1993, stipulated that postal ballots would now determine the continuation or introduction of political funds. Trade unions were given the option to choose between postal or workplace ballots in 1985–86. New elements in legislation required the conduct of the ballot and operation of political funds to be approved by the Certification Officer for Trade Unions and Employers' Associations.[19] The Labour Party would again perform no formal role in the TUCC campaign, as the strategy focused on the need to maintain political funds to assist trade union campaigning on political issues and the need to influence politicians of every political persuasion. The average number of votes in favour of retaining political funds remained relatively static over the two periods. For the 1985–86 ballots, support stood at 78 per cent, and in the 1993–97, ballots it was 82 per cent.[20] As a result of the successful campaigns, trade unions affiliated to the Labour Party were able to continue exercising political action and making political donations to the Labour Party.

In a further development during the political fund ballots (1994–96), TUFL was reconfigured into TULO in 1994.[21] The parameters of the mechanism at its inception were forcefully articulated: "The committee will not have a formal role in the party's decision-making procedures".[22] TULO's creation illuminated the progressive focus of Labour Party–affiliated unions through the party's internal mechanisms. The process was also representative of the gradual sidelining of the TUC by the largest trade unions in the country. Lord Morris, on this facet, stated the following:

> The fact that we then had to establish TULO is a manifestation that the Liaison Committee was no longer judged on results or delivering because if it were then we would have stuck with it. So, there are different constraints. One, was Labour Party affiliates, the other was all TUC affiliates. That's the dilemma and I don't have an answer as to how you bridge that gap because all things are political.
> (Extract from Lord Morris, Interview 7)

Former Prime Minister Gordon Brown offered his perspective on the progressive focus by affiliated trade unions on internal party mechanisms.

Brown drew attention to the need to have a mechanism involving Labour Party affiliates exclusively and another involving the TUC:

> The TUC is not officially linked to the Labour Party and it does represent a number of unions who are not affiliated. Indeed, the TUC can represent unions that are hostile to the Labour Party in some cases. Therefore, the relationship will not be exactly the same. So, you have to have a mechanism whereby the unions that are represented under the TUC if you like and the Labour Party as a government can meet.
>
> (Extract from Gordon Brown, Interview 9)

New Policy-Making Processes

'Labour into Power: A Framework for Partnership' (1997) transferred further policy-making power away from trade unions through the creation of the NPF.[23] The process gave the affiliated trade unions 17 percent of the voting power (i.e. thirty seats out of one hundred and seventy-five). Tony Blair (2010: 102) unashamedly stated that the document was designed to centralise greater power into his office. The Labour Leader perceived party mechanisms such as the NEC and Annual Conference as the "equivalent of the government's moral inquisitor, trying to keep it straight and narrow". The former Prime Minister was contemptuous of internal mechanisms, writing the following in his autobiography:

> The Party Conference became the focal point for dissension and a battleground for resolutions that usually asked the government to something electorally suicidal. The 'Party into Power' document effectively altered the rules so as to ensure that the routine resolutions didn't happen just by tabling a motion, but instead grew out of a managed process that required long debate and discussion in policy groups, and the NEC powers were sharply curtailed. We had to get the unions on board for the changes, and it was here that Tom Sawyer was invaluable as a former trade unionist.

McIlroy (1998: 545–546) remarked that 'Partnership in Power' was targeted at "enhancing leadership control, diluting the authority of the executive and the union's voice on it, diminishing Conference as a decision-making forum and weakening the impact of trade unionists on policy". Rodney Bickerstaffe, former General Secretary of UNISON, offered a complementary perspective which illuminates his concerns about the procedural management by the Labour leadership:

> Well I was never happy with the process, Robin Cook who I liked very much did Chair it for quite a bit, I never ever went to a meeting. I didn't think it was a good idea and I thought we would be corralled.
>
> (Extract from Rodney Bickerstaffe, Interview 10)

Lord Sawyer, General Secretary of the Labour Party at this juncture, identified the attempts by various union leaderships to exert greater degrees of control in response to the centralisation of power under Tony Blair:

> Also, the general secretaries of the unions during the Blair regime they had to pull as much power back into the centre as they could because Blair was riding roughshod over things. So, they couldn't really afford to delegate power to the NEC and they had to pull it back to themselves. In the end, it is all about power really.
>
> (Extract from Lord Sawyer, Interview 11)

John Edmonds complemented the prior remarks by drawing attention to efforts of the GMB to exert greater control on the NEC of the Labour Party in response to the progressive centralisation of power in the Labour leadership:

> The two representatives during my period always reported to each Executive Council of the union and they were cross-questioned on what happened and at every stage they were required to vote for union policy. Other unions did not have anything like that and they regarded it as legitimate for the person who sat on the Labour Party NEC to take a different position. We didn't do any-thing like that.
>
> (Extract from John Edmonds, Interview 6)

The contributions from trade union actors intimately involved in the transition from formal to informal processes through successive Labour leaders all emphasise the centralisation of power and detachment which emerged under Blair's leadership. The opportunity and ability to exert trade union policy influence on the key institutional mechanisms in order to constrain the Labour leaderships' desires were significantly constrained. As part of this equation, there was a concomitant effort to decrease the party's financial reliance on the trade unions. Rueda (2006: 393), for example, highlighted that the trade union share of Labour Party financing decreased from the 90 per cent averaged in the early 1980s to around 50 per cent at junctures under Blair's leadership. The Labour Party in the summer of 1996 also ended direct trade union sponsorship of individual MPs. The system was replaced by the funding of CLPs, which was a move designed to circumvent curbs on MPs initiating any parliamentary activity linked to trade unions as required by the Nolan Committee's standards in public life report.[24] The cumulative effect of the internal party reforms in conjunction with the liberal market reforms enacted by successive Conservative Governments demonstrated that in a historical context, there was now an "unprecedented degree of freedom" for Labour leaders (Quinn, 2004: 346).

Agency and Diminishing Trust

In an era of greater centralisation in the Labour leadership in sync with the weakening of formal internal party mechanisms, informal processes became more important as certain institutional routes were closed off. An important dynamic which is implicitly, if not explicitly, implied by actors, is the importance of personal relationships. The relational dynamics are a critical component directly influencing the strategic choices of union leaders. Lord Monks emphasised the shifts in personal relationships which were to occur under different Labour Party leaders by illustrating the modus operandi of Tony Blair in relation to the diminishing frequency of the Contact Group meetings:

> He {Blair} said 'Look I will always talk to you but you aren't getting any co-decision making and don't get any ideas. My door is always open' and so and so on. It still continued right up until the 1997 election. David Lea pressing for meetings, 'we have got to have a joint approach and we will fall apart if we don't' etc. John Edmonds too, but John Edmonds looking to deal on a party basis as well, which could bring Blair and Brown to account. He was having a major row with Brown in particular over economic policy since the early 1990's, a bit less so with Blair.
>
> Once Smith had his heart attack and Brown took over and then became Shadow Chancellor, the relationship—talking about prudence and other things—relations all round were pretty bad. I mean I had good relations with nearly everyone in this game and I became a bit of a hub for contacts, relationships and sorting out and so on. It staggered on until 97 with meetings and the Contact Group.
>
> (Extract from Lord Monks, Interview 3)

Sir Brendan Barber, Deputy General Secretary of the TUC during the period of 1993–2003, also identified the greater union-party detachment strategy pursued by Blair and its knock-on consequentials:

> So, he {Blair} wanted to create that distance in way that John Smith, you know, John Smith was comfortable with the union relationship and not worried in the same way that Tony proved to be. So, that undoubtedly influenced the atmospherics of the relationship. The unions felt this. They perceived here was a new leader of the Labour Party who unlike most of his predecessors really wanted to keep them rather at arm's length. And, that produced a human reaction on their part of some resentment and frustration and feeling that they were being unfairly excluded from proper influence on the way the party's thinking was developing on the key policy issues at the time.
>
> (Extract from Sir Brendan Barber, Interview 12)

In this context, Lord Sawyer highlighted that the pursuit of political and industrial objectives by the trade union UNISON also 'unravelled' under Blair's leadership:

> I can't recall the exact figures but in principle, health and education were our two biggest blocks of membership. We put a paper to the NEC which was basically two sides of paper on everything we wanted and we would get through what we could in the NEC. Thereafter, we would turn these commitments into a leaflet and send it out to members saying that this was party policy and this is what you will get if you vote Labour . . . but in the Blair years all this began to unravel and it was really up until John Smith when we had a leadership who were willing to agree to really solid policies for us and to get those commitments.
>
> (Extract from Lord Sawyer, Interview 11)

John Edmonds expanded upon his personal relationship with the Labour Leader, Tony Blair, and the relational detachment that arose when policy friction emerged:

> My job was not to deliver a position for the Labour Party that my union did not like. Tony Blair didn't understand this and he doesn't understand union representatives. I tried to explain, and I'm sure others did also many times, I said: 'You ask me to deliver something and I tell you I can't get this through my union and sometimes I don't want to get this through my union'. But, he regarded this as a non-sensical excuse and that if I tried hard I could get whatever I wanted through the union executive.
>
> (Extract from John Edmonds, Interview 6)

Edmonds added:

> So, like many others, I went through a process with Tony Blair where I started off as his great pal. I went to his house and had meals and so on until the first point when I said, 'sorry Tony I can't do that' or 'I don't agree with you Tony' and from that point I went from being a friend to being an obstacle.
>
> (Ibid)

The relational drift between the leaderships of the major trade unions, the TUC and the Labour Party under Blair's tenure can be further illustrated in the former Prime Minister's Press Secretary, Alastair Campbell, diaries 'The Blair Years' (2007: 58):

> (1 May 1995) Rodney Bickerstaffe {General Secretary of UNISON} came round for another general whinge. He said TB (Tony

Blair—author's insertion) had to realise he would need the unions at a later stage. I reported back to TB who said they can just fuck off.

Charlie Whelan, former Spokesperson for Gordon Brown as Chancellor, complemented the damaging assessment of the prevailing climate. Whelan added that a 'ruthless' attitude prevailed in key sections of the New Labour leadership towards trade unions:

> It's fair to say that Gordon Brown was very focused on having a policy developed by himself and Tony {Blair}, which was coherent and in some ways looking back on it in fact pandered more to the City than what some of the trade unions were looking for. They had become at the time pretty ruthless in just ignoring the demands of some trade unions.
>
> (Extract from Charlie Whelan, Interview 13)

The extensive dilution of trade union power and influence inside the Labour Party's structures in conjunction with frayed personal relationships set the scene for the unfolding negotiations surrounding the cornerstone elements of the employment relations framework as the Labour Party entered power in 1997.

Notes

1. The Conservative Party won the General Election on 3 May 1979 with 43.9 per cent of the vote and 339 seats in contrast with Labour's 36.9 per cent and 269 seats.
2. For a more extensive analysis of the Conservative Government's legislative measures to curtail trade union power see the Institute of Employment Rights, 'A Chronology of Labour Law 1979–2010'.
3. National Union of General and Municipal Workers (NUGMW) from (1924–74) and from 1974–82 the union was called the General and Municipal Workers' Union (GMWU). For the purposes of consistency in this chapter and the remainder of the book, the union will be referred to as the GMB (General, Municipal, Boilermakers and Allied Trade Union), which it has been called since 1989.
4. This is illustrated by Labour's support among manual trade unionists falling by a substantial 25 per cent between 1964 and 1987. It correspondingly fell by 7 per cent among manual non unionists (Marsh, 1992: 145).
5. Trade Union Coordinating Committee letter by Bill Keys, The Society of Graphical and Allied Trades (SOGAT), Chairman, 12 December 1984.
6. In 1985–86, the average turnout for workplace ballots was 69 per cent, but for postal ballots, it was 39 per cent (Leopold 1986 cited in Leopold, 1997: 29).
7. A further seventeen trade unions held political fund ballots for the first time and secured substantial majorities in favour (Grant and Lockwood, 1999; Leopold, 1997). In only one instance—the First Division Association—a union of

civil servants voted against. Approximately 80 per cent of union members were in unions with approved political funds by the end of the 1980s.

8. Three of Labour's most prominent figures—former government ministers David Owen, William Rogers and Shirley Williams—stated they could not remain in a party that championed left-wing policies, leading to a split known as the 'Gang of Four'. The group also included Roy Jenkins. The Gang of Four announced the new Social Democratic Party in 1981, after outlining their policies in what became known as the Limehouse Declaration on 25 January 1981.

9. The Conservatives won 397 seats on 42.4 per cent of the vote. with Labour gaining a total of 209 on 27.6 per cent of the vote. In 1979, Labour had 36.9 per cent of the general election vote. The Social Democratic Party gained 25.4 per cent of the vote.

10. Due to the growing role of the white-collar and public sector unions the TUC in 1982 reformed to reflect these economic structural changes so that automatic representation to the TUC General Council was secured for unions with 100,000 or more members leading to greater representation for white-collar and public sector unions.

11. Membership Statistics as reported in TUC Annual Report of 1979 and Membership Statistics as reported in TUC Annual Report of 1987.

12. Each Policy Review Group had seven to ten members chaired jointly by a member of the Shadow Cabinet and representative from the NEC. The 'People at Work' group dealt with industrial relations

13. In relation to the contentious area of picketing in industrial disputes, it was agreed that there would be a right to picket but only "peacefully, in limited numbers, in accordance with a statutory code of practice" (Marsh, 1992: 160).

14. The Social Charter included a number of minimum rights such as women being entitled to fourteen weeks' statutory leave, twelve weeks' redundancy allowance, a 48-hour maximum working week and part-time and temporary staff who work at least eight hours a week to be given the same employment rights as full-time workers.

15. Labour lost the 1992 general election, which it was predicted to win by many commentators, by 34.4 per cent (271 seats) to the Conservatives' 41.9 per cent (336 seats). The Liberals gained 17.8 per cent of the vote and twenty seats.

16. Trade unions and CLPs were required to ballot members individually, with results being allocated proportionately in leadership elections. The weighting of votes in the electoral college was changed to give each section (CLP, PLP and trade unions) a third of the share of votes. The role of trade unions was also reduced (and socialist societies) to 70 per cent of the vote (from 90 per cent) and the CLPs 30 per cent following the 1992 general election (i.e. 1993).

17. Tony Blair secured 57 per cent of the electoral college vote in contrast with John Prescott (24.1 per cent) and Margaret Beckett (18.9 per cent). Interestingly, in the trade union section, Tony Blair won an outright majority (52.3 per cent of all votes). Source: House of Commons Library. Leadership Elections: Labour Party (6 October 2010) by Kelly, Lester and Durkin.

18. The definition of political activity covered by the legislation was extended to include "the production, publication or distribution of any literature,

document, film, sound recording or advertisement the main purpose of which is to persuade people to vote for a political party or candidate or to persuade them not to vote for a party or candidate" [Trade Union and Labour Relations (Consolidation) Act 1992 (section 72(1) (f))]. In the 1987 general election period, NALGO ran a 'Make People Matter' campaign, which was judged to be in breach of the 1984 Act because the material urged members to vote against the Conservatives even if it did not explicitly state vote Labour.

19. The 1993 Act covered independent scrutineers and counting officers. To assist unions with the complexity of the law in this area, the Certification Officer produced a set of model rules.
20. Leopold (1997: 28–29) presents slightly different statistics based on a more representative weighted average of all votes, but it doesn't change the fundamental dynamics which is that 80 per cent of members voted 'yes' in 1994–96 compared with 82 per cent in 1985–86. Turnout was at 38 per cent in 1994–96 which was lower than the 'adjusted 1986' average of 63 per cent for these unions. The author attributes this to the change in the law permitting only postal ballots in the second round, whereas in 1985–86, unions could choose either postal or workplace ballots.
21. It consisted of the general secretaries of all the affiliates, the Leader and Deputy Leader of the Labour Party, the NEC Chair, the Treasurer and the chairs of all NEC committees.
22. Labour Party (1994: 1), NEC Report Supplementary report, the Union-Labour Party Link cited in McIlroy (1998: 546).
23. A Joint Policy Committee (JPC) was established with representatives of the Shadow Cabinet and the NEC, to be chaired by the Party Leader. The JPC was a new executive body overseeing a new process of party policy-making. Policy would be created through a two-year rolling programme, with the areas of policy to be addressed by the party as determined by the JPC. The JPC would also decide the policy areas and thereafter would consult with the National Policy Forum (NPF). The NPF would then establish policy commissions to assess the specified policy areas. CLPs, trade unions and members were entitled to make submissions, proposals and amendments to the policy commissions who, in turn, would produce reports on the policies under review. The process would then entitle the JPC to discuss these reports with the Policy Forum and to be debated by Labour Party Conference. In the second year, amendments would be considered by the JPC and the NPF. The JPC and the NEC would then publish final reports; however, voting at conference would be restricted to three policy motions.
24. In December 1983, there were ninety-five union sponsored MPs (45 per cent), and in 1992, there were 152 (56 per cent) (Alderman and Carter, 1994: 336).

Bibliography

Alderman, K. and Carter, N. (1994). The Labour Party and the trade unions: Loosening the ties. *Parliamentary Affairs*, 47(3), pp. 321–337.

Basset, P. (1991). Chapter 16: Unions and labour in the 1980s and 1990s. In: B. Pimlott and C. Cook, eds., *Trade unions in British politics: The first 250 years*. 2nd ed. Harlow: Longman House.

Blair, T. (2010). *A journey*. London: Hutchinsons.

Bodah, M., Ludlam, S. and Coates, D. (2003). The development of an Anglo-American model of trade union and political party relations. *Labour Studies Journal*, 28(2), pp. 45–66.

Brown, W. (1991). Chapter 14: The changes political role of unions under a hostile government. In: B. Pimlott and C. Cook, eds., *Trade unions in British politics: The first 250 years*. 2nd ed. Harlow: Longman House.

Campbell, A. (2007). *The Blair years: Extracts from the Alistair Campbell Diaries*. London: Hutchinsons.

Denman, J. and McDonald, P. (January 1996). Unemployment statistics from 1881 to the present day. *Labour Market Trends*, 104(1), pp. 5–18.

Freeden, M. (1999). The ideology of New Labour. *The Political Quarterly*, 70(1), pp. 42–51.

Golding, J. (2003). *Hammering the left: Defeating Tony Benn, Eric Heffer and Militant in the battle for the Labour Party*. London: Politico's.

Grant, D. and Lockwood, G. (1999). Trade unions, political funds ballots and party political funding. *Policy Studies*, 20(2), pp. 77–94.

Harrison, M. (1960). *Trade unions and the Labour Party since 1945*. Museum Street, London: George Allen and Unwin Limited.

Hayter, D. (2005). *'Fightback: Labour's traditional rights in the 1970s and 1980s'*. Manchester: Manchester University Press.

Howell, C. (1998). Restructuring British public sector industrial relations: State policies and trade union responses. *Policy Studies Journal*, 26(2), pp. 293–309.

Howell, C. (2005). *Trade unions and the state: The construction of industrial relations institutions in Britain, 1890–2000*. Princeton: Princeton UP.

Kelly, R., Lester, P. and Durkin, M. (6 October 2010). *Leadership elections: Labour Party*. House of Commons Library Note.

Labour Party (1986). *People at work: New rights and responsibilities*. London: The Labour Party.

Leopold, J.W. (March 1997). Trade unions, political fund ballots and the Labour Party. *British Journal Industrial Relations*, 35(1), pp. 23–38.

Ludlam, S. and Taylor, A. (December 2003). The political representation of the labour interest in Britain. *British Journal of Industrial Relations*, 41(4), pp. 727–749.

Marsh, D. (1992). *The new politics of British trade unionism: Union power and the Thatcher Legacy*. Houndmills, Hampshire: Macmillan Press.

McIlroy, J. (December 1998). The enduring alliance? Trade unions and the making of New Labour 1994–7. *British Journal of Industrial Relations*, 36(4), pp. 537–564.

Minkin, L. (1992). *Contentious alliance: Trade unions and the Labour Party*. Edinburgh: Edinburgh University Press Limited.

Quinn, T. (2004). Electing the leader: The British Labour Party's electoral college. *British Journal of Politics and International Relations*, 6(3), pp. 333–352.

Rueda, D. (2006). Social democracy and active labour-market policies: Insiders, outsiders and the politics of employment promotion. *British Journal of Political Science*, 36(3), pp. 385–406.

Taylor, A. (1987). *The trade unions and the Labour Party*. Burrell Row, Beckenham, Kent: Room Helm Ltd. (Provident House).

Taylor, A. (1989). *Trade unions and politics: A comparative introduction*. Houndmills, Hampshire: Macmillan Education Ltd.

Taylor, R. (October 1987). Trade unions and the Labour Party: Time for an open marriage. *The Political Quarterly*, 58(4), pp. 424–432.

The Institute of Employment Rights. *A chronology of labour law 1979–2017*. Available at: www.ier.org.uk/resources/chronology-labour-law-1979-2017 [Accessed 18 June 2017].

Trade Union Group of Labour Members of Parliament. Minutes of Meeting dated: 12 December 1984, 7/8 February 1990 and 13 April 1994.

TUC (1979). *TUC annual report of 1979*. London: TUC.

TUC (1983). *TUC annual report of 1983*. London: TUC.

TUC (1987). *TUC annual report of 1987*. London: TUC.

TUC (1989). *TUC annual report of 1989*. London: TUC.

Undy, R. (2002). New Labour and New Unionism, 1997–2001: But is it the same old story? *Employee Relations*, 24(6), pp. 638–655.

United Kingdom Government (1992). *Trade Union and Labour Relations (Consolidation) Act 1992*. London: Her Majesty's Stationary Office.

4 The National Minimum Wage (1998)

Introduction

New Labour's political and economic reforms, despite accommodation with the liberal market economy, were distinctive in comparison with the Conservative Governments' (1979–97) (Howell, 2004; Heffernan, 2011). There was a focus on individual employment rights which were designed to ensure that those employees in decollectivised and low trade union density areas of the economy had recourse to legal minimum rights and pay. New Labour's differentiated approach was advanced through the notion of social partnership. It represented a more inclusive approach towards trade unions in policy-making after the long period of hostility and exclusion under the Conservatives.

Social partnership was premised on the notion that firms are most successful when employers, managers and employees (and their representatives) work together, which should be supported by the state. The approach focused on supply-side initiatives such as skills, training and flexibility in the labour market. Heery (2005: 3) identified social partnership as a "key break in public policy", whereas Metcalf (2005: 27) added that it represented a shift from 'hostile forces' to an enabling environment for trade unionism. New Labour's employment relations approach also found ideological compatibility with the TUC's 'New Unionism' agenda (McIlroy, 1998; Maass, 2001; Smith and Morton, 2001; Ludlam and Taylor, 2003). The strategy was supported to varying degrees by the largest trade unions such as the AEEU, GMB and TGWU, who were three of the four largest affiliates all with significant private sector memberships.[1] It was in this context that the unfolding negotiations over the employment relations framework took place, as Labour secured a landslide victory achieving 43.2 per cent of the vote, winning 418 seats and giving the party a majority of 179 seats.

The Development of the NMW

The minimum wage was historically one of the most contentious policy issues and vociferously opposed by powerful sections in the trade union movement. The ideological underpinnings of the position are elucidated in Webb and Webb (1913: 296), whereby trade unions "fiercely resented any attempt to interfere with their struggle with employers, on the issue of which, they were told, their wages must depend". When the Independent Labour Party in 1926 launched its concept of the 'Living Wage' it provoked 'hostility' from Ernest Bevin, TGWU General Secretary, who "gave notice of the problems which would eventually be in store for a Labour Government if it attempted to intervene in 'a very intricate and involved wage system'" (Labour Party Annual Conference Report, 1929 cited in Minkin, 1992: 13). Resistance persisted in the post-war period as supporters of a minimum wage argued that it should be considered in the context of wartime economic controls being relaxed. The suggestion was opposed by the TUC as the ideological dominance of collective laissez-faireism prevailed.[2] Yet it would be misleading to suggest that all trade unions had an aversion to the state introducing regulatory measures and supportive institutional architecture. Smaller unions, white-collar unions and public sector unions were more positive about state regulation, hence collective laissez-faireism was never 'hegemonic' within trade unionism (Howell, 1998: 304). Lord Sawyer contributed insightful comments on the prevailing ideological dominance of free collective bargaining, which elicited unsympathetic attitudes towards the minimum wage from inside the trade union movement:

> So, as a union we {NUPE and UNISON} really focussed on what we really wanted and the minimum wage was a massive policy issue for us. I don't know if Bill Morris would agree with this but Rodney {Bickerstaffe} by any fair account led on the minimum wage while a union like the TGWU was opposed to it as it interfered with free collective bargaining. Most of the unions would go to the rostrum and oppose Rodney forcefully. They liked Rodney but would say to him 'you are wrong on this and we don't want state interference'.
>
> (Extract from Lord Sawyer, Interview 11)

NUPE did succeed in 1986 as the Labour Party officially adopted the minimum wage as policy within the 'Low Pay: Policies and Priorities' document. The position 'broke' with traditional TUC policy (Minkin, 1992: 412). The policy stated that it would start at 50 per cent of men's median earnings and thereafter be upgraded gradually to two-thirds (Coates, 2005). Due to the policy's contentiousness, it did not feature prominently in the general election of 1987. Marsh (1992) added that the lack of prominence was attributable to the divisions among trade unions over the policy. The minimum wage increased in prominence as trade union leaders engaged more in the Labour Party's structures to promote the policy. Rodney Bickerstaffe, former General Secretary of NUPE and UNISON, outlined his participation in the Labour Party's Economic Policy Review Group Subcommittee in 1989. Bickerstaffe illuminated the centrality of informal discussions, which were used to advance the union's policy objective. As the largest affiliate to the Labour Party, after the creation of UNISON, the union became the most powerful advocate of the minimum wage. Bickerstaffe would be described as the 'midwife' of the policy (Metcalf, 1999: 192). The former general secretary said:

> Well I was almost press-ganged and it had to be seen that I was involved. Tom Sawyer said to me that I had to be involved and John Edmonds was involved because the economy was his specialist subject. However, this was all about power play at the end of the day. You didn't need too much knowledge. I wouldn't have naturally gone on to it and I can't recall the number of times I actually attended, which is something you would have to check. It's not that I think the Labour Party is not important but I never thought it was my baby. It was an area where you could very easily compromise and it's important that these compromises are made.
>
> In 1991, I went to Oxford University at Magdalene College and spent an evening there with John Smith, Tony Blair, my researcher and Derek Robinson from Oxford. The five of us were trying hammer out an understanding on the minimum wage. If I had an issue, I would much prefer to meet on this and conduct talks like this. The broader issues, which are important, need to be discussed although not necessarily by me.
>
> (Extract from Rodney Bickerstaffe, Interview 10)

A key objective of the book is to evaluate the follow-through in outcomes arising from 'agreements' in informal processes. Bickerstaffe highlighted that 'vague promises' often manifest from informal spaces. This facet was brought into sharp focus in the transition of party leaders:

> It was a compromise on this by the way because we had a line. A TUC line and a party-conference line. We wanted a two-thirds minimum income target but at the end of the meeting, I had to accept that John Smith was not going to go forward with this. The understanding reached and what we tried to use as a compromise on the minimum wage was that over time, this would rise to two-thirds of average earnings but of course, John {Smith} died, and then Tony Blair changed things. This was despite Tony being at the meeting with John where we agreed a 50 per cent minimum rising to two thirds over time.
>
> (Ibid)

Lord Sawyer offered insight into the informal discussions inside NUPE and then UNISON, specifically on the rate of a minimum wage. Sawyer drew attention to the differences in public statements and internal institutional positions:

> I could say to him {Bickerstaffe}, 'I know you might not be very happy about this but we do have to think about this issue'. He would quite often say 'right this is the union policy'. So, for example, on the minimum wage it was five pounds an hour but I recommended that we agree to £3.50, as that's the best we can get. So, Rodney would say 'let's support this and then campaign for more as that's what Tom is arguing for with the leadership {Labour} because that's the best we can get just now'. So, on that basis I would argue with the leadership and say well the union policy is this and Rodney will argue for this. So, we played quite a good double act.
>
> (Extract from Lord Sawyer, Interview 11)

The Labour Party's manifesto for the 1992 general election pledged to deliver a £3.40 an hour minimum wage. The figure was based on Labour's commitment to introduce a rate starting at the 50 per cent of median men's earnings, which would rise to two-thirds of the median male hourly rate 'over time'.[3] However, in the aftermath of the election defeat, John Smith reportedly stated to the Labour Party's NEC that the electorate "remained to be convinced" on the issue (Clement, 1994). Smith was said to have opined to senior colleagues that the Labour Party was vulnerable to arguments by the Conservative Government that a statutory national minimum wage would create unemployment. Sir Bill Callaghan as the TUC's senior economist at this juncture complemented this perspective:

> I would draw attention to a number of developments. Firstly, the Conservative Government's decision to scrap Wages Councils brought about an increase in interest in regulation of the labour market. There was much debate subsequently in the Labour Party and the TUC on a Minimum Wage. One of the factors in Labour's defeat in the 1992 election was the attack on a national minimum wage based on a formula. In my view, Labour did not have a satisfactory rebuttal to claims that the national minimum wage would destroy jobs. Subsequently, at the TUC, we put a lot of effort into developing the case for a national minimum wage.
>
> (Authorised notes by Sir Bill Callaghan, 13 September 2018)

The tensions between trade unions and Tony Blair's leadership were immediately reflected in the minimum wage debates (Leopold, 1997; Undy, 2002). At a private meeting in July 1994 of the 'Contact Group', the TUC leadership purportedly extracted a commitment from Blair that the minimum wage would be a central policy for the next election.

The price for the commitment was dropping the half-male median earnings formula (Coulter, 2009). The position brought the TUC leadership into conflict with a number of its affiliates, in particular UNISON as the largest trade union (see Table 4.1). Those trade unions in favour of a higher rate continued to press the TUC to formally adopt a figure significantly over £4 an hour based on the earnings formula. This position was now supported by the TGWU. In April 1994, half-median male earnings amounted to £4.15 an hour and two-thirds amounted to £5.53. Lord Morris, General Secretary of the TGWU, argued that the Labour leadership should commit itself to a rate of £4.05 an hour. However, sectional divisions persisted as Bill Jordan, President of the AEEU, contended that it would be 'wrong to place demands' on the Labour Party ahead of a general election (Clement, 1994). At the 1995 Labour Party Annual Conference, a motion was remitted which specified a minimum wage level at £4.15, in favour of a figure being set by a commission involving trade unions and businesses post-election (Leopold, 1997). The divisions continued at the September 1996 TUC Congress as a UNISON and the NUM motion proposed a minimum wage level of half-male median earning set at £4.26 an hour, which faced 'strong opposition' from the TUC General Council (McIlroy, 1998: 548–549). John Edmonds, General Secretary of the GMB, argued that support for a £4.26 minimum wage level could negatively affect the Labour Party's election prospects. In response, Rodney Bickerstaffe illustrated the ongoing tensions as he said: "We are not in the pockets of the Labour Party" (Ibid).

Table 4.1 Largest TUC-Affiliated and Labour Party–Affiliated Unions 1997

TUC Affiliation	1997	Labour Party Affiliation	1997
UNISON	1,374,583	UNISON	700,000
TGWU	884,669	GMB	700,000
AEEU	725,097	TGWU	500,000
GMB	718,139	AEEU	400,000
Manufacturing, Science and Finance (MSF)	425,103	USDAW	260,159
USDAW	290,170	Communication Workers Union	224,888
Top 6 % of Total	52.1%	Top 6 % of Total	85%
Total Unions	75	Total Unions	23
Total Affiliated Membership	6,756,544	Total Affiliated Membership	3,286,133

Source: Membership Statistics as reported in TUC Annual Report of 1997a and Table 5.1 of McIlroy (2009: 168).

Bickerstaffe emphasised that the divisions between trade unions based on sectoral lines hindered policy agreement on many areas including the minimum wage:

> Each group, for example, the public sector unions would take a particular line. The private sector another and there wasn't always agreement between the unions obviously. The AEEU and NUPE did not have a meeting on minds on a lot of areas.
>
> (Extract from Rodney Bickerstaffe, Interview 10)

Tony Dubbins, former General Secretary of the GPMU, acknowledged the lack of organisational emphasis placed on the minimum wage similarly to the AEEU. Both aforementioned unions contained strong craft membership compositions. This is not to suggest the minimum wage was not viewed as an important policy issue but that it was not a policy priority in the same way as it was for UNISON. Dubbins said:

> Frankly, as far as the GPMU was concerned, the national minimum wage was neither here nor there for us, although it latterly became very important when we started to face the issue of agency and temporary workers. That was not to say it was not important to the trade union movement as a whole, it was vital and fundamental to it but for us it was not priority issue. We certainly put more emphasis on legislative changes to protect the industrial base than setting up the national minimum wage.
>
> (Extract from Tony Dubbins, Interview 8)

Sir Bill Callaghan highlighted that following the publication of a TUC document titled 'Arguments for a National Minimum Wage', the divisions between trade unions had begun to 'soften' in the run-up to the 1997 general election:

> In 1995 the TUC published a document 'Arguments for a National Minimum Wage' and this was discussed at a conference that year. By this time the traditional arguments between the unions were beginning to soften and the national minimum wage has to be seen as part of the wider range of issues that the TUC was in discussion with the Labour Party.
>
> (Authorised notes by Sir Bill Callaghan, 13 September 2018)

The Labour Party general election manifesto in 1997 pledged to introduce new machinery through a commission that would set the minimum wage, "not on the basis of a rigid formula but according to the economic circumstances of the time and with the advice of an independent low pay commission" (The Labour Party, 1997). The TUC, in its 1997 general election campaign document 'Partners in Progress', complemented the pledge by affirming its commitment to social partnership: "The TUC recognises that the minimum wage will need to be set following discussions with the social partners and in line with the economic conditions at the time" (TUC—Partners for Progress, 1997b: 20). Nevertheless, splits continued as the FBU, UCATT and UNISON—all party affiliates—reiterated calls for a specified rate of £4.42 an hour in the run-in to the general election (Coulter, 2009: 10, Footnote 7). The TUC would eventually set out a wage target in the negotiations for all workers by the end of 1997 on over £4 per hour being a 'practical proposition' for those over the age of 18 (TUC General Council Report to Congress, 1998: 45). The CBI sought to exploit the fault lines among trade unions as the business group argued "even a low minimum wage would reduce job opportunities and create major problems for wage structures in a wide range of companies" (Metcalf, 1999: 173).

Sir Ian McCartney was put in charge of Labour's preparatory work for the minimum wage in advance of the 1997 general election. McCartney was subsequently appointed the Government Minister responsible at the Department of Trade and Industry (DTI) for policy implementation. Two groups were established to develop the proposals between 1994 and 1997. The first of these groups met weekly to work on implementation issues. The second group looked at the policy mechanics including coverage. The introduction of statutory minimum was extoled as ending the "scandal of poverty pay" (Coates, 2005: 87). A statutory minimum wage, it was argued, would also protect quality producers from being undercut on the basis of lower wages and terms and conditions. The approach followed on from the Trade Boards established at the turn of the 20th century, which were designed to provide a legally enforceable bottom-floor particularly in areas of the economy where trade unionism was weak (Howell, 2005: 69). McCartney reiterated the importance of the process, which engaged all social partners in advance of the 1997 general election:

> With the unions we established one—a body—which met on a weekly basis to think through the first 72 hours of a Labour Government to present to the Cabinet basically a draft Bill because I felt if we had not done this it would be a year or more wasted on just trying to draft a Bill. Do the thing now. We have waited 100 years we don't want to wait 100 days. That work was ongoing and I had to coordinate and develop it.
>
> (Extract from Sir Ian McCartney, Interview 14)

McCartney added:

> We also in the run up to the election created a body, not a shadow Low Pay Commission, but it was a group of people from the trade

union movement, the co-operative movement and from academia and social affairs who had an interest in low pay. We brought them all together. We did the final work on what the National Minimum Wage Bill would look like and that was important.

(Ibid)

Sir Brendan Barber, Deputy General Secretary of the TUC at this juncture, complemented McCartney's comments on the preparatory work through the following remarks:

> So, that period between '93 and '97 there was a lot of joint working with the Labour leadership to try and collaborate exactly how could these two flagship initiatives be shaped {National Minimum Wage and Employment Relations Act}. What was the best basis on which legislation could be framed and I had a lot of contact with people around the Labour leadership. A lot of people in the TUC were involved in this work not just John {Monks} as General Secretary and myself as Deputy General Secretary. Some other colleagues were particularly working on the minimum wage issue for example and some of the arguments that had to be addressed about that. What would the impact be on the labour market and on jobs and so on and so forth. Doing the backup research and intellectual work to support the position. And we worked closely with people like Ian McCartney who was particularly tasked on the minimum wage for example to kind of chair a working group to flesh out the proposals.
>
> So, there was a lot of work to actually do the kind of serious thinking like exactly what would the legislation look like. Exactly how might it work. So, it wasn't just a headline commitment there was some serious underpinning planning work that was done throughout that period so that when Labour came into office in '97 they were actually in a position to say to the officials in their department 'this is how we want to do it, we know what we're going to do and this is exactly how we want to do it and we've thought through the issues to a sufficient level of detail to be confident we've got a solid basis for proceeding'.

(Extract from Sir Brendan Barber, Interview 12)

Former Prime Minister and Chancellor Gordon Brown also emphasised the importance of the preparatory work during Labour's time in opposition with respect to the minimum wage:

> I recall prior to 1997 that the TGWU was not in favour of the minimum wage and it took some time for the union movement to agree with the NUPE and then the UNISON position on the national

minimum wage. This then moved on to become part of our manifesto. When we moved into government we moved with massive speed and the Minimum Wage Act came in very quickly. . . . This all showed, however, the process of consultation when being in opposition that when we moved into government these issues were being dealt with very quickly with a result that two million people had their wages raised when that legislation was in use.

(Extract from Gordon Brown, Interview 9)

The Low Pay Commission

The LPC would be the embodiment of the social partnership model of employment relations, which the Labour Party was attempting to foster (McIlroy, 2000; Undy, 2002; Ludlam and Taylor, 2003). The LPC's remit was designed to take into account the minimum wage's impact on the economy, competitiveness, low-paying sectors, the youth labour market and small firms. The government chose the members of the LPC and set its terms of reference establishing "almost complete freedom of action for the government" (Labour Research Department, April 2000a). The membership of the LPC, which was initially set up on a non-statutory basis, consisted of equal numbers of trade unionists, employers and academics (as independent members)—three of each (see Box D). The composition was designed on the basis that it would 'avoid polarisation' of the social partners (Brown, 2011: 408).

Box D **Initial Composition of the Low Pay Commission (July 1997)**

- Professor George Bain (Chairman) President and Vice-Chancellor, The Queen's University of Belfast.
- Professor William Brown Professor of Industrial Relations, University of Cambridge.
- Bill Callaghan, Chief Economist at TUC.
- John Cridland Director of Human Resources Policy, Confederation of British Industry.
- Lawrie Dewar, M.B.E. Chief Executive, Scottish Grocers' Federation.
- Rita Donaghy, UNISON Executive Council.
- Paul Gates, General Secretary, National Union of Knitwear, Footwear and Apparel Trades.
- Professor David Metcalf Professor of Industrial Relations, London School of Economics.
- Stephanie Monk Director of Human Resources, Granada Group plc.

According to Howell (2004: 7), the design and composition of the LPC "guaranteed that the level would be set well below what trade unions were asking for". The government also explicitly rejected the prospect of 'automatic uprating', which was prevalent in European nation states (Gennard, 2002: 584). It was in this context that the LPC was described as being "nothing more than a short-term tactical manoeuvre and a device to abandon the rather unhelpful 'half male median' formula" (Coats, 2007: 24). However, Sir Ian McCartney explained the rationale underpinning the government's approach:

> So, the creation of a Low Pay Commission was really very important. One, it got unions off the hook in having a percentage figure and that was the campaign and on to an approach on engagement with employers in advance of the election to campaign for a business case for the minimum wage because employers were wanting to treat their employees in the labour market fairly got undermined by employers who didn't. So, it was important we had a social and economic case for the minimum wage—so the 'Fat Cats' campaign became the popular bandwagon for that to happen—in the end people were too scared to campaign against because they would be called 'Fat Cats' and the unions played that role.
>
> (Extract from Sir Ian McCartney, Interview 14)

Tom Watson, Political Officer for the AEEU during the first-term Labour Government (1997–2001), highlighted the union's strong support for the social partnership approach. The AEEU position illustrated the fault lines between the largest unions in advance of any rate being set. Watson said:

> So, though there was a slight wariness about what the impacts of the minimum wage would be in the labour market chain. There was certainly space for an institution to resolve what the rate should be. It was considered the right way that the employers and unions should sit around a table with the government to resolve it. Of course, this was different to a lot of the other unions who were very concerned that the employers would try and water down or someway undermine the rate.
>
> (Extract from Tom Watson, Interview 15)

Dave Prentis, General Secretary of UNISON, drew attention to the differences between trade unions but emphasised that the government's overriding concern was how a wage rate might affect the government's relationship with the business community. Prentis added:

> The challenges were well one for a number of years before we got it a number of trade unions were against they were worried about

the effects on differentials {rates of pay}. The Labour leaders were worried about the cost and that's why we finished it with the Low Pay Commission, which had academics, employers as well as trade unions.

(Extract from Dave Prentis, Interview 16)

The LPC launched its wide-ranging inquiry into low pay after its terms of reference were announced on 23 September 1997. The process involved gathering over 600 pieces of written evidence and visiting different parts of Great Britain and Northern Ireland to examine the practicalities of the minimum wage for those involved in its implementation and enforcement (Taylor, 1998). These dynamics cumulatively contributed to the 'extreme caution' by which the government would approach the rate and extent of cover as the negotiations developed over the details of the minimum wage (Towers, 1999: 83).

Policy Contestation and Division

Within 'days' of Labour's election victory, Tony Blair reportedly 'mobilised' social partners due to the leadership's concerns over the impact of the pledge. There emerged a view in key sections of the government that the Labour Party had been 'bounced' into the policy by previous Labour Party Annual Conference commitments (Brown, 2011: 406). Flowing from this perspective, Peter Mandelson MP, Trade and Industry Secretary, was reported to have launched an "extensively reported behind-the-scenes campaign for a variegated national minimum wage: one sensitive to the differing needs of firms of different size, region and sector" (Coates, 2005: 89). Cabinet papers leaked to *The Guardian* newspaper in November 1997 appeared to substantiate these claims as Margaret Beckett MP, President of the Board of Trade, purportedly 'clashed' with Mandelson over the proposal that ministers should have the flexibility to introduce wide-ranging exemptions (Milne, 1997).

In a successful outcome for trade unions, the efforts to consider the ability to vary the rate according to region, sector, occupation or company size were ruled out. This outcome was perceived as a 'clear victory' for Sir Ian McCartney as internal debates played out inside the government (Taylor, 1998: 298). However, manoeuvres to challenge the scope of the minimum wage persisted. In October 1997, John Monks as TUC General Secretary described attempts to apply a lower national minimum wage to under-25s as 'dynamite'. The remark was in response to Monks sharing a platform with Mandelson at a Labour Party Annual Conference fringe meeting, with the latter stating that a different statutory minimum 'will' apply to young workers. Mandelson added that the Labour Government's policy could provide a 'disincentive' for young people to stay on in education and training, and curtail employment (Clement, 1997).

In this contested environment, Frank Doran, who was the Parliamentary Private Secretary to Sir Ian McCartney at the DTI, noted the importance of the TUG in parliament as a key mechanism in conjunction with informal processes. These informal and formal processes were essential to exercising political pressure on the Labour leadership to prevent policy dilution. Doran said:

> There was a process, which had been agreed, which was to set up the Low Pay Commission and there were issues regarding the appointments to the Commission and who was the Chair. So, they were getting to set the rate and that helped take the issue out of the debate to a certain extent. Then there was the mechanism, once legislation is drafted and published, there is a huge process of feedback and regular meetings were held with the unions. Most of these meetings were formal but there were informal processes that we used as well. To be fair most of the battles we had were not with the unions but they were with our own people. There were ministers who had been briefed by their officials that such and such a section of the legislation could damage a particular part of their brief and they were obliged to present these views. There was a lot of toing and froing with Downing Street and a lot of the time Ian {McCartney} and myself—sometimes with officials and sometimes without them—would be locked in a room with one of the emissaries from Downing Street and we would argue these issues through.
>
> We did set up a form of informal processes with the Trade Union Group of Labour MPs and Gerry Sutcliffe was the Chair at the time and either Ian or I would talk to Gerry if we had a particular issue with Downing Street. We would arrange to have a meeting with the Trade Union Group and key people would be invited. We always had John Monks who was the main contact in the trade union side on this and of course there were individual unions with their own area of interest on this. But, I got the impression that the unions were relatively relaxed about the process which we had put in place. As I said, the main issue was going to be the level. We had these meetings when there was any difficulty and I think we had six of them and these were on areas when we had difficulty in getting our point across let me put it that way.
>
> (Extract from Frank Doran, Interview 17)

The National Minimum Wage Bill was published on 27 November 1997. The Bill confirmed that there would be a single national rate applicable to all regions, sectors and sizes of firm. The draft legislation although did permit the possibility for a lower rate or exclusion for young people aged under 26, which the LPC would consider and report to the government on its final recommendations by May 1998. Any exceptions or modifications to the draft legislation would be made by secondary legislation.

The pay arrangements of service personnel and reservists would be excluded on this basis as 'clause 34' was removed from the Bill. The Armed Forces Pay Review Body would now deal with this aspect. The President of the Board of Trade, Margaret Beckett, had initially written to John Redwood, the Conservatives' industry spokesman, in January 1998 to indicate that the Bill would cover "all workers in the United Kingdom above compulsory school age". Sir Ian McCartney informed the standing committee on the National Minimum Wage Bill on 3 February 1998 that an exemption would be forthcoming. The amendment to the Bill was reportedly a 'defeat' for the DTI in the face of demands from the Ministry of Defence (Abrams, 1998). However, McCartney offered an alternative perspective on this aspect of the negotiations:

> But, we did have to on some occasions outwit people. The one that sticks in my mind. The minimum wage covered non-officer ranks in the armed forces. There has always been a running theme of not allowing trade unions to have a foothold in the armed services. I knew if we inserted a clause in the Bill to cover the armed services it would be immediately flagged up. We got the clause in through the Cabinet and Number Ten. But, then we started getting the phone calls in quite early on from the Secretary of State for Defence, George Robertson. He wasn't threatening but basically he said the armed forces leadership were very concerned and worried about this. There were two strategies. One, to resist and the second one was once we had done that the Ministry of Defence would be amenable to me offering them something—and that's what I did. We resisted them over a few days.
>
> (Extract from Sir Ian McCartney, Interview 18)

McCartney added:

> Margaret Beckett was excellent and very supportive and then our agreed strategy was to say that we would put our hands up at some point and say: 'Ok if you are asking me to take this clause out, then OK but let's be clear then we want a letter put into the debate in parliament clearly stating that the pay review bodies who are responsible for these areas will be required to acknowledge they won't pay less than the minimum wage in the future'. So, this gave us the opportunity to do something, which allowed them to think that they had won but we established a key area with a problematic employer.
>
> (Ibid)

Agricultural workers would also be exempted, as the wages for those working in the sector were to be set by the Agricultural Wages Boards under the Agricultural Wages Orders. In a similar fashion to the armed services, where the agricultural minimum wage was higher than the minimum wage, the agricultural worker would be entitled to that higher rate but at a rate lower than the minimum wage, then this would have to be raised to the forthcoming statutory levels. In May 1998, the first report of the LPC recommended a minimum rate of £3.70 per hour to be introduced in June 2000 with an interim rate of £3.60 from April 1999. The LPC further proposed for those aged 18–20 a development rate of £3.20 per hour from April 1999 increasing to £3.30 in June 2000. All those aged 16 and 17 together with those on apprenticeships it was proposed should be exempt.

George Bain, Chair of the LPC, who incidentally served on the Bullock Committee as part of the Social Contract process, stated a number of critical differences existed between the two processes. In contrast with the Bullock Committee, Bain identified that the LPC produced a unanimous report signed by all its members. In addition, unlike the Bullock report, the recommendations of the LPC received a comparatively favourable reception from the media, business and the trade unions. A further factor acknowledged by Bain as a tactic deployed by the government was the commissioners were not leaders of their organisation, in particular on the trade union side (Bain, 29 November 2001). The ambition of the approach was to dilute the potential for rigid lines on a rate and to potentially avoid leaders from the trade union side who were ambivalent towards the policy supporting a lower rate due to pressure from elements in the Labour leadership.

As feared by strong proponents of the NMW, the attempts to apply a lower minimum wage to the under-25s proved successful. Rodney Bickerstaffe further noted that more than 40 per cent of the UNISON's members earned less than £4.42 as he cited government pressure put on the LPC to dilute the extent and rate of the minimum wage. The UNISON leader said,

> The Commission has had unparalleled pressure put on them by the government to ensure it's a low figure. I hope it doesn't take as long to get a decent level as it took to get the minimum wage established in the first place.
>
> (BBC, 1998)

Lord Monks welcomed the proposals as "a milestone in twentieth century industrial relations" and intimated that without consensus, the interim rate would have been less than £3.60 (*Financial Times*, 1998 cited in Metcalf, 1999: 193). Sir Bill Callaghan, as one of the three trade union appointees to the LPC, acknowledged the veracity of Monks' comments in the following remarks:

> The view of the three trade union members on the Low Pay Commission was that better to have unanimous agreement on the initial level

of the National Minimum Wage as a starting point on which to build on, rather than have an open split which could have jeopardised the long run future of the Low Pay Commission.

(Authorised notes by Sir Bill Callaghan, 13 September 2018)

Margaret Beckett MP, in response to the LPC's recommendations, outlined some key changes from the LPC's recommendations in parliament on 18 June 1998. The changes entailed an adult minimum wage for those aged 22 and over at £3.60 per hour. The government decided to set an initial youth rate for 18–21-year-olds at £3.00 per hour, which would increase to £3.20 per hour in June 2000. The LPC was asked to 'review' the position of 21-year-olds in 1999 and provide further advice on whether from June 2000 "they might move to the full adult rate". A £3.20 per hour rate was introduced for accredited trainees. The government's basis for modifying the LPC's recommendations was as follows:

> We are however at a critical point in the economic cycle. The Government is determined to proceed with all due caution with the introduction of that rate, especially for the crucial group of those aged 18–21.
>
> (Beckett, 18 June 1998)

On the basis of the prior terms, the National Minimum Wage Act was passed in July 1998. The statutory rates at introduction were provisionally estimated to positively impact 1.9 million workers the equivalent to 8.3 per cent of the total workforce with the majority of those to benefit being low-paid women (1.4 million). Ludlam and Taylor (2003: 737) cited the 'sharp disagreements' which persisted after the introduction of the legislation. The most contentious element was the decision to implement the youth rate of £3.00 an hour, which was condemned by trade union leaders as "an endorsement of workplace poverty" (McIlroy, 2000: 7). The TUC General Council Report (1998: 4) underlined its disappointment with the extent and scope of the legislation as it stated "the rates agreed by the Commission fall short of what we believe the economy can afford as well as what the low paid deserve. And the Government's modifications to the rates for young people were very disappointing". The TUC unanimously agreed a £4.61 target figure. The TGWU also in response launched a '£5 now' campaign as Lord Morris declared "thank you for the principle, shame about the rate" before adding that taxpayers would continue to "subsidise bad employers, while the low paid sink deeper and deeper into the poverty trap" (People Management Editorial, 1998). Sir Ian McCartney responded to the criticisms over the differentiated age rates and the introductory levels by providing revelatory insights into the inter-departmental government differences in relation to the rates and the role of the LPC itself:

> There were people in Treasury including Ministers in the Treasury who wanted the Low Pay Commission to be a temporary body. So, we ensured in the Act that it was statutory body and it's still here today.[4] It is absolutely true that the Treasury and its leadership took a very active interest in what the level of minimum wage would be. But, the fact that we argued and won the case in opposition to firstly establish a Low Pay Commission meant that it was critically important that the body was able to put forward proposals that fundamentally the government would accept. In the end the recommended rate was £3.60 but the Treasury wanted a rate between £3.20 and £3.50 so the Treasury didn't get its way. The £3.60 was a victory for the TUC and also the CBI resisting pressure, not from me as I had pressure on me from other places, but they stuck to their guns.
>
> (Extract from Sir Ian McCartney, Interview 18)

McCartney added:

> During the process, we had regular meetings with the Treasury, sometimes a Minister with their special advisor, who was Ed Balls, they were worried and concerned that the minimum wage would be inflationary. This was a failure of the party at every general election not to put an economic case for the minimum wage and we couldn't robustly challenge Tory allegations on job losses and all the rest of it. In the end, around 10,000 people who should have qualified for the minimum wage didn't, which is what I pointed out to Gordon {Brown} and others on the 21 years old and under aspect. It wasn't worth a candle to the Treasury but from my point of view it was 10,000 people against the bigger picture of 1 1/2 million to 2 million people benefiting from the minimum wage. So, in the end it went through in the way it did.
>
> (Ibid)

Evaluation and Reflections

The recommendations of the LPC were evidently "closer to the original stated position of business" (Howell, 2004: 7). The observation is based on a low initial level for the minimum wage, an exemption of young people 16–17 years old and an 18–21-year-old rate youth rate. Bewley (2006: 358–359) added that the government's rejection of the LPC's recommendation to reduce the age at which the adult minimum wage was applicable "implied that addressing discrimination against the young was not a priority". Further concerns over the strength of the framework related to the fines for non-compliance also being set at a low level and an associated lack of inspectors for enforcement purposes (Smith, 2009). The offences included refusal or wilful neglect to pay the NMW, failing to keep records, keeping false records, producing false records, intentionally obstructing an enforcement officer and refusing to give information to an enforcement officer. In addition, a third party who commissioned any refusal to pay the NMW or a failure to keep records was guilty of an offence. Metcalf (1999) identified that despite enforcement officers having the power to prosecute six criminal offences, the maximum fine for each offence being set at only £5,000 did not act as an effective deterrent.

The LPC complemented these emergent weaknesses citing a 'significant number' of workers who had been dismissed due to demanding the relevant rate. The commission reported 23 per cent of callers to its minimum wage advice line said they either had been denied the rate or had some reduction in terms and conditions due to receiving £3–£3.60 per hour (Kelso, 1999). The LPC's concerns were substantiated by the helpline statistics as over 200,000 calls by November 2000 had been received with 5,500 registered complaints of underpayment since it opened in January 1999. According to the published annual report (1999–2000), hairdressing and hotels (16 per cent) and catering and other services (14 per cent each) accounted for the largest proportion of complaints. A further 300,000 jobs were reportedly paid less than the minimum wage rates in April 2000 (Labour Research Department, November 2000). The impact on prices arising from implementation was also negligible as the annual rate of inflation fell to 1.8 per cent in February 2001. This was the lowest level since the current system of measuring consumer prices began in 1976 (*BBC*, 2001). The LPC noted "employment effects were reported in only a small minority of firms" (Labour Research Department, April 2000b). The pay body drew attention to the fact that in some of the sectors disproportionately affected by the implementation of the minimum wage—retail, hospitality and business services—employment increased in the year to June 1999. The statistics gave legitimacy to the assertion that the framework was representative of a minimalist approach by the Labour Government.

Concerns grew within the trade union movement that the NMW was being allowed to 'wither on the vine' due to there being no index link and automatic uprating process (Coates, 2005: 89–90). In this context, the TUC General Council Report to Congress (2000: 45) reiterated its "strong disappointment that the initial rate was set so low". Accordingly, the TUC raised its minimum wage target to £5 per hour. The position in Britain mirrored another classic LME—the United States—where no automatic system of adjustment existed. In the United States, there were long periods such as between January 1981 and April 1990 when the minimum wage was not increased. In real terms in 2000, it was worth only four-fifths of what it was worth in 1979. The position in another LME—Canada—was similar in that there was no indexation or automatic updating. These points lent support to the view that "movements in the minimum wage maybe more susceptible to the composition of government than otherwise" (Metcalf, 1999: 187).

Box E European Minimum Wages in April 2000

- **France**—the wage was raised by inflation plus at least half the average increase in earnings; interim increases if prices have risen by more than 2 per cent since the last rise. In April 2000, the last rise was 1.24 per cent.
- **Netherlands**—increased in line with average pay deals. The last rise in 2000 was equivalent to 2.6 per cent over twelve months.
- **Luxembourg**—the wage increased in line with other pay settlements, which were index-linked to prices. The government regularly reviewed the overall level taking account of "the development of general economic conditions and incomes". In January 1999, the rate was put up by 1.3 per cent and the index-linked rise was put up a further 2.5 per cent in 1999.
- **Spain**—the government had to take account of a number of factors including prices, economic growth and labour's share of the national income. In practice, the minimum wage increased by the government's estimate of inflation for the coming year. In January 2000, this meant a 2.0 per cent increase.
- **Portugal**—the government took into account a number of general economic factors, but also it had to reduce existing differentials. This led to increases in the minimum wage above inflation—4.1 per cent in both January 1999 and January 2000 at a time when price rises were 2.5 per cent (1999) and 1.9 per cent (2000), respectively.
- **Belgium**—the wage increase depended on the national framework pay deal for the economy. There was a rise of 5.9 per cent over two years from January 1999. This included subsequent pay increases index-linked to prices.
- **Greece**—in April 2000, increases were agreed in the national agreement, which were 'normally' negotiated every two years. In 1998–99, the agreement provided for a 1.4 per cent rise in the first half of 1999 and a further 1.4 per cent increase in the second half.
- **Ireland**—increases were included in the national deal—'Programme for Prosperity and Fairness'. A national minimum wage of Irish Pound £4.40 per hour was introduced in Ireland in April 2000 under the National Minimum Wage Act 2000. As part of the agreement, on 1 July 2001, the minimum wage was increased to £4.70 per hour.

Source: Labour Research Department (April 2000a).

The position in Britain, however, contrasted strongly with most other European states at the juncture of its implementation where there were established rules and guidelines governing the uprating process (see Box E). In this context, trade union disappointment was fuelled by the government's failure to uprate the minimum wage in line with inflation as occurred in European states. In October 2000, the minimum wage increased by 2.78 per cent, which was equivalent to an annual increase of 1.85 per cent. The figure was below the level of price increases (2.0 per cent January 2000) and below increases in overall earnings (6.2 per cent December 1999) (Labour Research Department, April 2000a). The 10p increase in October 2000 provoked an angry response from trade unions. The resultant effect was that in October 2001, the government approved an increase by 40p to £4.10 but only after trade union lobbying in the run-up to the 2001 general election as part of the Exeter Labour Party NPF process, as Chapter 6 on the Warwick Agreement will discuss.

Box F **National Minimum Wage Rates in 2000–02**

- In October 2000, the adult rate was raised to £3.70 and the development rate to £3.20.
- In October 2001, the adult rate was increased to £4.10, and the development rate to £3.50.
- In October 2002, the adult rate was further increased to £4.20, and the development rate to £3.60.

The TUC General Secretary, John Monks, described the 40p increase as "another significant step towards a decent minimum wage" but reiterated the adult rate should be extended to over-18s. The AEEU 'welcomed' the decision to uprate the minimum wage, which was slightly at variance with other major trade unions such as UNISON who warned—correctly, as it would materialise—that the rise to £4.10 would be achieved at the expense of future rises (Labour Research Department, April 2001). The 40p rise was followed by a post-election 10p rise in October 2002 (see Box F). Thereafter, the adult rate rose to £4.85 per hour for adults from October 2004 and to £4.10 for 18–21-year-old workers preceding the 2005 general election. A new £3.00 an hour rate was also introduced for 16–17-year-olds, as coverage was also extended to homeworkers. Regulation 2 of the NMW had originally exempted work done by a member of the family, either in the form of domestic chores in the family household, or as a contribution to the family business. The exemption had also covered workers (such as au pairs) who were not family members but, nevertheless, lived with a family. It would take until October 2010 for the adult rate to be finally extended to workers aged 21 at a rate of £5.93

per hour by which point Labour would be out of power. Dave Prentis, General Secretary of UNISON, reflected on the minimum wage framework, viewing it as a qualified success but lamented the level at which it was originally set:

> So, although we achieved the minimum wage and it's statutory, it applies to everybody which is a big achievement, it was set at a level which was too low. The argument was that jobs would go. The truth is that jobs increased in the years after the minimum wage. It was a false argument. It meant that the minimum wage was set at a low level and it also didn't really account for the cost of living in London compared with somewhere else which was a major issue for us. But, the reality was we achieved an objective. But, the level was not what it should have been and ever since then we've campaigned for the 'living wage'. So, UNISON started the campaign for a living wage and then it's taken up gradually. We started it in 1999/2000, and gradually it's getting some traction now. But, we wouldn't have had to have the campaign for the living wage if the minimum wage had have been set at the right level.
>
> (Extract from Dave Prentis, Interview 16)

Sir Ian McCartney in response to the criticisms over the initial rates cited the divisions between trade unions as being a contributory factor:

> It is true that some unions legitimately would like to have seen the minimum wage being set for those eighteen years and over but there were other unions such as craft unions who at the last minute agreed to go along with the minimum wage as part of the process of winning the general election but had little or no sympathy for the minimum wage. So, it was about managing all of this including those who said 'so far but no further' in terms of collective bargaining.
>
> (Extract from Sir Ian McCartney, Interview 18)

McCartney added:

> It was caution {initial rates}. I don't think people realise how scarred we {Labour} had become with previous situations in election after election where the party had failed to be robust enough to put the case for the minimum wage. There was the case of a hairdresser who was put up to ask a question to Tony Blair and he couldn't answer the question about the impact of the minimum wage in the hairdressing sector regarding the effect on employment. John Prescott was previously put up in the 1992 election and basically said if we lose jobs due to the minimum wage 'so be it' and companies who don't want to pay the minimum wage 'shouldn't be in business', that's a

loose paraphrase of what was said. In many ways, we gave up the argument and proved the Tories were right.

(Ibid)

The Labour Government's endeavour to cultivate a strong relationship with the business community advanced through the social partnership approach was paramount. John Edmonds of the GMB identified Tony Blair's resistance to strengthening the framework due to its perceived negative impact on the interests of business: "He [Blair] was so reluctant to introduce the minimum wage but it didn't stop him boasting about it afterwards when belatedly he realised it was popular" (Extract from John Edmonds, Interview 6). Dave Prentis complemented this perspective in the following remarks:

> So, near towards the end the unions had come on board, whether or not we put enough pressure on the Labour Government to put it high enough I don't think unions argued against it being at a high level, it was more the Labour leadership who didn't want to upset big business.
>
> (Extract from Dave Prentis, Interview 16)

Jon Cruddas also drew attention to the policy contestation over the terms of the LPC and the minimum wage regulations, which played out inside the government as the negotiations evolved. As part of the internal-party bargaining process, Cruddas identified the role of the TUG in parliament, TULO and informal processes as key levers of pressure on the Labour leadership. These levers counteracted further policy dilution. Cruddas echoed McCartney's previous comments on the role of the Treasury and the Prime Minister's Office with respect to debates over the statutory role of the LPC:

> Some elements within Downing Street, the CBI and Treasury wanted to wreck the Low Pay Commission but we had people in there to keep it together and to keep a united position. All of those things which are the product of normal negotiations. Strategically, I think we did alright, and to be honest I think it was the high watermark of union influence on the Labour Government in terms of delivering durable policy outcomes.
>
> (Extract from Jon Cruddas, Interview 19)

Cruddas added:

> So, from time to time, to put it bluntly, there was a need for the Trade Union Group in parliament and the TULO processes as well to put the pressure up. So, there was a series of informal and formal

mechanisms, customs and networks. How this actually works is a very interesting and elusive thing but it does work through protocol but also informal processes and lateral relationships. The hidden hardwiring of it all: personalities and how people perceive their own role.

(Ibid)

Gerry Sutcliffe, as former Secretary of the TUG in parliament during the first -term, added that if the body were not in situ alongside other pressure levers then there would have been greater opportunities to dilute the NMW's scope in terms of cover and rates. In Labour's first term, over 350 MPs belonged to individual unions' parliamentary groups. The TUG regularly met with the national TULO committee, which included the general secretaries of all affiliated unions and as such "provided unions with a lever in parliament to exercise influence" (Ludlam and Taylor, 2003: 735). Sutcliffe indicated that group contestation ultimately influenced the Labour leadership's approach:

Yes, we were able to influence the Prime Minister's thinking on employment issues such as the National Minimum Wage, Family Friendly policies, and there were a whole raft of policy areas that Labour did in principle want to introduce but the Trade Union Group ensured that we were able to push harder for those successes.

(Extract from Gerry Sutcliffe, Interview 20)

There is a strong body in the academic literature, which argues that the NMW was a "reflection of the industrial weakness of trade unions" (Simpson, 1999: 30). Ludlam et al. (December 2003: 611) further argued that the legislation was illustrative of a 'weaker' labour movement as trade unions "sought refuge in more subordinate roles under the banner of 'social partnership', and in the pursuit of statute-based protection for individual workers". Moreover, Howell and Kolins Given (2011: 247) emphasised that the NMW framework "perfectly exemplifies the replacement of a collective institution with an individualised one, one focused on protecting the floor rather than negotiating a higher ceiling". Despite these cogent academic critiques, it cannot be refuted that partial re-regulation is to be found in the NMW. The contributions by actors also illustrate the significance of informal processes and forms of group coordination, which positively shaped the NMW outcomes from a trade union perspective. The legislation is viewed as a qualified success by leading trade union actors, despite disappointment over its extent and scope. By 2001, the LPC in its 'Third Report Volume One' (2001) reported that the policy had benefited around 1.3 million workers with around 70 per cent of the beneficiaries estimated to be women. The policy had contributed towards a narrowing of the gender pay gap between men and women. Ewing (2005: 15) perceptively noted that the NMW illustrated the role of collective bargaining through a regulatory process, which in the "past was performed in part by national bargaining and wage councils". Viewed through this wider economic lens, trade union political action did influence the terms of the framework and can be considered critical to attaining employment relations outcomes in a liberal market economy. In a fascinating contribution, Sir Ian McCartney responded to criticisms over the lack of progress in regard to elements in the NMW framework after its implementation and the role of the LPC. McCartney acknowledged the frustrations of trade unions regarding the failure to learn and build upon the legislation in a more speedy fashion. Specifically, McCartney attributed this to a lack of 'intellectual awareness' in the Labour Government as its time in power progressed:

> I think we [{Labour} got ourselves into the situation where before the end of Gordon Brown's tenure in government a significant number of people in the front bench did not have any intellectual awareness of the case for the minimum wage.[5] We got ourselves into the situation in 2013 under Ed Miliband where we were claiming the successes of the policy but were also offering up a policy of a poorly paying employer agreeing to set up on the basis of an incoming Labour Government giving tax incentives. Alongside this was a statement saying we wanted to reduce in-work benefits. It was a ludicrous position whereby we were giving a cash incentive to a bad employer and at best the really poor employee wouldn't receive a single extra penny for their work—and a huge proportion would earn less. That for me was the moment when people in the movement forgot what the fight was about.
>
> (Extract from Sir Ian McCartney, Interview 18)

Labour Leader Ed Miliband, in November 2013, planned to offer firms a 12-month tax break in 2016 if they agreed to pay the 'living wage'. At the juncture, the 'living wage' was set at £8.55 an hour in London and £7.45 an hour in the rest of Great Britain and Northern Ireland. The national minimum wage was at £6.31 an hour for adults and £5.03 for those aged 18–21 (*BBC*, 2013). The policy featured in Labour's general election manifesto 'Britain Can Be Better' (2015: 23), as the party pledged to increase the NMW to more than £8 an hour by October 2019 and to introduce 'Make Work Pay' contracts to provide tax rebates to firms becoming living wage employers.

The presentation of the NMW has provided insightful perspectives from actors intimately involved in the negotiations, implementation and regulation of the framework. The perspectives support the assertion that the terms of the NMW framework would have been weaker without group pressure. Through formal and informal processes, trade unions working in partnership with supportive Labour ministers and advisors achieved checks on efforts to further dilute the framework. Concomitant with this observation is the palpable sense of disappointment with the strength of the initial framework by trade union actors. The principal factors of influence identified as shaping the development of the NMW are trade union ideology, the strategic choices of union leaders and the strategy of the state. The cumulative effects of these factors contributed to fault lines and collective action problems among trade unions. Ultimately, these factors combined to produce a weaker framework than many trade union and Labour Government actors sought.

Notes

1. In 1992, the AUEW merged with the EETPU. The new union took the name Amalgamated Engineering and Electrical Union (AEEU). For the purposes of consistency, AEEU will be used through chapter.
2. Vehicle Builders union resolution in 1946 called for a statutory minimum wage, which received 2,657,000 votes, whereas those opposing the resolution cast 3,522,000 votes to defeat it—TUC Congress Report 1946 cited in Panitch (1976: 17–18).
3. Opportunity Britain. Labour's better way for the 1990's' (1991) cited in Lourie (17 January 1995: 6).
4. The role of the LPC was confirmed in legislation by the NMW (1998).
5. Gordon Brown succeeded Tony Blair as Labour Leader on 24 June 2007 and as Prime Minister on 27 June 2007 in an uncontested leadership election process until the general election defeat in 2010.

Bibliography

Abrams, F. (4 February 1998). *Armed forces will be exempt from the minimum wage after Whitehall row.* Available at: www.independent.co.uk/news/armed-forces-will-be-exempt-from-the-minimum-wage-after-whitehall-row-1142773.html [Accessed 15 Mar. 2018].

Bain, G. (29 November 2001). *Speech on The Bullock Committee and the Low Pay Commission: Some reflections.* University of Warwick. Available at: www.instituteforgovernment.org.uk/sites/default/files/sir_george_bain_minimum_wage_speech.pdf [Accessed 12 Sept. 2016].

BBC (28 May 1998). Low Pay Commission recommends £3.60. Available at: http://news.bbc.co.uk/1/hi/uk/101783.stm [Accessed 22 Sept. 2015].

BBC (13 February 2001). UK inflation at record low. Available at: http://news.bbc.co.uk/1/hi/business/1167696.stm [Accessed 30 Sept. 2015].

BBC (3 November 2013). Ed Miliband pledges living wage tax breaks for firms. Available at: www.bbc.co.uk/news/uk-24786397 [Accessed 4 April 2018].

Beckett, M. (18 June 1998). *The government's response to the first report of the low pay commission.* Statement by Margaret Beckett, President of the Board of Trade, on the Low Pay Commission Report. Available at: http://webarchive.nationalarchives.gov.uk/20030524052609/http://dti.gov.uk/er/lowpay/response.htm [Accessed 12 Sept. 2016].

Bewley, H. (2006). Raising the standard? The regulation of employment, and public sector employment policy. *British Journal of Industrial Relations*, 44(2), pp. 351–372.

Brown, W. (2011). Industrial relations in Britain under New Labour, 1997–2010: A post mortem. *Journal of Industrial Relations*, 53(3), pp. 402–413.

Callaghan, B. (12 September 2018). Authorised written notes via email communication.

Clement, B. (10 May 1994). *Labour delay on minimum wage rate.* Available at: www.independent.co.uk/news/uk/politics/labour-delay-on-minimum-wage-rate-1434866.html [Accessed 15 Jan. 2016].

Clement, B. (2 October 1997). Labour conference: Minimum wage to be lower for younger workers. *The Independent.* Available at: www.independent.co.uk/news/labour-conference-minimum-wage-to-be-lower-for-younger-workers-1233428.html [Accessed 16 Jan. 2016].

Coates, D. (2005). *Prolonged labour: The slow birth of New Labour Britain.* Houndmills, Basingstoke: Palgrave Macmillan.

Coats, D. (2007). *The national minimum wage: Retrospect and prospect.* London: The Work Foundation.

Coulter, S. (March 2009). Lobbying for change: Labour market policymaking in a liberal market economy. Paper for LSE Conference, *Emerging research in political economy and public policy.* Available at: www.lse.ac.uk/europeanInstitute/events/2008-09/Coulter.pdf [Accessed 12 Oct., Dec. 2015].

Ewing, D.K. (March 2005). The function of trade unions. *Industrial Law Journal*, 34(1), pp. 1–22.

Gennard, J. (2002). Employee relations public policy development 1997–2001: A break with the past? *Employee Relations*, 24(6), pp. 581–594.

Heery, E. (2005). *Trade unionism under New Labour.* The Shirley Lerner Memorial Lecture 2005. Manchester Industrial Relations Society.

Heffernan, R. (2011). Labour's New Labour legacy: Politics after Blair and Brown. *Political Studies Review*, (9), pp. 163–177.

Howell, C. (1998). Restructuring British public sector industrial relations: State policies and trade union responses. *Policy Studies Journal*, 26(2), pp. 293–309.

Howell, C. (March 2004). Is there a third way for industrial relations? *British Journal of Industrial Relations*, 42(1), pp. 1–22.

Howell, C. (2005). *Trade unions and the state: The construction of industrial relations institutions in Britain, 1890–2000.* Princeton: Princeton University Press.

Howell, C. and Kolins Givan, R. (June 2011). Rethinking institutions and institutional change in European industrial relations. *British Journal of Industrial Relations*, 49(2), pp. 231–255.

Kelso, P. (2 October 1999). Workers still losing out on minimum wage. *The Guardian.* Available at: www.theguardian.com/uk/1999/oct/02/paulkelso [Accessed 3 Nov. 2015].

Labour Party (1996). *Press office: Voting strength and delegation size at Labour Party Conference.* London: The Labour Party.

Labour Party (1997). *New Labour, because Britain deserves better.* London: The Labour Party.

Labour Party (2015). *Britain can be better.* London: The Labour Party.

Labour Research Department (April 2000a). *How Europe raises its minimum.* London: Labour Research Department.

Labour Research Department (April 2000b). *Minimum wage fears unfounded.* London: Labour Research Department.

Labour Research Department (November 2000). *Ups and downs of national minimum wage.* London: Labour Research Department.

Labour Research Department (April 2001). *Unions mixed on minimum wage.* London: Labour Research Department.

Leopold, J.W. (March 1997). Trade unions, political fund ballots and the Labour Party. *British Journal Industrial Relations*, 35(1), pp. 23–38.

Lourie, J. (17 January 1995). *A minimum wage.* Research Paper (95/7). Available at: http://researchbriefings.files.parliament.uk/documents/RP95-7/RP95-7.pdf [Accessed 15 Nov. 2015].

Low Pay Commission (March 2001). *Third report volume one.* Available at: http://webarchive.nationalarchives.gov.uk/20130708093628/www.lowpay.gov.uk/lowpay/report/pdf/report3.pdf [Accessed 2 Mar. 2018].

Ludlam, S. and Taylor, A. (December 2003). The political representation of the labour interest in Britain. *British Journal of Industrial Relations*, 41(4), pp. 727–749.

Ludlam, S., Wood, S., Heery, E. and Taylor, A. (December 2003). Politics and employment relations. *British Journal of Industrial Relations*, 41(4), pp. 609–616.

Maass, G. (Winter 2001). Trade unions and the British model of industrial relations in a fragile period of transition. *European Review of Labour and Research*, 4(1), pp. 740–745.

Marsh, D. (1992). *The new politics of British trade unionism: Union power and the Thatcher legacy.* Houndmills, Hampshire: Macmillan Press.

McIlroy, J. (December 1998). The enduring alliance? Trade unions and the making of New Labour 1994–7. *British Journal of Industrial Relations*, 36(4), pp. 537–564.

McIlroy, J. (2000). The new politics of pressure—the Trades Union Congress and New Labour in government. *Industrial Relations Journal*, 31(1), pp. 2–16.

McIlroy, J. (2009). Under stress but still enduring: The contentious alliance in the age of Tony Blair and Gordon Brown. In: G. Daniels and J. McIlroy, eds., *Trade unions in a neoliberal world: British trade unions under New Labour.* London: Routledge.

Metcalf, D. (1999). The British national minimum wage. *British Journal of Industrial Relations*, 37(2), pp. 171–201.

Metcalf, D. (2005). *British unions: Resurgence or perdition?* London: The Work Foundation.

Milne, S. (28 November 1997). Beckett wins pay fight. *The Guardian.* Available at: www.theguardian.com/politics/1997/nov/28/past [Accessed 12 Oct. 2015].

Minkin, L. (1992). *Contentious alliance: Trade unions and the Labour Party.* Edinburgh: Edinburgh University Press Limited.

Panitch, L. (1976). *Social democracy and industrial militancy.* Cambridge: The Labour Party, the Trade Unions and Incomes Policy, 1945–1974.

People Management Editorial (1 October 1998). *TUC conference—union bosses despair at minimum wage 'betrayal'.* Available at: www.cipd.co.uk/

pm/peoplemanagement/b/weblog/archive/2013/01/29/4572a-1998-10.aspx [Accessed 3 Oct. 2014].

Simpson, B. (1999). A milestone in the legal regulation of pay: The National Minimum Wage Act 1998. *Industrial Law Journal*, 28(1), pp. 1–32.

Smith, P. (2009). New Labour and the commonsense of neoliberalism: Trade unionism, collective bargaining and workers' rights. *Industrial Relations Journal*, 40(4), pp. 337–355.

Smith, P. and Morton, G. (2001). New Labour's reform of Britain's employment law: The Devil is not only in the detail but in the values and policy too. *British Journal of Industrial Relations*, 39(1), pp. 119–138.

Taylor, R. (June 1998). Annual review article 1997. *British Journal of Industrial Relations*, 36(2), pp. 293–331.

Towers, B. (1999). Editorial: ' . . . the most lightly regulated labour market. . .' The UK's third statutory recognition procedure. *Industrial Relations Journal*, 30(2), pp. 81–95.

TUC (1997a). *Annual report of 1997*. London: TUC.

TUC (1997b). *Partners for progress: Next steps for the New Unionism*. London: TUC.

TUC (1998). *TUC general council report to congress (1998)*. London: TUC.

TUC (2000). *TUC general council report to congress (2000)*. London: TUC.

Undy, R. (2002). New Labour and New Unionism, 1997–2001: But is it the same old story? *Employee Relations*, 24(6), pp. 638–655.

Webb, S. and Webb, B. (1913). *Industrial democracy*. Printed by The Authors for the Trade Unionists of the United Kingdom. London: Longmans Green and Co.

5 The Employment Relations Act (1999)

Introduction

The ERA (1999) chapter will further scrutinise the emergent employment relations regime under New Labour. The chapter will focus on key elements of the legislation such as the size of the bargaining unit eligible for trade union recognition, which will illustrate that the ERA proved to be more contentious and divisive than the NMW (1998). The policy outcomes arising from an emphasis on the available formal processes by trade union leaders due to the fractured role of informal processes will also be analysed. Due to weak coordination mechanisms in conjunction with the manipulation of informal process by the Labour leadership, these dynamics would combine to have profound implications for the legislation as the chapter will evaluate.

Fairness at Work (May 1998)

Labour's business paper prior to the general election of 1997, 'Building Prosperity—Flexibility, Efficiency and Fairness at Work', contained a commitment to union recognition but no firm details. In this context, Lord Monks highlighted that the majority of trade unions in the TUC and Labour Party were broadly 'cohesive' around ending the closed shop, but in relation to statutory recognition there were a number of differences. Lord Monks said: "What we were not cohesive about was that Blair said 'I am going to give you trade union recognition', which we hadn't agreed that we really wanted" (Extract from Lord Monks, Interview 3). According to Lord Monks, these concerns were also shared by Lord Morris of the TGWU, as the former drew attention to concerns both individuals had over trade union recognition procedures: "We didn't think that after a while it would work because after the initial boost it would get buggered up by the company lawyers and the union busters and so on" (Ibid). In contrast, John Edmonds, former GMB General Secretary, highlighted that the only area of major concern from his perspective pre-election was on secondary action during an industrial dispute. Edmonds added:

Secondary industrial action, which by and large I supported, was getting close to an issue which could have a big effect on a general election not because of the policy itself but because it would be a substantial platform for the Tories to argue that this is 'giving the trade unions back their power' and so on.

(Extract from John Edmonds, Interview 6)

These nuanced positions would be illustrative of the fault lines that would emerge in relation to the development of the new employment relations framework. Sir Ian McCartney outlined Labour's approach in advance of the proposals being published. McCartney contributed the following remarks on the general preparatory work in partnership with the TUC on the government's forthcoming White Paper 'Fairness at Work':

On the employment side, this was an area where a number of us were given different tasks by Tony Blair and to be honest with you the politics of this was to outflank some of my colleagues and get the unions into a position where we could have an engagement. In the run up to the 1997 election, we had a common agreement not to get into the situation of having a long list of union demands and a long list of Labour promises. What we had to do was concentrate on a range of very important policy areas and to put a coherent political strategy together—a coherent legislative programme in advance of the general election. So, we had a whole range of groups, which I established to work on a weekly basis but were linked to the party—they had to be accountable.

(Extract from Sir Ian McCartney, Interview 14)

Frank Doran complemented McCartney's comments in relation to the engagement with trade unions:

Prior to the 1997 general election back to around 1994 there had been a dialogue with the unions and Ian [McCartney] was a key part of that. The talks in opposition were based on getting an agreement on what an agenda should be for a Labour Government in employment relations. A lot of this was carried through the TUC and it was extremely successful.[1]

(Extract from Frank Doran, Interview 17)

Jon Cruddas, as the trade union liaison contact in Downing Street, described his role as the employment relations framework developed:

I saw my role as representing labour in those negotiations. We had another guy there at the time called Geoff Norris and his role was basically to do the equivalent job for the CBI with the business community.

Blair to his credit, and this is often underestimated, he would assume
that everybody went and fought the issues out.[2] So, it was not as if the
whole of Downing Street was against the unions. There was in fact a
whole multitude of interests and contributions. My role was to help
build an entry point into Downing Street and build it into the forums
of union representation. This took the form of formal meetings with
the TUC and the trade union liaison forums within the party.

(Extract from Jon Cruddas, Interview 19)

Illustrative of the different 'forums' of representation, Tom Watson
acknowledged a process involving representatives from the four largest
affiliates to the Labour Party (AEEU, GMB, TGWU and UNISON). The
identification of various groupings involving trade unions through the
TUC and the party's structures alongside informal processes that involved
the largest trade unions is illustrative of the coordination challenges that
would prove significant. Watson said:

TULO was a formal structure by which the Labour Party and the unions
held discussions. But, when in government there was obviously a government machinery of formal consultation and then there are always
these informal relationships. What became apparent, very early on, was
there needed to be a sort of medium order level—my level—where there
was a degree of candour with our colleagues in the other unions about
what was achievable and what wasn't within the negotiations.

Actually there was a small group convened, an informal group convened by the TGWU that had the big unions just meeting informally.
So, I went on behalf of the AEEU {with representatives from unions
including the GMB and UNISON}. It got nicknamed the 'Sushi Club'
because the TGWU office was near a sushi bar at that time {we'd have
takeaway sushi}. And, it was an informal meeting where we could
talk about where each General Secretary was coming from within the
negotiations and where the bottom lines were. Really it was useful
for us because it gave us a much greater clarity on where the fault
lines in government were so who in the administration was more
positive about the legislation and who was less supportive. Very often
in those negotiations Jon Cruddas would often say things like 'if you
want X, you can't push Y'. So, what he gave us was a candid view
of how far we could push on some things and we would give him a
candid view of what we could swallow within the framework.

(Extract from Tom Watson, Interview 15)

As the negotiations developed, Lord Monks wrote to the Prime Minster
on behalf of the TUC as the trade union movement was informed that
the Labour leadership was influencing the forthcoming White Paper proposals in line with the CBI's views. Lord Monks was moved to publicly

warn the government that the TUC "could not support decisions along these lines and if they were introduced would campaign against them" (McIlroy, 2000: 7). However, as part of the process of "trying to move matters forward" due to the vigorously contested nature of the forthcoming proposals, the TUC in principle acceded to the 'case' for a minimum 'yes' vote in a trade union recognition ballot. This was to ensure that there was a "basis for sustainable collective bargaining". The TUC further acknowledged that it also "might not be appropriate in the smallest of firms, say those with fewer than 10 employees" (TUC General Council Report to Congress, 1998: 9). The nature of these statements reflected the intense behind-the-scenes negotiations. The TUC's formal position over recognition bargaining units remained that the process should be presided over by a new agency; there should be no exclusion of small firms and recognition should be automatic where more than 50 per cent of the externally defined bargaining unit agree.

The Labour Government's proposals were formally set out in the White Paper 'Fairness at Work' (DTI, 1998: 2), which was published in May 1998. The key objective of the draft legislation was to facilitate an employment relations 'settlement' for a generation. In a much-cited Foreword (1998: 2) to the White Paper, the Prime Minster wrote the following:

> There will be no going back. The days of strikes without ballots, mass picketing, closed shops and secondary action are over. Even after the changes we propose, Britain will have the most lightly regulated labour market of any leading economy in the world.

The recognition procedures emerged to be more complex than the automatic right to recognition assumed to be agreed in principle in the run-up to the 1997 general election by trade unions. Several controversial escape routes would be inserted into the draft legislation, principally, a majority of those voting and at least 40 per cent of those eligible had to vote in favour of trade union recognition. Workers in small firms under-21 employees were excluded from a right to trade union recognition. A central facet of the government's approach was an endeavour to create a climate that would minimise industrial conflict. It was envisaged that this would be achieved through establishing forums and procedures which were designed to encourage trade unions and businesses to negotiate with each other. Sir Ian McCartney outlined his perspective on the White Paper, which drew him into 'frank' negotiations with trade unions:

> I wanted to try and ensure we didn't get competition between unions trying to bar each other from the workplace or gain access to the workplace at the expense of another union. It was important that this didn't happen. The background to this was not just history but there was indeed a range of disputes at that time 98–99 where there

was trade unions competing against each other and I got the senior leaders in and spoke to them frankly, put it that way, about how they were doing down the legislation by this continuing dispute between themselves about who represented the workplace—that should be a right for the workforce to decide.

I was going to ensure that built into the process for them a disadvantage—not an advantage to the employer—but a disadvantage so it would ensure that they worked cooperatively in gaining access to workplaces. I think that was important so although a friend of the unions I had to stand back from them. I wasn't their tool, not that they expected that of me. We had very good working relationships and great respect between us all. So, we had to work in a way to get this very complex and large agenda off the ground.

(Extract from Sir Ian McCartney, Interview 14)

'Fairness at Work' (1998: 18) focused on a series of supply-side initiatives such as training, skills and a flexible workforce, which was illustrative of its social partnership underpinnings. The draft legislation introduced a number of family-friendly proposals that delivered core statutory minimum rights.[3] However, this aspect is not the primary focus of the chapter, which has elected to focus on the trade union rights elements of the legislation, principally, collective bargaining, recognition, unfair dismissal and disputes procedures. The White Paper proposals emphasised that in the liberal economic environment, trade union growth would be dependent on the ability of unions to "convince employers and employees of their value—how much help they can bring to the success of an enterprise for employers, and how much active support they can offer employees" (Section 4.11). In this context, Howell (2004: 19) claimed that collective bargaining, union recognition and statutory rights would be "justified by their contribution to the construction of partnership in the workplace in the quest for global competitiveness".

The trade union movement secured what was perceived as a qualified success in that the threshold of firms with twenty plus employees eligible for union recognition was significantly lower than the CBI's target of fifty. Moreover, a demand that firms themselves should define the bargaining unit by sections of the business community was rejected in favour of the CAC, which would adjudicate on this matter (Lourie, 1998: 38). Tom Watson identified the role of the AEEU, specifically in regard to the exemption for trade union recognition in small firms. In doing so, Watson illuminates the fractious nature of negotiations and divisions between trade unions arising from the strategic choices of union leaders:

There was actually quite a lot of hostility internally in the unions on that, in particular the GPMU, who were very vexed about the 'twenty plus one'. They said it would rule out a lot of potential representation for small printers—and this is the bit that I think you may find interesting in terms of a journalist would call it 'colour'—Downing Street itself did not have a common position. What you had was Jon Cruddas who was in the sort of gearbox between Downing Street and the unions, who was also involved in internal negotiations with people in the Blair Administration and who tried to improve the outcome of the legislation into the benefit of the unions.

It came to a head over the bargaining unit where behind the scene negotiations nearly broke down when the GPMU got all the other unions to refuse to accept the position. I was authorised to negotiate on behalf of the union on this. So, informally to negotiate, but what actually happened was when they realised that I was holding the line on behalf of the union, somebody and I don't know who it was, reached Ken Jackson directly and Ken conceded the position. This essentially meant the unions' negotiated hand was weakened and ultimately we ended up with the twenty plus one. There was not a common position in the unions and we were easily outmanoeuvred in the negotiations and that's partly because there was very little respect paid to the TUC in its role and these bilateral negotiations that built up.[4]

(Extract from Tom Watson, Interview 15)

Furthermore, Tom Watson identified the key role of corporate lobbyists and business organisations as part of a matrix of interests contesting and shaping the terms of the employment relations framework:

The second point on that is, and of course this is of interest to me personally, there was an extraordinary amount of time spent on the bits of the legislation that would allow Rupert Murdoch the ability not to agree to unions at Wapping. Whenever there had been progress behind the scenes between unions and Downing Street there was never sign-offs until News International had got their line in. And, in the end when we got the legislation it allowed for News International to organise its affairs such that the unions could not go for a recognition ballot.

(Ibid)

Reflective of the policy contestation between stakeholders, the TUC General Council Report to Congress (1998: 4) reported that in "the months leading up the White Paper Fairness at Work were ones in which the complexities of dealing with Government were all too apparent". The report added that the process leading to the White Paper was "one of intensive activity". Coates (2005: 83) complements this assessment by suggesting that the government's proposals were not published until May 1998 precisely because "its agenda was so contested by the relevant social partners, and because its consequences in terms of its new industrial relations framework were so hard to settle between 'old' and 'new' Labour elements in Tony Blair's first Cabinet".

The TUC did gain some 'concessions' on individual rights relating to trade union representation at disciplinary hearings and unfair dismissals (Coulter, 2009: 15).[5] Schedule 4.22 of the White Paper, for example, proposed employees dismissed for taking part in lawfully organised official industrial action should have the right to complain of unfair dismissal to a tribunal. The caveat was any tribunal should not get involved with "looking at the merits of the dispute; its role would be to decide whether the employer had acted fairly and reasonably taking into account all the circumstances of the case". The response from sections of the business community was scornful, as the Institute of Directors (IoD) attacked the White Paper as representing "a significant swing towards the employee" (Lourie, 1998: 15). In contrast, the CBI had shifted their position from outright opposition to one of engaging and contesting key clauses of the proposals. Specifically, the CBI focused on the element that to gain recognition 40 per cent of the workforce must say 'yes'. The industry body also argued that there should be procedures for derecognition and prohibitions on industrial action to secure recognition (McIlroy, 2000: 7). These policy positions were reflected in the published White Paper as a testament to the pressure the business community brought to bear on the framework.

Lord Monks on behalf of the TUC responded to the proposals stating that they represented a 'big improvement' for trade unions. However, a number of key concerns remained over the White Paper, in particular the 40 per cent threshold which was described as 'too stiff' (*The Guardian*, 1998). Monks also expressed disappointment at the exclusion of an estimated 5 million employees in small firms from union recognition rights. John Edmonds, GMB General Secretary, argued that the proposals were a 'flawed jewel' due to the government listening to the 'siren voices' of the CBI. Edmonds pledged that the GMB union would campaign to change the 40 per cent threshold (Ibid). The 'Fairness at Work' offered the prospect of review on this aspect in Schedule 4.18. The proposed framework was described by Howell (2004: 9) as being 'fairly limited' in nature, which was accentuated by the family-friendly rights aspect being 'heavily influenced' by existing or proposed EU legislation. In the areas the Labour Government had freedom of manoeuvre over the framework could be viewed as even more minimalist in this context.

Trade union actors involved in the 'Fairness at Work' process attribute disappointment over the extent of the proposals as deriving partly from competing organisational priorities and a lack of trade union coordination among the largest trade unions (see Table 5.1). The latter aspect stemmed from the multilateral and bilateral processes in action involving the TUC, the four largest trade unions and key trade union actors, in particular the AEEU General Secretary. John O'Regan, as a political

Table 5.1 Largest TUC-Affiliated Unions 1979 and 2001

TUC-Affiliated Membership	1979	2001	% Change
TGWU	2,086,281	858,804	−59
AEEU	1,661,381	728,211	−56
UNISON[6]	1,657,926	1,272,470	−23
GMB	1,096,865	683,680	−38
MSF	701,000	350,974	−50
USDAW	470,017	310,222	−34

Source: Membership Statistics as reported in TUC Annual Report of 1979 and 2001.

officer for the printers' trade union—the GPMU—outlined a number of the challenges in trying to achieve coordination in the trade union movement in the following terms:

> There was not one union agenda. The public sector unions, UNISON in particular, they didn't have the same problems on recognition and at that time on the issue of strikes. So, that wasn't the big issues for them. It was better conditions for public sector workers and now they had a Labour Government who they could work with to get things done much more readily than they could with the Tories. That was their [UNISON] agenda. The AEEU agenda was strange to say the least.
>
> (Extract from John O'Regan, Interview 21)

Dave Prentis, Deputy General Secretary of UNISON in 1999, acknowledged the divergence of organisational importance placed on policy items. Prentis agreed that the 'Fairness at Work' proposals were not viewed as an organisational priority, in contrast with the minimum wage. This point, however, should not be confused with not appreciating the importance of the proposed legislation for other trade unions. Nonetheless, the policy emphasis would be to an extent a mirror image of the GPMU and AEEU position in relation to the NMW (1998) not being considered an organisational priority. Prentis said:

> I mean, probably we didn't put as much emphasis on this as we [UNISON] did the minimum wage and a lot of the things that were being talked about. They weren't directly relevant to us because we did have recognition throughout public services and because we had national agreements. We had recognition even when our density was low.
>
> (Extract from Dave Prentis, Interview 16)

The extracts illuminate the policy nuances—implicit or explicit—that government ministers concerned with specific elements of the prospective legislation sought to expose through bilateral negotiations with individual trade union leaders. The observation lends credence to the contention that the opportunity for trade union leaders to act in greater coordination was limited by what Frege and Kelly (2003: 14) characterised as an 'individualist leadership structure'.

Employment Relations Bill

On 4 November 1998, Peter Mandelson MP, Trade and Industry Secretary, at an appearance before the Trade and Industry Committee, heightened trade union concerns over the proposed recognition procedures. There was an implication through Mandelson's use of the words 'in the place of work' that the government could dilute the original proposals by applying a '50 per cent plus one' threshold to every site of a company rather than across the firm as a whole (Assinder, 4 November 1998). Senior trade union leaders met with the Prime Minister and Mandelson on 17 November 1998 to discuss the details of the draft legislation as the White Paper moved into the Bill stage. Coates (2005: 86) reported that Tony Blair appeared more concerned about the impact which the new regulations could have on the government's pro-business agenda "that at his [Blair] key meeting with the TUC General Secretary, John Monks, when the controversy was at its peak, he apparently spent most of the 45 minutes promoting the CBI case to Monks". In the aftermath of the meeting, the TUC felt compelled to publicly state:

> its strong concern at reports that the Government is giving sympathetic consideration to employer lobbying aimed at sabotaging clear principles set out in the White Paper. The employer agenda is not concerned with mere detail but persuading the government to water down the White Paper and destroy the careful balance it established.
> (TUC, 18 November 1998)

Despite the public protestations from trade unions, the government gave notice that there would be a number of changes following the results of the consultative process. The DTI received more than 470 responses from employers, individuals, lawyers, trade unions and employer organisations. In a letter to Lord Monks and Adair Turner, Director General of the CBI, from Peter Mandelson (dated 17 December 1998), the government set out the forthcoming 'main decisions', which diluted the strength of the original proposals. The government confirmed that it had in principle agreed to a £50,000 limit on unfair dismissal compensation, whereas the White Paper (Section 3.5) stated it planned to 'abolish' the maximum limit on compensation for unfair dismissal. The CBI had urged

Mandelson to raise the limit from £12,000 to £40,000 and that a cap on awards should remain (*BBC*, 1998). Mandelson added the qualifying period for unfair dismissal would also be reduced from two years to one. The dismissal of people taking legal industrial action would be judged unfair for the first eight weeks of a dispute. The trade union movement was described as being particularly 'incensed' by the Labour Government's refusal to honour John Smith's 1992 commitment to extend protection from unfair dismissal to workers from the first day of their employment (Coates, 2005: 92).

Trade unions would have to demonstrate 10 per cent membership in the bargaining unit in order to trigger a recognition ballot. An employer or a group of employees could also apply to the CAC for derecognition after three years. The CAC could order derecognition ballots if recognition was considered to be "not in the interest of good industrial relations". The decision could be arrived at if the CAC judged that employees did not want the recognised trade union to collectively bargain on their behalf on the basis it was satisfied the applicant was more than likely to win and if union membership was judged to have fallen below 50 per cent (Lourie, 1999; Gennard, 2002). Trade union frustrations deriving from the changes to the Bill from the White Paper to accommodate employers' concerns spilled over publicly. A week before the official publication of the Bill, Lord Morris, General Secretary of the TGWU, in a New Statesman interview on 22 January 1999 stated: "We were promised, before the election, fairness not favours. Well, we haven't had the fairness, but the employers have certainly had the favours". Morris added the 50 per cent 'yes' threshold requirement, which must amount to at least 40 per cent of the total workforce rather than a simple majority, was "a threshold level that is unique to any democratic institution and it can't be fair" (Wilby, 1999). Tony Dubbins, former General Secretary of the GPMU, reflected on the dilution of the Bill from the White Paper proposals:

> Again and again, it was quite clear that the CBI and employer groups were watering down the type of legislation and its content that we thought had been agreed in the manifesto. So, there were various stages to this and various outcomes some of which we agreed with, and some quite frankly we were disappointed with. Much to our concern there was a great deal of influence by the CBI and the people who were around in the DTI at the time.
>
> (Extract from Tony Dubbins, Interview 8)

In the aftermath of the Bill's publication, the fault lines that emerged between trade unions during the process were now in full public display. Ken Jackson, General Secretary of the AEEU, welcomed the Employment Relations Bill as "a major step forward for social partnership. It is an opportunity for trade unions to demonstrate that partnership is the right way forward" (Labour Research Department, February 1999). The public affirmation of social partnership by the AEEU reinforced its leadership's ideological accommodation with the government's approach. Watson on the significance of the strategic choices of trade union leaders with respect to the ERA negotiations added the following:

> I mean the General Secretary was satisfied with the outcome. He {Jackson} thought it would bring broad benefits to the union but didn't particularly make a big song and dance about it. A lot of trade unions would say it didn't go far enough because it didn't give an automatic right to access to workers which is really what everyone was after. But, from the public face of the AEEU, Ken Jackson expressed satisfaction and it didn't really matter what anyone else said.
>
> (Extract from Tom Watson, Interview 15)

The Employment Relations Bill was published on 27 January 1999. The proposals retained the family-friendly component of the White Paper, principally due to the incorporation into law of European obligations under the Social Chapter and the implementation of the European Commission Directive on Parental Leave. The Directive gave all parents (men and women, including those who adopt a child) the right to three months' parental leave and introduced a right to time off for urgent family reasons. As identified in Mandelson's letter, the ability for trade unions to seek and maintain union recognition from the original proposals was weakened. Three routes to trade union recognition were proposed: voluntary, by ballot and automatic. The White Paper did not mention a specific figure as evidence of a reasonable level of support. The CBI had proposed a threshold of 20 per cent membership over the preceding 12 months. The Bill would determine that trade unions would have to show 10 per cent union membership in the bargaining unit to trigger a ballot. If there were disagreements about the bargaining unit, this would be resolved by the CAC. On this aspect of the draft legislation, Sir Ian McCartney outlined the compromises that were made to enshrine an automatic right to recognition:

> On the issue of automatic recognition I sat in the garden at Number Ten with the Prime Minister one morning. I persuaded him to agree a mechanism which would allow automatic recognition—which is now in law. I remember right after it getting a call from Tony Blair asking me 'did I just agree this aspect with you' and I responded 'yes' and I asked 'why?' to which he responded 'well my advisors are having a go at me' and I said 'well we agreed it' and I asked 'are you going to go back on it?' Tony responded and said 'Oh no, I'm happy to agree'.

The reality was there were a number of unions who weren't interested in recruiting people in small employers and preferred to organise in the sectors of the economy with large employers they were already in. It was right to ask for clarity around what was the government trying to do and how could we achieve it in terms of creating an environment that made it easier not harder for unions. We tried our best to create this and make it easier. But, this was in a context whereby unions should act responsibly and fairly towards each other. I kept all these incentives in.

(Extract from Sir Ian McCartney, Interview 18)

The Bill permitted employers and employees to reach individual contracts even when a trade union was recognised in the bargaining unit but simultaneously protected employees from being forced to do so. The industrial action ballot provisions would remain, but a number of changes designed to protect the privacy of union members and simplify ballot procedures were included. In relation to the period of an industrial ballot's effectiveness, negotiations could continue beyond the four weeks 'expiry date' when both sides agreed, but this period should not exceed eight weeks. The White Paper had remained silent on the dismissal of those involved in industrial action other than indicating support for remedial procedures in principle. In contrast, the Bill stated that the government intended to make the dismissal of people taking legal industrial action unfair for the first eight weeks of a dispute as outlined in Mandelson's letter on 17 December 1998. After the eight weeks, the dismissal would be unfair only if the employer had not taken all procedural steps as would have been 'reasonable' to settle the dispute. Lord Morris complained the prior aspect offered employers an incentive to sit out a strike (Wilby, 1999). The cap on unfair dismissal awards at £50,000 was confirmed, as was the qualifying period for unfair dismissal being reduced from two years to one. This would be achieved by using an existing Order-making power to vary this period.[7] Employers were also prohibited from forcing employees sign away rights to protection against unfair dismissal in contracts of employment. It was further proposed that trade union members would also be protected against discrimination by blacklisting when applying for jobs.

The TUC raised further concerns in relation to the remit for employees being eligible for trade union representation in disciplinary hearings and serious grievances as being 'drawn too narrowly' (TUC, 26 January 1999). The trade union body added that the Bill did not appear to cover discrimination on grounds of age and there was no clear obligation on employers to have grievance procedures. Furthermore, in what can be judged to be a major omission in the Bill, the Labour Government decided not to bring forward measures to regulate the use of 'zero hours' contracts. An estimated 780,000 people in June 2018 were estimated to be on zero hours contracts (Office of National Statistics, 2018). The issue was originally raised for consideration in the White Paper in Section 3.14 where the government estimated around 200,000 people were working on zero hours contracts.[8] The official response to the Bill by Lord Monks on behalf of the TUC was as follows:

> Of course, the Bill does not go as far as we would like. And we are worried that concessions given to employer lobbying may lead to unnecessary legal action and openings for US-style union busting consultants. But these disappointments should not distract from the historic gain for people at work that this Bill represents.
>
> (TUC, 26 January 1999)

Sir Ian McCartney, who highlighted his personal efforts to 'outflank' ministerial colleagues on employment relations matters, drew attention to the challenges of government. McCartney reasoned the proposals must be viewed in the context of multiple interest groups seeking to shape the employment relations framework:

> The White Paper set a baseline and we added to this and refined it the whole way through because, remember, no specifics were agreed to in the manifesto. So, we would get on a regular basis massive amendments being put forward in Whitehall, which we had to see off, or if we couldn't win on an area then how did we protect the underlying principles of what the Bill was trying to do rather than lose it completely? Of course, not just the CBI but every large business organisation was in this process. It got to the point where Margaret Beckett had gone and Peter Mandelson came in, and in fairness to Peter, he worked closely with me on the employment relations agenda. He {Peter} was always open with me and if there were issues that came up we resolved them.[9] All through the Bill, to the committee process, we added things. We tried to sit down with unions and resolve the recognition process. There wasn't a common front among unions. I couldn't turn up and tell Tony Blair every union was behind this because that wasn't the case.
>
> (Extract from Sir Ian McCartney, Interview 18)

The rationale of McCartney's comments from a governmental perspective is important to illuminate. The employment relations environment had undergone substantial structural changes over the previous twenty years. In a pluralist policy context, trade unions are only one albeit a major socioeconomic interest group. Nevertheless, the significant changes included in the Bill from the White Paper must be viewed as "a victory for employers" (Lourie, 1999: 8). Moreover, McIlroy (2000: 8) cogently noted that from a trade union perspective, the "already modest proposals were circumscribed". Tom Watson reinforced these observations, concluding that the fruits of the negotiations should be viewed as a policy success for employer interests and those sympathetic to them in the Labour Government. Watson also identified that the minimalist outcomes were partly attributable to a lack of trade union coordination: "And, where I would say that Downing Street absolutely won on this was there was not a unified position across the unions on key points within the Bill" (Extract from Tom Watson, Interview 15).

ERA (1999)

The legislation reflected the influential impact of employers' organisations through each stage of the process. The ERA did not reinstate the promotion of collective bargaining within the terms of reference of ACAS. This facet was included in the Employment Protection Act (1975) as part of the Social Contract but was removed by the Trade Union Reform and Employment Rights Act (1993). Given the ballot thresholds required for statutory recognition, this maintained the 'dominant position' of employers in the employer-employee relationship according to Smith and Morton (2001: 126). The mechanical disadvantages in relation to the pathways for trade union recognition were intensified in those instances where there was an absence of any trade unionism in a workplace in the first instance, which gave employers an 'inestimable advantage' (Ibid). Despite these disadvantages, Howell (2004: 10) identified the statutory right to union recognition as the 'biggest surprise' in the legislation because recognition could be automatic where a trade union could demonstrate a majority of a firm's employees were members of the union. Baccaro and Howell (2011: 538) added that statutory recognition was the "one major collective innovation" of the Labour Government. This perspective was complemented by Brown (2011: 406), who noted that the 'main innovation' in the proposals was the statutory recognition procedure. Employers could be compelled to cooperate with a recognition ballot and to provide the relevant trade union with access to the workforce during the period of a ballot. If an employer failed to do so, the CAC could issue a declaration stating that a union can be recognised to conduct collective bargaining on behalf of the bargaining unit (para. 27(2)). However, in a significant qualification, the access proscribed to trade unions would be restricted to the period of the ballot. In contrast, there were no restrictions on employers in the period prior to the ballot thus raising the spectre of union-busting tactics cited in particular by Lord Monks.

Undy (2002: 653) importantly draws attention to the positive and inclusive signals of the Labour Government's discourse, contending the employment relations framework enabled the potential for trade union growth. Undy stated that a change in the political environment "made employers think twice about emulating the aggressively anti-union behaviour of some large and influential employers in the 1980's and early 1990's". The assertion echoed the 'demonstrative effect' in reverse as identified by Howell (1998) in relation to the state's exclusionary and hostile measures from 1979–97. The more favourable climate created by the Labour Government can be empirically located in trade union density and membership statistics remaining relatively static during the party's first and second terms. The relative stability should be considered a significant outcome in light of the trend over the previous eighteen years. Trade union membership, in fact, rose in 1998 for the first time in twenty years, as total membership increased by 50,581 to 7.8 million (Labour Research Department, July 2000a). The Labour Research Department (July 2000b) also reported that trade unions secured seventy-five new recognition deals covering 21,366 workers in ten months. Nonetheless, the mechanical disadvantages associated with the recognition procedures are illustrated by trade unions signing 166 recognition deals in 2003, which was around half of the 307 signed in 2002 and around a third of the 470 signed in 2001. Moreover, of the 166 recognition agreements in 2003, more than four out of five (137 out of 166) were voluntary.

The TUC suggested that one reason for the recognition slowdown was that some companies were effectively using the legislation to enact 'union busting tactics' as predicted by trade union actors (Labour Research Department, April 2004). However, the threat of the statutory route is cited as a positive influence in trade unions attaining voluntary agreements. In 32 per cent of cases, trade unions considered that the right to statutory recognition was influential in securing a voluntary deal (Ibid). It is also worth noting that the TUC reported an upward trend in recognition agreements with the anticipation of the Labour Government's legislation in the period from July 1997 to February 1998. Recognition deals outpaced derecognition in terms of numbers of employees affected by forty-five to one (Lourie, 1998). Therefore, the 'shadow of the law' did stimulate an increase in voluntary agreements (Moore, 2004: 11).

The positive influences of the legislation were counteracted by the negative components and the various escape routes in-built for employers to exploit. Howell (2004: 17) observed that the Labour Government appeared "willing to accept collective representation where it can be voluntarily negotiated between employer and employees". Simpson (2000: 222) echoed these points by drawing attention to the "absence of any state commitment to collective bargaining". There was an expectation by the government in light of the new framework that trade unions and employers would in partnership agree to trade union recognition if a majority of the workforce desired such an arrangement. If not, then there was a statutory route to recognition available to trade unions in the face of a hostile employer. This was a far more neutral position adopted by the Labour Government than trade unions had wished for in the context of twenty years of neoliberal reforms and legal restrictions on trade unions.

Smith and Morton (2001) highlighted the restrictions on applications for recognition as the ERA stipulated that an application from a union(s) is inadmissible unless trade unions demonstrate that "they will co-operate with each other in a manner likely to secure and maintain stable and effective collective bargaining arrangements" (para. 37(2)). The CAC could not accept an application from a trade union if there was a collective agreement in existence. Hence, the in situ trade union remained entitled to bargain on behalf of any workers in the bargaining unit (para. 35(1)). The maintenance of so-called sweetheart deals (non-independent unions), therefore, were not 'completely debarred' by the legislation (Gall and McKay, 2001: 103). The ERA contained a number of 'problematic' aspects according to Heery and Simms (2008: 34). In particular, this included

> the scope for employers to use sweetheart or company unions to block recognition, contest bargaining units to make it harder to secure majority support, delay decisions by the CAC to demoralise workers, limit organiser access to workplaces, and mount counter-organising campaigns.
>
> (Ibid)

The White Paper had proposed that there would be a 'broadly similar' procedure available for derecognition as for recognition.[10] The ERA would specify that an employer or a group of employees could apply to the CAC for derecognition after three years. In these circumstances, the CAC was enabled to order a ballot if it was satisfied that the applicant was more than likely to win and at least 10 per cent of the workers constituting the bargaining unit favoured an end of the bargaining arrangements (para. 110 (a & b)). The TUC would judge this outcome as a qualified success in the context of the significant shift towards employers (TUC General Council Report to Congress, 1999: 17–18). In a further example of the policy dilution, there was an absence of the three-year moratorium for an application by employers to change the bargaining unit. The CAC could, at any juncture, decide that the "original unit is no longer appropriate" (Schedule A1 para. 66 (1)).

The ERA provided employers with the ability to offer financial inducements to workers to opt out of collective agreements, which was aptly described by Wedderburn (2000: 10–11) as the 'sweeteners' clause. According to Wedderburn, this clause was tantamount to "leaving the door open to a variety of discriminatory derecognition moves by employers".[11] Collective bargaining was also narrowly defined as "negotiations relating to pay, hours and holidays" (Schedule A1 para. 3.3). This was at variance with the wider definition, which embraced the whole pay-effort.

The victory for employers was most obvious and damaging to the interests of trade unions in relation to the 'twenty plus one' rule, in particular for smaller craft-based unions. The clause contained in Schedule A1 excluded an estimated 31 per cent of the workforce, which was equivalent to omitting up to 8.1 million workers from trade union recognition (Simpson, 2000: 196). John O'Regan expanded upon the major concerns for small craft-based unions over the employee thresholds for statutory recognition and highlighted divergent trade union positions:

> This is one of the issues, which didn't affect quite a few unions and I remember the TGWU saying 'this isn't a problem for us as we don't organise in workplaces less than fifty'. Now the GPMU on the other hand in ninety-one percent of workplaces we organised in, they were small workplaces under fifty. It was something like 80 per cent under twenty-one employees.
>
> (Extract from John O'Regan, Interview 21)

Howell (2004: 10) viewed the recognition thresholds as an indication that "employers won most of the battles for the application of the statutory right". Gerry Sutcliffe expanded upon the balance, which had to be struck from the government's perspective:

> Well, it was very difficult and we did counter balance in other pieces of legislation that helped on recognition. But, you are right because at the end of the day when you are a government minister, you have to respond to the collective principle of being in government and I didn't win the argument when I put the case for recognition for under twenty employees. So, then I was caught with the collective position in which we were in and I knew the union's aspirations because they were my own aspirations when I was a full time official.
>
> (Extract from Gerry Sutcliffe, Interview 20)

The final component in the ERA, which is worthy of further consideration, pertains to the caveats inserted into the legislation regarding workers participating in lawful strikes. In the Notice of Industrial Action Section 11 of Schedule 3, it specified that trade unions proposing industrial action had to provide "such information in the union's possession as would help the employer to make plans and bring information to the attention of those of his employees". Wedderburn (2000: 130–131) observed that the inequity of this aspect meant that there was "no complementary duty on the employer to tell the union how he aims to win the dispute (perhaps by recruiting another workforce which is regulated in many other countries)".

Evaluation and Reflections

Without fundamental and sustainable structural reform in the employment relations arena, the social partnership approach was destined to be institutionally weak. Gordon Brown, former prime minister, acknowledged that the approach was not as successful as desired by the government:

> When I was Chancellor we had a forum, which involved the unions, business and the government to look at issues such as jobs, competitiveness and productivity in the economy. We asked the unions to prepare papers and employers to prepare papers at these discussions. It was an attempt to find consensus on industrial policy. I can't say it was as successful as it should have been but it did raise a lot of big issues for the future of British industry.
>
> (Extract from Gordon Brown, Interview 9)

The institutional weakness of the social partnership approach should be taken in conjunction with two central dynamics. First, the government retained the key elements of the employment relations reforms enacted by successive Conservative Governments. Second, there was an emphasis by Labour that in a liberal market economy, trade union growth would be dependent on the ability of trade unions to "convince employers and employees of their value".[12] In this context, Smith and Morton (2001: 134–135) judged the legislation's effect along with the prevailing body of restrictive legislation as an outcome "comparable to, and in some areas worse than, the Industrial Relations Act 1971".

In the transition from the preparatory discussions to the White Paper's publication through to the legislation, McIlroy (2000: 9) considers the TUC as having "failed to achieve justified goals". The weaknesses associated with the ERA outcomes from the trade union perspective can be traced to the fault lines prior to the 1997 general election. The ERA did not automatically strengthen trade unions collectively, albeit trade unions and the workforce had a legal route to achieve trade union recognition. Rather, the primary focus of the legislation was based on statutory rights for individual workers hence the appropriateness of *regulated individualism* as the descriptor of New Labour's employment relations model. To the present day, the same recognition procedures are in place. For critics of the legislation, the continual contraction of trade union density and collective bargaining, particularly in the private sector, highlights the ineffectiveness of the legislation. In contrast, collective bargaining coverage and trade union density has remained relatively stable in a number of advanced industrialised nations due to institutional support from the state (see Tables 5.2 and 5.3). Therefore, despite the ERA removing hostile and exclusionary measures on trade unionism, it did not establish the necessary supportive institutional framework to facilitate trade union growth.

Table 5.2 International Collective Bargaining Levels From 2000 to 2016

Country	2000 (%)	2005 (%)	2010 (%)	2016 (%)
Austria	98	98	98	98
Belgium	96	96	96	96
Britain	36.4	34.9	30.9	26.3
Finland[13]	85	87.7	77.8	89.3
Germany	67.8	64.9	59.8	56
Spain	82.9	76	76.9	73.1
United States	14.2	13.1	12.6	11.5

Source: Visser (2015) and ILOStat (2018).

Table 5.3 International Trade Union Density From 2000 to 2016

Country	2000 (%)	2005 (%)	2010 (%)	2016 (%)
Australia	24.7	22.4	18.3	14.5
Austria	36.9	33.8	28.9	26.9
Belgium	56.2	53.7	53.8	54.2[14]
Britain	29.8	28.6	26.6	23.5
Germany	24.6	21.5	18.9	17
Italy	34.4	33.3	35.5	34.4
Sweden	79	75.7	68.2	67[15]
United States	12.9	12	11.9	10.3

Source: Visser (2015) and ILOStat (2018).

Sir Ian McCartney reflected on the successes of ERA from the government's perspective by advocating that in the context of trade union divisions and minimal details set in advance of 1997, the legislation did significantly enhance individual and trade union rights:

> I do recognise people's frustrations but try to balance these feelings. I can honestly say there were things trade unions could do about enhancing and utilising their lot in the workplace with existing or new members. There was a significant amount done in the legislation, which should be taken in the context of very little in detail being said in the 1997 manifesto.
>
> (Extract from Sir Ian McCartney, Interview 18)

In response to the criticisms that the employment relations framework established in the ERA was not supportive enough to enable trade unions to grow, Sir Ian McCartney added:

> No {I don't agree} and I will tell you why. After eighteen years, the circumstances in which trade unions worked in not just in the UK

{United Kingdom}, but America and other places had significantly changed. Unions had contracted substantially. However, some unions and their officers were averse to recruiting members. So, once the Tories changed the law to remove the closed shop and in reality the closed shop meant adding an employee to the workplace and simultaneously to the union but this all stopped. Very few unions understood the changes that were taking place.

So, what we tried to do in government was set up a partnership fund—an education and training fund—the only government in the world doing this.[16] These funds were designed for trade unions to restructure and to give them time to be able to recruit in areas of difficulty. This was important and lots of good work was done here and funded. This was tens of millions of pounds straight to unions in order to enhance their members' skills. The truth was that union officials couldn't be in every single workplace so we provided funds in order for to help members at the workplace to recruit and organise.

We wanted to help. We restructured the employment tribunal system as the Tories had been systematically sacking good trade union officials and I intervened as a minister to reappoint independently qualified trade unionists who had been taken out the system, as Tory ministers didn't like what they were doing. What we couldn't do was roll back two decades in terms of membership loss. A lot of this loss came through deindustrialisation and the removal of the closed shop.

(Extract from Sir Ian McCartney, Interview 18)

Jon Cruddas complements McCartney's more positive assessment of the ERA. In doing so, Cruddas illuminates the role of informal processes engaging actors in the transition from the White Paper through to the enacted legislation. These processes were utilised by trade unions to prevent even further policy dilution in favour of employers' organisations. Cruddas said:

At that time, Gerry Sutcliffe was Secretary of the Trade Union Group and basically we had informal arrangements whereby we made sure meetings would take place to apply pressure when agendas were emerging. The agendas and the priorities were fairly seamlessly interlinked to the internal negotiations that were occurring. Similarly, I worked very closely with Ian McCartney and others worked very closely with other relevant ministers. So, there was this parallel other operation and it's fair to say there were a number of outcomes that we weren't unhappy with and our priorities which we really focussed on such as the bargaining unit and automatic recognition—although we never put these things up in lights and tried to downplay the significance of those things, But, the final shakedown meant that we had proximity and access. I think the general agreement was that this was a fairly good agreement.

Firstly, this was all consolidated into a major juggernaut piece of legislation rather than a series of discreet initiatives, which some wanted and second, in terms of the architecture of the recognition procedure, there was less damage to it than there might have been. I think the unions' strategy throughout was very creative because it was very much above the line and below it such as the regular meetings between McCartney and Sutcliffe. It was quite a tight operation.

(Extract from Jon Cruddas, Interview 19)

Tom Watson offered an alternative perspective of the negotiations from a different vantage point as he reflected on the 'ad-hoc' nature of the negotiating process. Watson described it in the following terms, "Looking back on it now, it was pretty ad-hoc given the significance of the negotiation. It was almost deliberately opaque and made it much harder to get a decent deal for the unions I would say" (Extract from Tom Watson, Interview 15). Nonetheless, it is evident that if political action processes designed to apply leverage were not in situ, then there would have been further dilution in the 'Fairness at Work' proposals, and in the legislation itself. The observation is presented despite the notable actions of trade union actors who undermined the efforts to maintain a coordinated policy front. Trade unions did achieve a shift in a liberal market economy through influencing the details of the Labour Government's employment relations model. For example, the IoD opposed statutory recognition outright and the CBI had originally argued that a union recognition claim should be accompanied by a demonstration of 30 per cent support—the latter's position would shift to 20 per cent. The law ultimately finished on the basis of demonstrating 10 per cent membership in the bargaining unit to trigger a ballot.

The ERA significantly decelerated the decline in trade union density and collective bargaining coverage. Both elements decreased proportionally by around 17 per cent over fifteen years (1998–2013) compared with the contraction of 40 per cent in union density and 49 per cent for collective bargaining coverage over the period of Conservative power (1979–1997) (Visser, 2015). To crystallise the predicament for trade unions: what other viable strategic options, other than political action, could have effectively promoted trade union interests in a liberal market? The proposition must be viewed in the context of eighteen years of deindustrialisation. As the first term of the Labour Government (1997–2001) progressed, it was accompanied with rising dissatisfaction at the minimalist extent of the employment relations framework. The Labour Party's Exeter NPF (2000) in advance of the 2001 general election would be a turning point for many leaders of the affiliated unions to the Labour Party.

The brewing tensions between the trade unions and the Labour Government were exacerbated by the review of the ERA in mid-2002 (Waddington, 2003: 354). The promise of a future review had contributed to the TUC and trade unions such as the GMB giving qualified support to the ERA on the basis that 'unsatisfactory aspects' of the legislation could be reviewed and amended in the future (TUC General Council Report to Congress, 1999: 19). These aspects specifically included the recognition procedures, exemptions for small firms, action on zero hours contracts and gaining employment rights from day one. In a twist of fate, the 'Review of the Employment Relations Act' (December 2003) was signed off by Gerry Sutcliffe, who had been at the forefront of campaigning to enact a stronger framework.[17] Wood and Moore (2003: Abstract) highlight the government's review specifically concluded that the "union [recognition] procedure was broadly working and confirmed that the Government would not be changing the procedure's basic features".[18] The failure to amend the legislation simultaneously highlighted the dependence on the Labour Government—and the state—to facilitate and promote trade union growth. Sir Brendan Barber supported the perspective that the restricted scope and 'loopholes' contained in the ERA fermented trade union dissent:

> Well, there's no doubt that there were aspects of the legislation, the Employment Relations Act in particular, less so the minimum wage I think, that did not go as far as many people in the union movement would have liked and some of the provisions within the recognition legislation for example, which left a loophole for sweetheart unions to be recognised by employers and so on. Some of the hurdles which unions had to get across to qualify for the legal entitlement were regarded by many people as too onerous and unnecessarily so, too protective of employers who were going to be opposing unions in some of the battles to come maybe. So, of course there were those grievances and they were important but in a broader way there was some satisfaction that the incoming Labour Government did have a programme with some key progressive features from a union perspective.
>
> (Extract from Sir Brendan Barber, Interview 12)

Lord Collins, former General Secretary of the Labour Party and TGWU Assistant General Secretary, also lamented the attitude of the Labour leadership with particular reference to the ERA (1999):

> The missed opportunities for me, and if I was to criticise the party leadership pre and post 1997, it was that there prevailed a culture, which thought trade unions were illegitimate. Trade unions were seen as a negative force whereas if you go to the United States even right-wing Republicans see the legitimacy of trade unions in a way that many politicians don't see it here. I think the Labour leadership mood music was too negative. It was a missed opportunity to

promote a much more modern response in the economic life of the country and the role of trade unions.

(Extract from Lord Collins, Interview 22)

Furthermore, Dave Prentis, UNISON General Secretary, contributed to the sense of disappointment over the scope of the ERA with particular reference to the failure to reform industrial action ballots:

> The line that came from the Labour leadership was that it was up to the unions to recruit. It wasn't up to the government to legislate for it, they would remain fairly neutral, that they'd deal with some of the anomalies. But, for us the biggest problem that we had was balloting for industrial action where it's virtually impossible to run a legal ballot and none of this was ever dealt with under Blair. He'd talk about individual rights, workers' rights and not trade union rights and this was probably the minimum that they could do.
>
> (Extract from Dave Prentis, Interview 16)

The context set the scene for a series of leadership changes in the largest affiliated trade unions to the Labour Party, principally during Labour's second term (2001–05). The leadership changes would be viewed as a rebuke of trade union accommodation with the government's social partnership approach and the 'close working relations' with New Labour (Waddington, 2003: 354). These factors would emerge to define the future trajectory of relations between the Labour leadership and largest trade unions affiliated to the Labour Party during the party's remaining tenure in government. It is to the final case event of the Warwick Agreement (2004) which the book will now turn.

Notes

1. Doran is cited in the TUC General Council report (1999: 15) as engaging with trade unions on 10 February 1999 on the Bill to corroborate his intimate involvement.
2. Geoff Norris was the Prime Minister's liaison with the business community. In May 1997, Norris was appointed Blair's Special Adviser responsible for Trade, Industry, Energy, Employment, and Planning.
3. Some of the family-friendly rights included up to three months' unpaid parental leave for men and women to be taken while the child is under 8. It was to be extended to adoptive parents (Schedule 5.11 and 5.15). The proposals included time off for urgent family reasons to help workers look after a sick child or deal with a crisis at home (Schedule 5.11). New mothers were entitled to eighteen weeks' maternity pay but only fourteen weeks' maternity leave. Leave was to be extended to eighteen weeks. The longer period was to be available after one year's service rather than two (Schedule 5.14 and 5.18).

4. Sir Ken Jackson was the General Secretary of the AEEU from 1995 until its merger with the Manufacturing Science and Finance union to form AMICUS in 2001. Jackson subsequently became one of the Joint General Secretaries of AMICUS. AMICUS became the second-largest trade union, and the largest private sector union. Two smaller unions, UNIFI and the GPMU thereafter joined in 2004.

5. The right to claim unfair dismissal was introduced by the Industrial Relations Act (1971). At that time, the qualifying period was two years. This was reduced to one year in 1974 and to six months in 1975 by the Trade Union and Labour Relations Act (1974). It was increased again to one year in 1979 by the Unfair Dismissal (Variation of Qualifying Period) Order 1979 SI No 959 and to two years for employees in firms with fewer than twenty-one employees in 1980 under the Employment Act 1980. It was raised to two years in all cases in 1985 by the Unfair Dismissal (Variation of Qualifying Period) Order 1985 SI No 782.

6. Consisting of NALGO, NUPE and COHSE in 1979.

7. Employment Rights Act 1996, section 209 (1) (c) and (5).

8. Schedule 3.4 of Fairness at Work (1998) stated: "These contracts do not specify particular hours: the person may be required at any or at specified times. These contracts maximise flexibility for employers and suit some people who want occasional earnings. Many employers ensure the contracts are used sensibly, but they have the potential to be abused".

9. After the election, Beckett was appointed President of the Board of Trade (a position the title of which would later revert to Secretary of State for Trade and Industry). Peter Mandelson succeeded Beckett in July 1998.

10. Fairness at Work (1998), Schedule 4.18.

11. The preamble to the Trade Union Recognition (Method of Collective Bargaining) Order (2000: 2) expressly states even if the CAC has imposed a collective method, it "does not prevent or limit the rights of individual workers to discuss, negotiate or agree with their employer terms of their contract of employment, which differ from the terms of any collective agreement into which the employer and the union may enter as a result of collective bargaining conducted by this method".

12. Fairness at Work (1998), Section 4.11.

13. Figure relates to 2015 as provided by the ILOStat (2018).

14. Figure relates to 2015 as provided by the ILOStat (2018).

15. Figure relates to 2015 as provided by the ILOStat (2018).

16. The Union Learning Fund was established in 1998, with its primary aim being to develop the capacity of trade unions, and learning representatives were tasked with working with employers, employees and learning providers to encourage a higher take-up of workplace learning. Between 1998–99 and 2006–07, around £70m of funding was estimated to have been allocated to support the ULF. Around a further £116m in total was estimated to have been distributed to ULF projects between the financial years 2007–08 to 2015–16. Source: Department for Business, Innovation and Skills (24 November 2015) in a Parliamentary Question Response.

17. Gerry Sutcliffe at this juncture was the Parliamentary Under Secretary of State for Employment Relations, Competition and Consumers.

18. The only significant changes were that the government proposed 'greater scope' for unions to exclude or expel individuals from membership whose offensive political conduct was protected by trade union law. In Section 3.37, the government reaffirmed its intention to leave the basic period of protection at eight weeks. However, the government proposed to legislate to ensure that lockout days are disregarded in calculating the end of the eight-week period as outlined in Section 3.38. The period would end only when 56 days have passed since the action began on which no lockout occurred. This was to ensure that employers did not try to sit out the eight weeks by using the lockout tactic (Section 3.39). This issue arose in the Friction Dynamics case where the employer participated minimally in conciliation.

Bibliography

Assinder, N. (4 November 1998). *Mandelson signals weaker union laws.* Available at: http://news.bbc.co.uk/1/hi/uk_politics/207824.stm [Accessed 3 Dec. 2015].

Baccaro, L. and Howell, C. (2011). A common neoliberal trajectory: The transformation of industrial relations in advanced capitalism. *Politics and Society,* 39(4), pp. 521–563.

BBC (24 November 1998). Workers to be given more rights. Available at: http://news.bbc.co.uk/1/hi/special_report/1998/11/98/queen_speech/221010.stm [Accessed 4 Dec. 2015].

Brown, W. (2011). Industrial relations in Britain under New Labour, 1997–2010: A post mortem. *Journal of Industrial Relations,* 53(3), pp. 402–413.

Coates, D. (2005). *Prolonged labour: The slow birth of New Labour Britain.* Houndmills, Basingstoke: Palgrave Macmillan.

Coulter, S. (March 2009). Lobbying for change: Labour market policymaking in a liberal market economy. Paper for LSE Conference, *Emerging research in political economy and public policy.* Available at: www.lse.ac.uk/european Institute/events/2008-09/Coulter.pdf [Accessed 12 Oct. 2015].

Department for Business, Innovation and Skills (24 November 2015). *Parliamentary question response.* Available at: www.parliament.uk/business/publications/written-questions-answers-statements/written-question/Lords/2015-11-24/HL3882 [Accessed 10 July 2015].

DTI (2000). *The trade union recognition (method of collective bargaining) order 2000.* UK Department of Trade and Industry. Available at: www.gov.uk/gov ernment/uploads/system/uploads/attachment_data/file/336130/Method_of_Collective_Bargaining_Statutory_Instrument.pdf [Accessed 2 Feb. 2016].

DTI (December 2003). *Review of the Employment Relations Act 1999 government response to the public consultation.* Available at: http://webarchive.nationalarchives.gov.uk/+/http:/www.dti.gov.uk/er/era_rev99_govresp.pdf [Accessed 6 Feb. 2016].

Frege, C. and Kelly, J. (2003). Union revitalization strategies in comparative perspective. *European Journal of Industrial Relations,* 9(1), pp. 7–24.

Gall, G. and McKay, S. (2001). Facing 'fairness at work': Union perception of employer opposition and response to union recognition. *Industrial Relations Journal,* 32(2), pp. 94–113.

Gennard, J. (2002). Employee relations public policy development 1997–2001: A break with the past? *Employee Relations*, 24(6), pp. 581–594.

The Guardian (22 May 1998). Scale of ministers' concessions on working rights surprises unions. Available at: www.theguardian.com/politics/1998/may/22/economy.uk [Accessed 8 June 2015].

Heery, E. and Simms, M. (2008). Constraints on union organising in the United Kingdom. *Industrial Relations Journal*, 39(1), pp. 24–42.

Howell, C. (1998). Restructuring British public sector industrial relations: State policies and trade union responses. *Policy Studies Journal*, 26(2), pp. 293–309.

Howell, C. (March 2004). Is there a third way for industrial relations? *British Journal of Industrial Relations*, 42(1), pp. 1–22.

ILOStat (2018). *Collective bargaining and trade union destiny statistics*. Available at: http://laborsta.ilo.org [Accessed 31 July 2018].

Labour Research Department (February 1999). *The employment relations bill: Introduction*. London: Labour Research Department.

Labour Research Department (July 2000a). *TUC welcomes upturn in union membership*. London: Labour Research Department.

Labour Research Department (July 2000b). *New law marked by record number of deals*. London: Labour Research Department.

Labour Research Department (April 2004). *Fewer recognition deals signed*. London: Labour Research Department.

Lord Wedderburn. (2000). Collective bargaining or legal enactment: The 1999 Act and union recognition. *Industrial Law Journal*, 29(1), pp. 1–42.

Lourie, J. (1998). *Fairness at work research paper* (1998/1999), Cmnd 3968. House of Commons Library. Available at: https://researchbriefings.parliament.uk/ResearchBriefing/Summary/RP98-99#fullreport [Accessed 7 July 2015].

Lourie, J. (5 February 1999). *Employment relations Bill 1998/1999 Bill 36*. House of Commons Library. Available at: http://researchbriefings.files.parliament.uk/documents/RP99-11/RP99-11.pdf. [Accessed 7 July 2015].

Mandelson, P. (17 December 1998). Letter by Peter Mandelson MP, Secretary for State for Trade and Industry to John Monks and Adair Turner, Director General of the CBI. House of Commons Library, Dep 98/1540.

McIlroy, J. (2000). The new politics of pressure—the Trades Union Congress and New Labour in government. *Industrial Relations Journal*, 31(1), pp. 2–16.

The Office of National Statistics (14 August 2018). *Dataset: People in employment on zero hours contracts*. Available at: www.ons.gov.uk/employmentandlabourmarket/peopleinwork/employmentandemployeetypes/datasets/emp17peopleinemploymentonzerohourscontracts [Accessed 19 Sept. 2018].

Simpson, B. (2000). Trade union recognition and the law a new approach. Parts I and II of schedule A1 to the Trade Union and Labour Relations (Consolidation) Act 1992. *Industrial Law Journal*, 29(3), pp. 193–222.

Smith, P. and Morton, G. (2001). New Labour's reform of Britain's employment law: The Devil is not only in the detail but in the values and policy too. *British Journal of Industrial Relations*, 39(1), pp. 119–138.

TUC (1979). *TUC annual report of 1979*. London: TUC.

TUC (1998). *TUC general council report to congress (1998)*. London: TUC.

TUC (18 November 1998). *TUC to step up fairness at work campaign*. Available at: www.tuc.org.uk/workplace-s/welfare-and-benefits/tuc-step-fairness-work-campaign. [Accessed 4 Dec. 2015].

TUC (1999). *TUC general council report to congress (1999)*. London: TUC.

TUC (26 January 1999). *TUC hails fairness at work*. Available at: www.tuc. org.uk/employment-rights/proposed-changes-law/tuc-hails-fairness-work [Accessed 28 Nov. 2015].

TUC (2001). *TUC annual report of 2001*. London: TUC.

United Kingdom Government (May 1998). *Fairness at work*. Presented to Parliament by the President of the Board of Trade by Command of her Majesty. Cmnd 3968. London.

United Kingdom Government (27 January 1999). *The Employment Relations Bill*. Available at: https://publications.parliament.uk/pa/cm199899/cmbills/036/ 1999036.htm [Accessed 28 Nov. 2015].

United Kingdom Government (27 July 1999). *Employment Relations Act*. Printed in the UK by The Stationery Office Limited.

Undy, R. (2002). New Labour and New Unionism, 1997–2001: But is it the same old story? *Employee Relations*, 24(6), pp. 638–655.

Visser, J. (October 2015). *ICTWSS database*. version 5.0. Amsterdam: Amsterdam Institute for Advanced Labour Studies AIAS. Open access database available at: www.uva-aias.net/nl/data/ictwss [Accessed 31 Dec. 2016].

Waddington, J. (2003). Heightening tension in relations between trade unions and the Labour Government in 2002. *British Journal of Industrial Relations*, 41(2), pp. 335–358.

Wilby, P. (22 January 1999). *The new statesman interview—Bill Morris*. Available at: www.newstatesman.com/new-statesman-interview-bill-morris [Accessed 20 Dec. 2015].

Wood, S. and Moore, S. (2003: Abstract). *Reviewing the statutory union recognition (ERA 1999)*. London: Centre for Economic Performance London School of Economics and Political Science, Houghton Street.

6 The Warwick Agreement (2004)

Introduction

The primary reason for selecting the Warwick Agreement (2004) is the significance of the strategic choices of trade union leaders in a liberal market economy. The chapter will evaluate the leadership changes in the largest 'Big Four' trade unions—AMICUS, GMB, TGWU and UNISON—which acted as a catalyst for concerted political action inside the structures of the Labour Party. The endeavours would be operationalised through greater degrees of trade union coordination and institutional reconfiguration after the 2001 general election. The two-strand strategy focused on reforming TULO, which involves all trade unions affiliated to the Labour Party, and a complementary process consisting of the leaders of the largest four trade unions. The strategic approach enabled trade unions to positively affect state legislation via an effective channel of influence in the Labour Party. The strategic pivot was also characterised by the sidelining of the historical role performed by the TUC as the primary channel of influence in favour of affiliated Labour Party trade unions, as the chapter will examine.

Exeter Policy Forum (2000)

The opportunity to attain positive employment relations outcomes in a liberal market was constrained by the progressive centralisation of institutional power in the Labour leadership. The underlying institutional tensions stemming from this position manifested at the Labour Party's Exeter NPF in July 2000. The event is identified as a critical juncture by actors, but its importance is insufficiently discussed in the literature, although there are some notable exceptions such as Heery (2005), Bewley (2006), Gennard and Hayward (2008) and Minkin (2014). Trade unions retained a significant voice in the party's policy-making structures despite internal reforms. Trade unions collectively held 17 per cent of the voting power in the policy forum.[1] However, trade union coordination was not evident in Exeter, whereby minimal progress was made to strengthen the employment relations framework.

Minkin (2014: 324), for example, draws attention to a tentative agreement made by the GMB, GPMU and Stephen Byres, Secretary of State of Trade and Industry, on extending trade union recognition to firms with fewer than twenty-one employees, only to be overruled by Downing Street. Gennard and Hayward (2008: 215) state that the 2001 Labour Party manifesto deriving from the Exeter process starkly illustrated the divisions between trade unions: "Instead of a common trade union position being adopted, the unions were 'picked off', one by one, as they did individual deals with the Labour Government in return for their continued support". Undy (2002: 652) supports this contention, concluding that the government chose to "deal more directly with more amendable individual union leaders of the mega union(s)". Sir Brendan Barber complemented the academic assessments, highlighting the individualistic and informal manner in which Tony Blair engaged trade union leaders:

> So, Tony {Blair} would prefer to meet individual leaders of the unions on an individual basis and they could plead their issues and highlight their particular priorities and twist his arm on things as they felt appropriate. . . . But he didn't want there to be a more systematic, more formal basis for these exchanges. He was more comfortable, in a sense, dealing with the personal relationship with individual general secretaries of his major affiliates.
>
> (Extract from Sir Brendan Barber, Interview 12)

Tony Dubbins, General Secretary of the GPMU during this period, expanded upon the lack of coordination manifesting from the individual and informal processes, noting that "a number of unions made representations to various government ministers and perhaps the Prime Minister himself on particular issues" (Extract from Tony Dubbins, Interview 8). Dubbins added:

> What became apparent in a very short period of time was that deals had already been done. Done by the CWU {Communication Workers Union} on the privatisation of the Post Office and that it would not happen, which was a separate deal. UNISON got guarantees on the two-tier work force and the TGWU had another priority. When it got to the voting the GMB were pretty much sidelined. The GPMU was sidelined, as was Jimmy Knapp at the RMT {Rail, Maritime and Transport workers' union} who was trying to get a deal on rail renationalisation. The voting worked on a basis that a number of unions because they had already got agreements with the government on their own particular areas voted in support of the government. Therefore, we could not get the necessary votes to make even minority issues appear on the Labour Party Conference. I made up my mind that if TULO was going to succeed in the future then

identifying core trade union issues and gaining agreement across all unions was essential.[2]

(Ibid)

John Edmonds confirmed that the Exeter NPF process acted as a 'catalyst' for a number of key trade unions to achieve greater coordination:

> This was really the catalyst for ensuring that we had a trade union caucus because some of us were not going to go through the Exeter experience ever again. We were in our meeting room having a trade union caucus meeting before the policy forum—strange things had happened. Brendan Barber, then Deputy General Secretary of the TUC, turned up which was absolutely unheard of in the Labour Party policy-making. I mean the TUC would always keep hands off.
>
> (Extract from John Edmonds, Interview 6)

Edmonds added:

> Then we had the discussion on employment rights issues and everybody was in favour of the trade union position. Well of course they were as they formed it but there was then a very exciting variety of thoughts and suggestions about how we might not press some of these things to a vote, or if we did vote it may go the other way or to seek some things withdrawn just in case we upset the party leadership. Maybe the timing isn't right and so on. This was three years after the last election, which meant we were only one away from the next, and so on—and we are moving into an electoral period allegedly. This was at a time when the Labour Party was so far ahead in the polls that you couldn't even see the Tories. The meeting went on and on and on and on, and we never reached an acceptable conclusion because as I said it was divided every way. People kept leaving the room I assume to talk on the phones to people close to the Labour Leader and so on. It was like a little puppet theatre.
>
> (Ibid)

The General Secretary of UNISON, Dave Prentis, and Assistant General Secretary, Liz Snape, similarly considered Exeter a seminal moment in relation to the costs associated with a lack of coordination. Both actors acknowledged UNISON's engagement with the Labour Government at this point being individualistic, as Snape remarked that during the Exeter negotiations people were as a result 'picked off' (Extract from Dave Prentis and Liz Snape, Interview 16). Jack Dromey, former Deputy General Secretary of the TGWU, complemented the observations on the management control by the Labour leadership, remarking that the policy-making process was "run from Number Ten" (Extract from Jack Dromey,

Interview 23). Furthermore, Tom Watson added that the individualistic approach of trade unions heightened the tensions between trade union leaders:

> the relationship between the general secretaries, remember at that time you've got Morris, Ken [Jackson], and you've still got John Edmonds and their personal relationship was not warm, not warm at all.
>
> (Extract from Tom Watson, Interview 15)

Watson expanded upon the AEEU's approach at Exeter, re-emphasising the lack of trade union coordination:

> However, you know we {AEEU} weren't really wed into much of it. There were no red lines and you know essentially things would just get crunched through at the last minute and it was administratively chaotic. So, you would actually not notice whether things went through or not, points of detail, but there was also no collective position amongst the unions.
>
> (Ibid)

John Edmonds complements Watson's analysis, attributing the divisions between trade unions as deriving from the strategic choices of union leaders:

> Really central to all this was the position of the AEEU and the position of MSF, to some extent USDAW, but particularly those two. We couldn't get a unified position and frankly, until the people who represented those unions moved on a unified position was just not possible.
>
> (Extract from John Edmonds, Interview 6)

From a governmental perspective, Sir Ian McCartney highlighted the relational dynamics but also drew attention to the evolving nature of the policy-making process itself as being a contributory factor to dissatisfaction:

> At Exeter, it was still evolving {National Policy Forum}. One, it was really important to the leadership that it didn't all fall apart and it being seen as the party being split on policy. On the unions' side, it was still very much at that time big individuals at the TUC but in particular at the head of each of the individual unions all with their own union agenda—all their own style of working.
>
> (Extract from Sir Ian McCartney, Interview 14)

In contrast, Jon Cruddas offered an alternative perspective on the Exeter process. Cruddas suggests that Exeter should be viewed through the lens of it being the 'high point' for trade union influence in the backdrop of the NMW (1998), ERA (1999) and European directives being enacted during Labour's first term. In October 1998, the Labour Government had implemented the Working Time Regulations giving workers the right to minimum rest breaks, paid annual leave, maximum weekly hours of work and special provisions for night time workers.[3] In this context, Cruddas said:

> At that stage, Geoff Norris was taking quite a proactive role because he felt under threat because of the Employment Relations Act, the National Minimum Wage and the Regulation of Working Time, irrespective of the opt-out, but due to the general shape of all this because it was quite a substantial first-term agenda. The question then was 'is it a foothold into a durable second term agenda?' But, it never really occurred. Why it didn't occur is a very interesting question. In a sense, Exeter was the high point of union influence in terms of the strategy and its relationship with outcomes.
>
> (Extract from Jon Cruddas, Interview 19)

The Labour manifesto in the run-up to the 2001 general election promoted a number of employment relations commitments. This included a rise in the minimum wage (adult hourly rate rose from £3.70 to £4.10 in October 2001), statutory backing for union learning representatives and further support for the ULF. The manifesto pledged to end the two-tier workforce in the public sector and to review TUPE regulations (Labour Manifesto, 2001: 34).[4] More generally, Labour committed to increase spending on public services in its prospective second term. The Chancellor, Gordon Brown, subsequently announced the first increase in direct taxation in 2002 with a 1p in the pound rise in National Insurance contributions to pay for the investment. To the chagrin of trade unions, Labour simultaneously committed itself to the 'fundamental reform' of the public sector, principally through privatisation. Tony Blair argued: "There should be no barriers, no dogma, no vested interest that stands in the way of delivering the best services for our people" (Coates, 2005: 93). The main thrust of Labour's manifesto (2001: 11) reinforced the minimalist regulatory approach as it acclaimed, "In the labour market, minimum standards for people at work offer dignity and self-esteem. Regulation should be introduced, where it is necessary, in a light-touch way". As such, Ludlam and Taylor (2003: 745) observed the Labour Government's approach continued to embody the 'Anglo-Saxon' model of capitalism.

The hostility to the privatisation strategy was attributed to the GMB withholding £2 million of its political fund from the Labour Party. The union declared it would spend the money on an advertising campaign against the Private Finance Initiative (PFI) strategy in 2001.[5] Key divisions persisted between the largest trade unions, as the PFI policy was supported by the AEEU section of AMICUS (Ludlam, 2003: 151). In the aftermath of Labour's election victory, as it gained 40.7 per cent of the vote and a majority of 166 seats, Dave Prentis of UNISON argued that there should be a 'marginal' role for private companies in public services. A survey conducted by UNISON of its members in privatised local government services in 2001 revealed that pay levels for new starters were worse than those of transferred staff in more than 90 per cent of cases (Labour Research Department, September 2002). Trade unions leaders accepted concessions from Labour ministers in return for delaying until 2002 a review over the privatisation of public services to avoid open conflict (Maguire et al., 2001). The Department of Transport, Local Government and the Regions promised to 'tighten up' the application of TUPE transfer regulations. The change would be achieved through the introduction of a code. This would require contractors to employ new starts on "fair and reasonable terms and conditions, which are, overall, broadly comparable to those of transferred employees" (Labour Research Department, June 2002). However, a row erupted over the failure of Labour ministers to stick to the 'no surprises' policy designed to forewarn trade unions over plans to extend the role of the private sector in the NHS. A TUC paper in December 2001 complained that compliance with this agreement had "been patchy at best" (Wintour, 2001).[6]

Degrees of progress from Exeter were made with a series of provisions being implemented in the Employment Act (July 2002) concerning 'family-friendly' working, the resolution of individual disputes at the workplace and equal treatment for fixed-term employees (See Appendix B). Howell (2005: 182) highlighted the limited nature of the legislation, observing that the "core of the legislation was aimed at a reform of the employment relations system, with the goal of reducing the number of cases handled by the tribunal system". There was an increase in tribunal system cases from 36,000 cases in 1990 to 104,000 in 1999–2000. McIlroy and Croucher (2009) further highlight that the statutory right for paid time off for union-learning representatives in the legislation was critically restricted. The new rights applied only to workplaces with union recognition, and employers were under no obligation to even consult over training.

The concerns of trade union leaders over the lack of progress in relation to the employment relations framework appeared justified when the Prime Minister at the Labour Party's Welsh Conference in spring 2002 used the word 'wreckers' to describe those opposed to public sector reforms (Ludlam and Taylor, 2003: 743). There was little doubt that the comments were aimed at newly elected left-wing union leaders in trade unions. The emergent policy effects of these new leaders manifested at the October 2002 Labour Party Annul Conference. UNISON successfully tabled a motion calling for a moratorium and review of PFI deals, which was backed by 67.19 per cent to 32.81 per cent. A statement by the

Labour Party's NEC supportive of PFI was overturned by 53.62 per cent to 45.38 per cent (Maguire, 2002). Yet, in naked example of the centralisation of power in the party, Charles Clarke MP, Labour Party Chairman, said: "The policy of the Labour Party is not the same thing as a resolution passed by the Labour Party conference" (Grice and Clement, 2002).

Leadership Dynamics

In a round of successive elections, candidates opposed to the New Labour project won the top leadership positions. The results included the general secretarial positions at the CWU, the RMT and the deputy position in the TGWU won by Tony Woodley in 2002. Woodley went on to win the general secretary position in 2003.[7] Derek Simpson was also elected General Secretary of the AEEU section of AMICUS in June 2002, beating Tony Blair's 'favourite trade unionist' Sir Ken Jackson (*BBC*, 2002). In the election in 2003 to succeed John Edmonds in the GMB, the winner Kevin Curran would continue the union's scathing analysis of a number of government policies, particularly on privatisation and PFI. The aforementioned elections followed Dave Prentis in 2001, succeeding Rodney Bickerstaffe as General Secretary of UNISON.[8] The leadership changes in the four largest trade unions over the course of two years in conjunction with the retirement of TUC General Secretary, John Monks, in March 2002 facilitated greater cohesion among trade unions: ideologically, personally and organisationally.

The emergent strategy developed by the largest trade unions was framed around 'reclaiming' the Labour Party. To illustrate the approach, Tony Woodley stated he would convene a meeting of like-minded general secretaries to consider how to put the "Labour back into the party" (Labour Research Department, July 2003). However, disaffiliation would be adopted by several smaller unions, principally the RMT (February 2004) and the FBU (June 2004) following a bitter nine-month industrial dispute in the case of the latter (Charlwood, 2004). A number of key policy areas are identified as fuelling intra-union dynamics and hostility to the New Labour project including the privatisation of public services. The attitudes were informed by an interpretation of accommodation to the Labour leadership and an inability to effectively challenge the social partnership policy agenda (Ludlam and Taylor, 2003). Trade union actors support this analysis as Derek Simpson offered the following contribution:

> This is in 2002 to 2003 after 1997. Labour in this period had been returned with three million less votes and there was a general dissent and general feeling that there wasn't enough being done. Maybe this manifested among union members. So, the type of rhetoric was appealing. For example, my rhetoric was that Ken Jackson was Tony Blair's favourite union leader and his stances on issues like pensions

were because Tony Blair wanted him to do this as they didn't want
to restore the link any more than they did to reverse the anti-trade
union laws.

(Extract from Derek Simpson, Interview 24)

Kevin Curran identified that the Labour Government's strategy directly
influenced the trajectory of the internal politics and ideological discourse
of trade unions:

> Absolutely, I think that people were looking for a more radical under-
> standing in what our purpose was and that's why a lot of organised
> workers being dissatisfied and disappointed with the Labour Gov-
> ernment because they could see that there was things that could be
> done to improve power and accountability at work and nothing was
> being done. In effect, the opposite was happening.

(Extract from Kevin Curran, Interview 25)

Speaking as the general secretary-elect of the TGWU, Tony Woodley
(July 2003), summed up the frustrations of the new leadership in the
largest trade unions as he acerbically judged that the employment relations agenda of the second term Labour Government could be "fitted on
the back of a postage stamp" (*Financial Times*, 2003 cited in Ludlam and
Taylor, 2003: 745).

The Big Four

It is critical to illuminate the strategising processes of trade union leaders, in particular how they interpret the constraints and opportunities
available in a liberal market. A key part of the interpretation process
is framed through the progressive centralisation of power in the trade
union movement (see Table 6.1). In 2006, the process of consolidation
would accelerate to the largest four trade unions, constituting 60 per cent
of the membership out of a total of sixty-three unions. The concentration
of resources, accordingly, facilitated an interpretation of what could be
possible if consensus between the largest trade unions could be arrived at.
It is in this wider context that the creation of the Big Four process involving AMICUS, GMB, TGWU and UNISON must be seen.[9]

The Big Four began a number of meetings over the summer of 2003
with the aim of adopting coordinated positions to maximise influence. Wintour and Maguire (2003) note the strategising would focus
on the forthcoming meetings of the Labour Party's NPF in the spring
and summer of 2004 at Warwick. The meetings would determine the
policy documents to be voted upon at the Labour Party Annual Conference in the autumn (27 September–1 October 2004). If approved, the
policies would go on to form the basis of the election manifesto. Dave

Table 6.1 Largest TUC-Affiliated Unions 2004–06

TUC-Affiliated Membership	2004	2005	2006
UNISON	1,301,000	1,310,000	1,317,000
AMICUS	935,321	1,200,000	1,200,000
TGWU	816,986	806,938	777,325
GMB	600,106	571,690	575,105
Top 4 % of Total	3,653,413 (57%)	3,888,628 (60%)	3,869,430 (60%)
Total Unions	70	66	63
Total Membership	6,423,694	6,452,179	6,463,159

Source: TUC Annual Reports (2004, 2005, 2006).

Prentis of UNISON stated that an alternative strategic response was necessary if the Labour Government's control of the policy agenda was to be challenged:

> When I became General Secretary about that time, we began to realise that the only way in which we were going to achieve anything was by working together. So, Unite was still separate, it was still the TGWU and AMICUS and then we had the GMB who we've got close relationships with and we decided that the only way in which we could play a full part in the Labour Party Conference and stop the manipulation was if we worked together and voted together and we met a number of times.
>
> We met very, very frequently, Liz {Snape} was one of the organisers of it, and it was really, when we did meet, it was about our political activity, not our industrial activity. And, we decided that each union would take a lead on certain issues and obviously our lead was on public services. The other unions took a lead on the different aspects. Each union was responsible then for putting in a motion and voting for the other motions as well and that changed the dynamics within the Labour Party Conference and it stopped individual unions being picked off and many times in the second term especially where we disagreed with Labour policy. It might be foundation hospitals, PFI and pensions and the unions would be able to vote together, and we did have a bigger influence on conference.
>
> (Extract from Dave Prentis, Interview 16)

Derek Simpson identified the ideological convergence and shared interpretation of the opportunities available among the leaders of the four largest unions as being central to coordination:

> The first thing was to bring the four unions together and make it into the Big Four. And, then to discuss common motions where we could

agree and to discuss what motions each union would like to push and then to in turn share it to see if any of us had problems with it so we could all support the motions. So, at TUC and Labour Party Conference, I don't think we have lost a vote. This in short is how the unions came together. Now whether this would have been possible if we didn't have common leaderships in honesty it would have been difficult.

(Extract from Derek Simpson, Interview 24)

Furthermore, Kevin Curran identified warm personal relationships as being an important dynamic in facilitating greater coordination:

What happened, which in my view was second best, we, as in me and a couple other general secretaries came together to articulate the reality that the four of us together could actually make a difference inside the TUC and inside the Labour Party . . . to make that work initially was personality based because, as in any walk of life, if you want to get people working together you have to be able to develop good relationships with them and so that wasn't always the case with general secretaries.

A lot of general secretaries had different ambitions; egos were always an issue. All those things I thought countermanded what we needed to, which was to get together. And, as history chanced it, I was elected then Tony {Woodley} was elected to the TGWU. Tony and Derek {Simpson} working closely together already. Dave {Prentis} in UNISON, as you probably know is an amenable guy, so we started talking basically and getting together.

(Extract from Kevin Curran, Interview 25)

As a by-product of trade union dissatisfaction, the Big Four process would not involve the leadership of the TUC. Sir Brendan Barber, former General Secretary of TUC, acknowledged the development of the Big Four as being partly attributable to weak coordination mechanisms:

So, in the absence of something like the TUC/Labour Party Liaison Committee, in the absence of any kind of real appropriate collective mechanism, increasingly unions looked to the Labour Party conference as the one opportunity each year to potentially really try and force a policy line through.

(Extract from Sir Brendan Barber, Interview 12)

Sir Brendan Barber judged the Big Four development to be an understandable reaction to the Labour Government's policies, yet remarked that the new strategic approach excluded other partners in the trade union movement as supportive levers:

I understood the frustrations and both John {Monks} during his period as General Secretary and I during mine had in different ways and at different times repeatedly tried to persuade Blair, then indeed Brown later on, that there needed to be a different basis for the conversation. Rather, than this punch up at the Party Conference every year which was just mutually hugely unsatisfying because even on those occasions where the unions kind of won the conference vote, the leadership just immediately made it clear that they had absolutely no intention at all of doing anything as a consequence. So, what's the bloody satisfaction in that kind of thing?

So, I certainly tried to persuade Blair to do something different and set up some kind of different basis for a conversation and not succeeded. So, I understood the union kind of frustrations but I was uneasy too. In part because it didn't look to me like it held a great deal of promise for actually genuinely building influence, which I've always thought is based on trying to develop some kind of mutually supportive, respectful relationships, that try to build some genuine consensus and understanding of different perspectives. To try to build towards some conclusions but that was the way you ought to be trying to make policy. Not, you know, by brute force on a 6/5 vote or something. So, I was not confident that it would actually be effective and I was certainly concerned that the dynamics of the Big Four being at the head of this process excluded an awful lot of other people in the wider trade union movement.

(Ibid)

The issue of encompassing a wider section of the trade union movement to garner support in partnership with the Big Four was a key part of the strategy towards the reform of TULO. Byron Taylor, Secretary of TULO during this period, stated that while the Big Four could act as the vanguard, those unions required wider support if policy objectives were to be attained:

In that sense, Tony Dubbins was the link between the Big Four and the other unions. What the Big Four wanted they usually got. However, the problem was that the Big Four on their own did not have the power to force the issues through Labour Party Conference or the National Policy Forum. These forums relied upon smaller unions to sustain that unity.

(Extract from Byron Taylor, Interview 26)

The reorientation strategy would entail a substantial shift in the historical modus operandi of TULO and its antecedents. The body had concentrated on fundraising, organising and campaigning among trade unions affiliated to the Labour Party to support it, particularly although not exclusively around elections. The strategy confirmed the marginalisation of the TUC as the primary channel of influence in favour of the Labour Party.

Institutional Reconfiguration: TULO

The opportunity for maximising leverage on the Labour leadership became greater as trade union financial contributions became proportionately more important as Labour entered its second term in office.[10] In conjunction, the role of TULO became progressively more important in persuading union members to support Labour as the party's electoral support diminished from 43.2 per cent of the popular vote in 1997 to 35.2 per cent in 2005. Evidence on electoral turnout and voting patterns suggested that the efforts trade unions made to encourage trade union members to vote Labour did have an impact in 2001. Trade union members were as much as 10 per cent more likely to vote than voters did in general and were far more likely than non-trade unionists to vote Labour (Ludlam et al., 2002).

It was in this context that reforming TULO alongside the creation of the Big Four and a reconstituted TUG in parliament represented the greatest strategic opportunity to maximise trade union influence since Tony Blair's election to the leadership in 1994. Undy (2002: 644) described a twin-track strategy of the TUC and the 'fall back route' of the Labour Party structures that were available to trade unions. The 'routes' would now switch, as the party route became the primary channel for exerting influence on the Labour Government for the largest trade unions. John Edmonds outlined the genesis of the steps to reform TULO after the 2001 general election initially through informal processes:

> It was in no sense just my initiative. It was the initiative of the people who I talked about Bill [Morris], Tony {Dubbins}, Jimmy Knapp {RMT General Secretary} and myself. Pent up frustration at the fact that we couldn't manage to punch our weight in the various Labour Party decision-making bodies because of the process I was talking about. So, more and more the move was towards discussing policy issues and discussing approaches towards the policy forums. It was more successful than having nothing but it was not successful as it might have been because the processes that were leading to these problems were still there. But, it was clearly necessary to have a forum where affiliated unions could form policy and it was even more important once the Labour Party Conference diluted the trade union vote and where the policy-making role of the conference was diluted. So, it became even more important that the trade unions had a collective position.
>
> (Extract from John Edmonds, Interview 6)

Dave Prentis emphasised the centrality of the Big Four to the reconfiguration of TULO:

> I mean, well we [Big Four] drove the agenda. So, I mean we wanted to. We realised only the affiliated unions could operate within Labour

Party democracy. The TUC could talk to ministers and, well there were ministers at the time, but if you wanted to change Labour Party policy you had to do it through the internal mechanisms. And, there was an issue as well for us, that in developing this idea of the 'Big Four' being united, there were quite a number of other unions affiliated and we didn't want to leave them out. You know we wanted everybody to be within the fold. So, this idea of coordination we developed it with the other unions and so we decided as well that we had to do more work through TULO, principally because we were going in a different direction to some of the Blairite policies.

(Extract from Dave Prentis, Interview 16)

The end of Lord Morris' tenure as Chair of TULO in September 2003 facilitated the opportunity for institutional reform. John Edmonds highlighted there was some initial 'resistance' from sections of the affiliated trade unions to the reform of TULO but emphasised that it was necessary in order to foster greater cohesion in an environment of centralised power in the Labour leadership. Edmonds said: "There was some opposition there but the trend was pretty clear that you had to do this otherwise some of the nonsense where you couldn't even get the trade union votes to vote for trade union policy" (Extract from John Edmonds, Interview 6). Tony Dubbins complements the previous perspective by identifying the 'lukewarm' support from specific union leaders. Dubbins outlined the informal steps taken to reform TULO as the body's new Chair from September 2003:

> I did see every single general secretary at the time and did talk it through and made it pretty clear what I wanted to do with TULO. So, no one could suggest or say that they were under any doubt about what I wanted to do when I took over as Chair of TULO. While it is true to say there was no public resistance to it, some of it was a bit lukewarm and some of it was left in the air with questionable degrees of support. So, it was going to be tested in that sense, and the first test came along at the very next conference {Labour Party} because of course you have to get a TULO agenda at conference also because it was not only an agenda for the National Policy Forum.[11]
>
> (Extract from Tony Dubbins, Interview 6)

In addition, Byron Taylor outlined the formal steps undertaken to facilitate the institutional reconfiguration of TULO as the body's coordinating secretary:

> In preparation for Tony Dubbins coming into the Chair of TULO I wrote a series of documents entitled 'Structures, Campaigning, Policy and Finance'. Each of those had a clear direction of where I thought TULO could go. On structures, I highlighted the fact that

there was no Executive function and attendances at TULO meetings were poor. Decisions at TULO subsequently carried very little weight. I made a proposal in light of this for an Executive and Tony Dubbins thought that was too formal and reduced this to the Contact Group, which was a much more informal body but in essence was the same thing. This was the general secretary of the eight largest unions meetings on an ad hoc basis out with the regular TULO meetings designed to discuss issues of importance and to meet with the government.

(Extract from Byron Taylor, Interview 26)

The reform of TULO received varied responses from those Labour ministers dealing directly with trade unions on employment relations matters. Gerry Sutcliffe reflected on his direct involvement with TULO in policy negotiations as a government minister describing the new process as more 'professional':

Well it was quite odd really because as Employment Minister I used to meet the TUC on a regular basis such as our quarterly meetings, which would involve usually the same people. Then we would go to TULO, which involved only affiliated unions to the party. So, it was quite odd that we had these separate meetings. The TUC meetings were very formal way much the same as with the CBI. However, within the TULO framework, we used to meet on a monthly basis and in addition to policy there were also wider discussions about what was going on in the party, constituencies and in the unions. I think TULO fostered a far more professional relationship, and, Ian {McCartney} and I particularly were keen to participate in this and give it a go.

(Extract from Gerry Sutcliffe, Interview 20)

Tom Watson reinforced the view that the reform of TULO induced a more 'professional' approach. Watson affirmed that the central dynamic in the reform process was the personal relationships in the Big Four unions being 'healed':

I think what Tony {Dubbins} did was demand a discipline from the unions in the way they processed their own policy-making but it didn't necessarily become the cohesive group until there was change at the top of the unions. And, the reason I think TULO is far more effective now is essentially because the leaders of Unite [TGWU and AMICUS], the GMB and UNISON have worked very, very hard to achieve common positions with each other, and where they can't get common positions certainly not undermine each other's positions.

And so, Tony certainly used the TULO mechanism to professionalise the way union research departments submitted content, the way the public positions of unions was made and was given to the press and the negotiation position they took. But, he didn't really have the authority to do it. TULO didn't really have the authority to negotiate with strength until the relationship with the general secretaries was healed.

(Extract from Tom Watson, Interview 15)

In an echo of Sir Brendan Barber's critique of the new trade union strategy, Lord Collins, Labour Party General Secretary (2008–11), argued that TULO reform in fact limited the scope for policy discussion:

I would argue that TULO very strongly should not be involved in policy-making not because I don't think trade unions should not have a right to be heard it's because if this sort of position is adopted then you actually deny unions the opportunity to put forward their own particular perspective to it. I think this is what has happened. The range of trade union issues and trade union voices has been diminished because TULO if you like has become the lobbying group.

(Extract from Lord Collins, Interview 22)

Furthermore, Sir Ian McCartney commented from the perspective as Joint Chair of TULO during this period. McCartney viewed the reform as 'flawed' and re-emphasised that the TUC should have remained the primary channel for dialogue with the government:

I think it is fundamentally flawed [TULO reform]. I was joint Chair of TULO. TULO was designed for a different purpose. TULO was designed to develop the campaigning strategy and tools for the unions and the party to campaign in elections. It was also for to campaign on issues and quite rightly so. There are other bodies where the dialogue on policies should take place, which are accountable and wider.

The relationship with the TUC is very important because in the end policy with the TUC is about affiliated and non-affiliated unions. It can't be just inclusive of affiliates. The problem is that they aren't actually part of the party but party machinery has to engage on policy, which is accountable. This has been on-going during the period when I was Joint Chair. There was increasing pressure to take issues, which were in the domain of the TUC quite frankly as the social partner and put into TULO. TULO is made up of large and small unions, and the large unions just dominated the discussion and the rest had to go along with it.

(Extract from Sir Ian McCartney, Interview 14)

In response, trade union actors involved in the process of TULO reform and the creation of the Big Four explain the strategic reorientation was judged as the optimum option in which to advance trade union objectives. In relation to the specific criticism of the TUC leadership's marginalisation, the leadership of UNISON offered the following explanation.

> Dave Prentis: I think it was just an arrangement that we knew each other and we were working well together and we had . . . there was an organisation around us that led us to do it through that forum. But, I don't think it, other people may think differently, but I don't think we sat down and said we're going to exclude the TUC.
> Liz Snape: No, I think it happened by default. We had all suffered or were suffering attacks within our unions, all unions, regarding disaffiliation and we really hadn't shown affiliation brought us influence, brought us access and policy changes and opportunities. So, we had a debate the year before [2003].[12]
> Dave Prentis: Yes a major debate the year before.
> Liz Snape: A major debate trying to disaffiliate us from the party. GMB had two goes at it. TGWU probably hadn't or AMICUS most definitely hadn't. But, there was a feeling that as the Left was growing in unions, questioning the value particularly of New Labour, as it was on the ascendency by this point. So, we just had to go hell for leather and showing what us all chipping in millions every year, blank cheques as they were called, that there was a bit of return because the TUC didn't put a penny in. So, we needed to differentiate ourselves.
>
> (Extract from Dave Prentis and Liz Snape, Interview 16)

Kevin Curran complemented this analysis adding that the marginalisation of the TUC leadership was not a deliberate exclusionary strategy but evolutionary in the context of Labour's tenure in office:

> I don't think it was conscious. It was just the way it evolved. No one sat down and planned the Big Four. It just made complete sense at the time. So, there was no strategy worked out like do we include this person, do we exclude that person. There was none of that. It was almost evolutionary—it just had to happen.
>
> (Extract from Kevin Curran, Interview 25)

The factor of financial donations as noted by Prentis and Snape (UNISON) by affiliated party unions was an important consideration in the respective leaderships of trade unions. The GMB as previously referred to had reduced financial contributions to the Labour Party due to policy disagreements such as PFI. The aspect of financial contributions to the party must be considered in conjunction with the decadal political fund ballots (2003–05). In the latest balloting round, there would again be a

Table 6.2 Labour Party–Affiliated Unions 1998 and 2004

Labour Party Affiliates	1998	2004
AEEU/AMICUS	400,000	571,600
Associated Society of Locomotive Engineers and Firemen (ASLEF)	15,260	15,500
Bakers, Food and Allied Workers Union (BFAWU)	20,100	5,100
Broadcasting, Entertainment, Cinema and Theatre Union (BECTU)	12,000	8,000
Ceramic and Allied Trades Union (CATU/ UNITY)	22,335	4,625
CWU	224,888	210,000
FBU	20,000	N/A
General Union of Loom Overlookers (GULO)	200	218
GMB	700,000	400,000
GPMU	70,000	49,500
ISTC/COMMUNITY (Formerly the Iron and Steel Trades Confederation)	48,000	50,173
MSF	135,100	N/A
Musicians Union (MU)	10,500	10,500
National Association of Colliery Overmen, Deputies and Shotfirers (NACODS)	1,000	450
National Union of Domestic Appliances and General Operatives (NUDAGO)	590	600
National Union of Knitwear, Footwear and Apparel Trades (NUKFAT)	41,000	2,537
NUM	5,001	5,100
RMT	50,000	N/A
TGWU	500,000	400,000
Transport and Salaried Staffs Association (TSSA)	30,000	27,338
UCATT	20,000	51,000
USDAW	260,159	314,143
UNISON	700,000	570,000
TOTALS	**3,286,133**	**2,696,384**

Source: Figures provided by TULO (October 2015).

resounding 'yes' vote, with the average being 78 per cent slightly lower than previous two rounds. The turnout was 28 per cent significantly lower than the 38 per cent achieved in 1994–96 (Leopold, 2006: 197).[13] The sidelining of the TUC, therefore, should be considered through the lens of trade union leaderships initiating strategic steps to substantiate the continuance of the party-union relationship in order to offset criticisms of party affiliation. Nonetheless, Kevin Curran did identify that there was a perception that the TUC strategy was 'too slow', which in the context of mounting internal-frustrations required a more assertive response:

> Unfortunately at the time, Brendan {Barber} got some flak for it, because there was so much impatience and anger in what wasn't happening and some general secretaries previously of the TUC have been too leaden, too slow, not dynamic enough if you like, and some of that criticism was fair, some was unfair.
> (Extract from Kevin Curran, Interview 25)

Lord Morris complements the previous point, suggesting that one channel for focusing policy efforts was strategically more advantageous than a fragmented process. In doing so, Morris identified that the TUC had also failed to 'grasp' the outsourcing and privatisation of public services. As such, this contributed to reservations over the body's effectiveness with the government:

> There was a universality of interest in that debate {privatisation}, which the TUC has never been able to grasp at all. Hence, you get different structures as alternatives. I don't think you can make a distinction by saying some issues in this forum and some others you don't because this fragments the process because some people are at both meetings and some people at only one. So you have to choose. It's a choice you have to make.
> (Extract from Lord Morris, Interview 7)

The Agreement

In May 2004, the Big Four held a conference titled 'Working Together for a Radical Third Term'. Leopold (2006: 198) considered the meeting as "evidence of a regrouping to reassert the link but demand something in return for it". Stronger employment relations laws would form the central policy platform for trade unions at the Warwick NPF in July 2004. Byron Taylor outlined the tactics adopted by TULO and the efforts to present the most cohesive policy front in advance of the forthcoming NPF meetings:

> There was a surprising level of determination by senior trade union officials. The changes in general secretaries had facilitated that process. . . . I asked all the trade unions to submit to me all the issues they would like to see and what they would consider to be their primary and secondary policies. This was done over a period of two months or so.
>   Then it was the responsibility of TULO to log, categorise, clarify, and then to assemble them into a coherent document. Once, we had

this coherent document of primary and secondary issues it was then our responsibility and literally we spent hours with all the political officers together working through the issues one by one and seeking to find where there were conflicts between trade unions. The rule was that wherever there was a conflict it was expelled from the document. In actual fact, there were only two issues, which came up where we couldn't reach agreement with all the unions. So, it was quite a straightforward thing to go to Warwick with a full agenda.

(Extract from Byron Taylor, Interview 26)

Derek Simpson, former General Secretary of AMICUS, emphasised that in order to foster commonality divisive policy items between trade unions had to be removed from the Warwick negotiations:

For example, why would we want to push motions on nuclear weapons when thousands of our members work in the defence industry when we know that UNISON who is pushing a green agenda will oppose it? Why then would UNISON want to push a motion on anti-nuclear weapons when they know we would oppose it for the opposite reason? Therefore, let's concentrate on the positive things we want and can agree on and leave out the contradictory ones and where we have differences.

(Extract from Derek Simpson, Interview 24)

John O'Regan complemented the previous contributions, as he also identified the importance of divisive policy issues being left off the negotiation table to prevent trade union splits:

There were a few issues by the way which were left off of that agenda because what we said was that unless all the unions could agree then that union could still put it on but we didn't want anything that we couldn't all get behind. There wasn't many issues just one or two such as the renationalisation of the railways but there wasn't many. We then had meetings with the government and Ian McCartney was the minister at the time and Gerry Sutcliffe was involved because he was also a minster at the DTI.

(Extract from John O'Regan, Interview 21)

As a participant in the negotiations through his role as TGWU Deputy General Secretary, Jack Dromey, identified the centrality of trade unions acting 'collectively and the months of preparatory work leading up to the Warwick negotiations':

So, in the run up to 2004 at Warwick, the unions were much more effective and coherent. They {trade unions} acted collectively and

I was part of the negotiating team. There were eight on the union side, two from the TGWU that was Tony Woodley and myself.

(Extract from Jack Dromey, Interview 23)

Dromey added:

For months before Warwick there was discussion around a trade union agenda. Inevitably there was a shopping list or a wish list. I think it started with fifty-eight in inverted commas—demands—but then we progressively focused on key issues. What was good about this is that we were not just going to leave it to the forum itself. . . . For example I met various people on the issue of pensions and some of the issues around workers rights. So, we would have these detailed discussions and then report back. Therefore, the ground was very effectively laid with government.

(Ibid)

As the Warwick negotiations between the trade unions and the Labour Government advanced, Byron Taylor drew attention to the fault lines that emerged between Labour ministers in advance of the NPF discussions at Warwick, and during the forum's deliberations. To an extent, this would represent a reversal from the trade union divisions which had prevailed during the NMW (1998), ERA (1999) and Exeter NPF (2001). Taylor offered the following observations on the negotiations:

In terms of the Parliamentary Labour Party it became obvious very early on that there were divisions over the trade unions. This point takes me back to when I referred to the divisions and the negotiating tactics. We had Ian McCartney and Gerry Sutcliffe offering the government perspective and who were very keen to strike a deal with the trade unions and very favourable towards the unions. Although aware their room for commitment and manoeuvre was limited. Often agreements could be struck with them and then taken off the table. Geoff Norris, Patricia Hewitt {Secretary of State for Trade and Industry} and Pat McFadden {Prime Minister's Political Secretary} I think were the key people from the government side. Occasionally other ministers would be brought in. I remember having quiet conversations with Gerry Sutcliffe in the Warwick Conference Centre trying to find out how far they could be pushed.

(Extract from Byron Taylor, Interview 26)

In addition, Taylor noted:

Most of the discussion was face to face. Matt Carter was also in there from the Labour Party I should say. The sessions lasted from eleven in the morning right thought to three and four in the morning.[14] The divisions in the Labour Parliamentary Party were extremely useful to us in identifying where we could and couldn't go.

(Ibid)

Gennard and Hayward (2008: 218) add that the professionalisation of TULO as previously highlighted by Watson, Sutcliffe and Dromey assisted the objectives of trade unions as the negotiations unfolded. The authors contend that due to the greater degrees of coordination, TULO was "better organised and resourced" than the government. Kevin Curran reinforced these academic assertions:

> There was always unity amongst the Big Four. The Labour Party knew they couldn't grab one general secretary's shoulder down the corridor and say 'by the way Kevin, do you think you could do this or do that'. That was the agreement's effect because they knew that we were together and that there was no way there was going to be any personality issues. Again, back down to relationship management. Relationship management was very important. We were really confident that we were negotiating with the support of trade unions and that TULO were our right hand if you like and doing it very well.
>
> (Extract from Kevin Curran, Interview 25)

Furthermore, Gerry Sutcliffe contributed the following comments in agreement with the importance of TULO reform to the Warwick Agreement negotiations:

> I think this {TULO reform} has actually helped trade union and government relations because we knew what the common list was going to be. When we got to Warwick, we reached an agreement based on the TULO representatives coming together in a common aim which in years gone by never happened.
>
> (Extract from Gerry Sutcliffe, Interview 20)

The emergent details from the Warwick NPF on 25 July 2004 would provide the basis for the Labour manifesto in 2005 (see Appendix C for more details). Dave Prentis heralded the Warwick Agreement as "the most comprehensive and far-reaching ever agreed between the trade unions and the party of Government" (Labour Research Department, September 2004). However, in a sign of the friction to develop over the coming years regarding the implementation of pledges, Labour ministers and advisers simultaneously briefed that many of the pledges were "a promise only to review issues" (Wintour, 2004). Reflective of the fault lines between the Labour Party leadership and the trade unions, both parties each produced documents setting out their different perspectives on what had actually been agreed to in the official policy document of the Labour Party titled 'Britain is Working' (September 2004).

Implementation

The Employment Relations Act reached the statute book in September 2004 with a cluster of its provisions brought into force in October with other aspects in April 2005. The legislation enhanced a number of employment rights. Protection against unfair dismissal was extended from eight to twelve weeks. Workers gained statutory protection against being offered inducements by their employer to be or not to be a trade union member, and to remove collective bargaining agreements. Smith and Morton (2009: 215) highlighted the specific case of ASDA, who were forced to pay 340 members of the GMB £2,500 each at a total cost of £850,000 in light of the company offering an inducement to remove collective bargaining in 2006 due to this clause. A union official allowed to accompany a worker at disciplinary or grievance hearings was expanded to include responding on the worker's behalf to any view expressed at the hearing.

The legal requirements concerning industrial action ballots and notices to employers were also simplified. Nonetheless, the legislation in relation to 'lists and figures' in sections 22 and 25 specifically instructed trade unions to provide employers with a list of members (by category and workplace) and the figures involved (total, number in each category and the number in each workplace). Simpson (2005: 333) remarked these amendments continued to "underline the function of the law . . . in assisting employers to limit the impact of any industrial action". A number of other measures were introduced designed to tweak the statutory trade union recognition procedures. This included prohibiting improper campaigning activity by employers and unions during recognition and derecognition ballots. Trade unions were now permitted to communicate with workers covered by recognition claims at an earlier stage in the process. In contrast, the ERA (1999) stated employers must provide the relevant trade union with access to the workforce only during the period of the ballot. The government added pensions-related issues to the topics for collective bargaining under a statutory recognition award (pay, hours and holidays). According to the TUC, the ERA (2004) contained 'significant union victories' as the TUC General Secretary, Sir Brendan Barber, welcomed the legislation, saying: "Trade unions will be able to recruit members in an environment free of underhand, US {United States}-style union-busting activities" (EurWork, 2004).

In March 2005, the Prime Minister confirmed that regulation to end the two-tier workforce in local government would be extended across the public sector including the civil service and the NHS. The announcement was part of pre-election steps to minimise tensions as trade unions announced a strike ballot of hundreds of thousands of public sector workers over an imminent rise in the retirement age for local government employees.[15] Sir Ian McCartney, as Labour Party Chair, sought to reassure unions that the government was adhering to the Warwick pledges, citing the protection against dismissal being extended before adding: "Warwick will be implemented—but only if Labour wins the historic third term we all cherish" (Wintour, 2005). Labour was returned to government in May 2005 with 35.2 per cent of the vote (40.7 per cent in 2001) compared with 32.4 per cent for the Conservatives. The vote share drop represented a reduction of nearly 4 million votes from 1997. The general election spending further illustrated the progressive financial influence of trade unions during successive Labour Governments (1997–2010), despite the efforts of the Labour leadership to reduce the reliance on trade union financial contributions. The Electoral Commission between July 2001 and December 2004 reported that the Labour Party centrally received a total of £41.1 million in donations and affiliation fees with affiliated trade unions accounting for £26.4 million of that figure (Labour Research Department, May 2005).

In the aftermath of the general election victory, the Trade and Industry Secretary, Alan Johnson, argued that the influence of trade unions on Labour Party policy should be curtailed, as he alleged the trade unions were "abusing their power by voting together and commanding policy" (Buckley, 2005).[16] The proposals were outlined in the Labour Party document 'A 21st century party' in the context of a proposed mega-merger involving AMICUS, GMB and TGWU. In conjunction with UNISON, the four largest trade unions controlled over a third of the total voting strength at the Labour Party Annual Conference.[17] The internal party manoeuvres increased trade union concerns in relation to implementation of the agreement. Derek Simpson, speaking in May 2006, noted:

> Some aspects of Warwick have been delivered. . . [but] the more contentious—and more important—issues have only partly been dealt with or not dealt with at all. In fact it seems almost as if there is an attempt to renege on Warwick.
>
> (Davies, 2006)

By the autumn of 2006, progress was being made on a number of policy issues such as maternity leave being further extended in the Work and Families Act (2006) (see Box G). TUPE protection for pensions affected by company mergers was strengthened, as two public bodies were created possessing powers in relation to private pension plans: the Pensions Regulator and the Pension Protection Fund.[18]

Box G Progress on the Warwick Agreement (2006)

- Protection from dismissal for strikers from eight to twelve weeks.
- TUPE-style protection for pensions affected by a company transfer or merger.
- Pensions for same sex partners.
- Pensions White Paper proposing restoration of the link between the basic state pension and average earnings and 3 per cent compulsory employer contributions.
- Increasing statutory maternity leave from six to nine months in April 2007.
- Corporate Manslaughter Bill, but without director's liability.
- Manufacturing—fostering an expansion of apprenticeships and an increase in the number of union learning reps.
- The government also implemented a Manufacturing Forum, similar to the existing Public Service Forum, in December 2004.
- Training for pension trustees.
- NHS cleaning contracts based on tests of cleanliness and not allocated on basis of price.
- Rolling out of two-tier workforce protection in local government across the public services.

Source: Labour Research Department (October 2006).

Following the creation of Unite the Union, a review of the Warwick Agreement was published in July 2008. The report was framed around a 'traffic light' system to indicate degrees of progress (green, yellow and red).[19] The report supported the wider concerns about the slow progress made in relation to 'contentious issues' cited by Derek Simpson. Items considered 'red' included support for a pilot in trade union recruitment in small firms and making pensions a bargaining issue for recognition purposes. Items considered 'yellow' included progress on the LPC examining differential pay rates for 18–21-year-olds and the implementation of the European Union Agency Workers Directive. Nonetheless, the report overall conveyed a sense that the Warwick Agreement represented a qualified success by the juncture of publication as Unite judged of 108 policy pledges agreed at Warwick 70 (65 per cent) were classified as 'green', 25 (23 per cent) 'yellow' and 13 (12 per cent) as 'red'.

Ewing (2005: 21) drew specific attention to the issue of sector forums, which was categorised as 'red' by Unite. Ewing considered the pledge the 'most important' element of the Warwick Agreement on the basis that forums "could become a new institutional form in which employer representatives and trade unions come together to develop common standards". Possibly due to these potential implications the Labour Government would never roll-out sector forums. Trade union frustrations persisted as McIlroy (2009: 197) highlighted that the 'seemingly straightforward' pledge to exclude bank holidays from employees' statutory leave entitlement took until October 2007 before it was phased in through the Working Time (Amendment) Regulations 2007. The government had also agreed to uprate redundancy pay, incorporating the commitment under section 14 of the Work and Families Act 2006. The uprate from £350 to £380 did not take effect until October 2009. A further area of frustration for trade unions was in relation to the Corporate Manslaughter and Homicide Act (2007), which came into force in April 2008. The law made it easier to prosecute firms for negligence following a work-related death. On conviction, an organisation faced an unlimited fine, a remedial order to remedy a fatal breach and a public order. To the disappointment of trade unions, prosecutions focused on the corporate body and not individuals. There was no change to the liability of directors, board members and other individuals under health and safety law or general criminal law.

The Unite-TGWU section presented a motion to the Labour Party's Prosperity and Work policy commission, which "stressed that the agency workers issue was the single biggest issue facing Britain today" (NPF Report to Annual Conference, 2008: 235). Following consensus on the motion in July 2008 through the NPF process, this facilitated an agreement between the government, TUC and CBI in September 2008. The deal entitled equal treatment of agency workers after twelve weeks in a job. However, it would take the European Union Agency Workers Regulations (2010) until 1 October 2011 before it came into force, seven years after the Warwick Agreement (2004). The directive was itself undermined by the Swedish Derogation.[20] Sir Ian McCartney acknowledged the frustrations over the Labour Government's delays in implementation on Corporate Manslaughter legislation and European Directives in particular:

> The other major area where I did agree with the trade unions and battled for them was the amount of time it took to implement European legislation. In terms of the time it took to negotiate with the European Commission. Quite frankly, I tried to get my hands on this when I was Chair of the National Policy Forum or when I became party chair. Also on the issue of Corporate Manslaughter, which was approved in 1997 based on a paper written by Paul Boateng and myself. The time wasting that went on regarding implementation.[21] Employers ended up not happy with these areas, nor were unions happy because what did get implemented wasn't near far enough for them. So, a situation was created where nobody was happy. That should be a big lesson for a future Labour Government.
>
> (Extract from Sir Ian McCartney, Interview 18)

The NMW (1998) rates were also finally extended to include from 1 October 2010 workers aged 21 at £5.93 (minimum rate per hour) and an apprentice minimum wage rate was set at £2.50 an hour. Labour by this point was no longer in office. The Labour Party lost the general election in 2010 in the aftermath of the global financial recession. The Labour vote collapsed to 29 per cent (8,609,527 total votes) from 43.2 per cent in 1997 (13,518,167 total votes), which constituted a loss of 4.9 million votes over its tenure in government.

Evaluation and Reflections

The evidence substantiates that trade unions affiliated to the Labour Party achieved significant policy outcomes through the Warwick Agreement. The manifestations of these successes were primarily arrived at flowing from informal processes such as the Big Four in the post-2001 period. The agreement to end two-tierism in the public sector and the halting of privatisation in the provision of health services are both cited as particular examples of the progress that was made from Warwick by the UNISON leadership. John Reid, as Health Secretary, gave a commitment to limit private sector involvement with the maximum private share of NHS work being no more than 15 per cent 'in my lifetime' due to trade union pressure (Carvel, 2005). From the perspective of UNISON, the Warwick Agreement was considered a qualified success, as Prentis said: "Yes it was more successful than we expected" (Extract from Dave Prentis, Interview 16). The UNISON General Secretary identified the run-in to the general election in 2005 as exercising degrees of constraint on the ability of trade unions to attain stronger outcomes. Prentis reflected:

> We could have always got more. What happens is in the year before an election pressure is put on you not to rock the boat. So, probably if we'd have started a little bit earlier we could have had far more pressure, or we could have put far more pressure on the party. But, this is just the reality of political life. In the run up to an election you don't want to make public your disagreements because the electorate won't vote for you and we all recognise that and perhaps we did accept things.
>
> I think on employment rights we should have pushed harder and again on foundation hospitals. We were probably within a few votes of stopping foundation hospitals happening and we just failed and it was the trade union vote that stopped us. So, there were issues where you think, you know, we opposed ideologically privatisation but we also oppose it because the user of the service gets a poorer service and it's not value for money. If we'd had our way, it would have stopped the privatisation and fragmentation that took place in the second term or the third term. I mean when we were formed as a union in 1993 we probably dealt with 2,000 employers at the most. We now deal with 22,000 employers directly because of the Blairite years in fragmenting public services. So, you've got to keep the success in perspective.
>
> (Ibid)

Kevin Curran, the former General Secretary of the GMB, agreed with the circumspect reflections of Prentis on the extent of the outcomes: "We did achieve a fair amount. Nowhere near enough as we could have achieved but you know the reality was that there was only so far we could go" (Extract from Kevin Curran, Interview 25). The strategic actions enacted by trade union leaders to reform TULO and create the Big Four were considered critical to ensuring the implementation of key elements of the Warwick Agreement. Derek Simpson added that the Big Four was pivotal in terms of positively shifting the trade union policy agenda forward stating the process 'moved the line-up' (Extract from Derek Simpson, Interview 24). If the aforementioned strategic steps had not been taken, Tony Dubbins concluded the Warwick Agreement would not have been as successful as it was for trade unions:

> So, I think the party came to a conclusion very quickly that as a result of changes in leadership and the success we had already demonstrated at two or three party conferences that they were not going to divide the unions and therefore it would be better to try and agree an agenda. I think it succeeded pretty well and Warwick would never have happened without those changes.
>
> (Extract from Tony Dubbins, Interview 8)

Jack Dromey (TGWU) supported the prior assessment as he emphasised the key ingredient to the successes at Warwick derived from the Big Four process:

> I don't want to overstate this but coming up to Warwick 2004 it tended to be the Big Four rather than TULO but having said that the Big Four were very influential in TULO. Actually, TULO was very effective in bringing together the Big Four agenda and the agenda of others so there was unity of purpose at Warwick. Now, was it right that TULO was used to achieve that kind of unity and for the development of a coherent agenda? Yes, it was right.
>
> (Extract from Jack Dromey, Interview 23)

In contrast, Jon Cruddas identified the limitations of the 'reorientation' strategy from his perspective, specifically citing the marginalisation of the TUC. Nonetheless, Cruddas ascribed the strategy as being a 'symptom' of the centralised power in the Labour leadership:

> Well I understand the reorientation of the strategy. It is a symptom of our failure to build upon the first-term because that is the failure of Blair and Brown. What they should have done is welcome the Monks strategy and to help him. Monks leaving the TUC was also symptomatic of this and he was the best possible General Secretary for a

New Labour Government. Partly as a result of the frustration of the leadership not to build a strong single channel through the TUC and everything moved into the institutions of the party, understandably, but this track failed too.

(Extract from Jon Cruddas, Interview 19)

On the basis of this perspective, Cruddas questioned the level of success in the Warwick Agreement despite acknowledging the greater coordination amongst trade unions: "Whilst there was a tighter union agenda it being translated into definable and discernible outcomes I am much less sure about" (Ibid). Sir Brendan Barber also reiterated that the shift away from the TUC channel was detrimental to the interests of the whole trade union movement, and ultimately the Warwick outcomes:

So, the hugely important issue of education never got a look in. You know the affiliated unions had a particular catalogue of kind of issues partly arising from their own sectorial concerns and so on, that they wanted a highlight button. Hang on a minute there are whole huge areas of policy on which apparently we had nothing to say or had no view at all.

(Extract from Sir Brendan Barber, Interview 12)

Accordingly, Barber observed that the Warwick Agreement's impact was 'mixed' in terms of the outcomes for trade unions:

Well, there were some issues that were highlighted there, where clearly the government moved to take the steps that were envisaged and implement the issues that were identified. And, there were some others though it seemed as if perhaps some of the points in the documentation were rather more aspirational and less worked through. Where it was hard to subsequently say well what actually happened as a result of those few sentences or the section of the document on this particular point or that point and so on. So, it was mixed. It was mixed. There were clearly some issues where I think from a union perspective, progress was made.

(Ibid)

Lord Monks also shared these circumspect observations as he questioned the overall impact on the employment relations framework deriving from the Warwick Agreement:

The CBI hated the Warwick agreement not because very much came out of it arguably nothing came out of it by the way. The work had been made to be so imprecise that nobody is clear exactly what they have agreed to when they leave like on the Working Time . . . as there is all different types of interpretations of what was done. The unions were frustrated, as was I—I mean why am I over here {Brussels} and not over there {Britain} with dealing with Blair and others and getting nowhere. The TUC had reached a kind of limit and they were frustrated. They {the largest trade unions} decided to start linking policy to their financial muscle with a bit of encouragement with friends like people such as Ian McCartney.[22]

(Extract from Lord Monks, Interview 3)

Sir Ian McCartney identified Tony Blair's announcement to stand down as Prime Minster on 10 May 2007 as a key juncture. In a sequence of fascinating reflections, McCartney acknowledged trade union frustrations over delays in the implementation of the Warwick Agreement suggesting this partly stemmed from Blair's decision to stand down, and the subsequent political manoeuvrings in government:

I do understand {the frustrations}. The truth is the government after 2005 completely lost its way in reality. There were still a lot of good things done but you have, one, a sitting Prime Minister leaving at some point, and two, someone else planning for the job and who wants it and due to this the government lost focus. You also get reshuffles and some Secretaries of State actually not seeing the importance of the Warwick Agreement. This is why it's critical that after passing a policy area or agreeing to it just isn't enough from my experience in government.

(Extract from Sir Ian McCartney, Interview 18)

McCartney further reflected on the 'in-house' politics which beset Labour's third term before the onset of the global financial crisis of 2008:

There were good people in that third-term who did not have a focus. The government became so political in the sense of personalities and with in-house government politics—and they lost the wider perspective. Crisis management after 2008 {the global financial crisis} but long before this it was happening. It was one of the reasons I left government. It wasn't because I was offered a job I didn't want far from it. It was because I just felt that being a minister at that point we weren't going to get the things done. Even promises may not get done. Some ministers became more interested in taking over from Gordon {Brown} or whether Gordon would stay on. We became like the Tory Party leading up to 1997. There was no focus by ministers at the time. It was gone. This is what happened to Labour in the third term. The truth was nobody was properly focused on a fourth term.

(Ibid)

Despite there being varying interpretations over the progress made through the Warwick Agreement, there were a number of positive impacts on the employment relations framework as even those critical of the agreement's economic functionality (supply-side policies) and the speed of implementation concede.[23] Brown (2011: 411) judged the Warwick Agreement as being "far from the 'corporatist' collaboration with union leaders so characteristic of the 1960's and 1970's". Although the previous point may be true, it is not particularly insightful to compare the outcomes associated with the Social Contract (1974–79) and the Warwick Agreement (2004) on an equivalent basis because they manifested in two structurally different contexts. Rather, the central aspect to reflect upon is the comparative degrees of success in a liberal market economy. Viewed through this lens, the Warwick Agreement in some senses can be considered contextually a greater success than the NMW (1998) and ERA (1999) from a trade union perspective. The proposition is based on the successes judged to have been associated with both the process and outcomes. This is despite an acknowledgement that the Labour Party failed to deliver the Warwick Agreement 'in full' as the manifesto stated it would.[24]

Notes

1. In 2018, there were 204 members of the NPF with affiliated trade unions having thirty seats.
2. The current position regarding NPF representatives is that they are able to propose amendments to the NPF Report. A minority option is formed where the amendment has less than 50 per cent support but more than 25 per cent support from those present. The 25 per cent threshold is underpinned by a minimum 20 per cent of the forum membership (forty votes).
3. There were a number of rights guaranteed under the working time regulations. Workers required working only a maximum of 48 hours a week (averaged over a reference period of seventeen weeks—or more in specified circumstances) unless they 'opt out'. The regulations also specified a minimum daily rest period of eleven consecutive hours in each twenty-four-hour period plus an uninterrupted minimum weekly rest period of twenty-four hours. Instead of providing twenty-four hours' rest in each week, employers can, if they choose, provide forty-eight hours' rest over a fourteen-day period. In a working day longer than six hours, a worker is entitled to a rest break of at least twenty minutes. Workers were also entitled to a minimum 5.6 weeks' paid annual leave. This consisted of four weeks' basic leave and 1.6 weeks' additional leave to ensure all workers benefited from public holidays. The 5.6 weeks was subject to a cap of twenty-eight days.
4. The ending of the 'two-tier workforce' related to the practice of private sector companies taking over parts of the public sector and paying new workers a lower wage than the transferred workers whose pay and conditions were protected under Transfer of Undertakings Regulations (TUPE) regulations (1981).

5. Central Government directly funded infrastructure works such as schools or hospitals through PFI. PFI entails a consortium of private sector banks and construction firms who finance, own, operate and lease them back to the UK taxpayer, over a period of thirty to thirty-five years. PFI deals have been criticised as not having value for taxpayers, as the initiative is 'significantly more expensive' than government-funded projects, with the cost of borrowing at least two times higher than government-financed works, according to a 2011 HM Treasury Report (Benjamin, 2014).

6. It was announced without any warning on 4 December 2001 that the private health firm BUPA was awarded the contract to run a new NHS treatment centre in Surrey.

7. For further reading see Waddington (2003) and Ludlam and Taylor (2003).

8. Dave Prentis secured 125,584 votes (55.9 per cent) in the UNISON election in February 2000. Tony Woodley was elected with 66,958 votes (44 per cent) in May 2003 in a contest of four candidates including future Deputy, Jack Dromey. Kevin Curran was elected with 60,590 votes (65 per cent) in April 2003. However, due to allegations of vote rigging, Curran would resign in April 2005. Derek Simpson was declared the winner after a fourth count in July 2002 when he polled 89,521 votes to Sir Ken Jackson's 89,115.

9. For purposes of consistency, AMICUS will now be used for the remainder of the chapter.

10. In 1999, Labour fought four sets of elections (Scotland, Wales, Europe, and local authorities) and operated at a loss. Seven large unions made additional donations totalling £6 million, on top of their affiliation fees, to assist with these elections (*Financial Times*, 2000 cited in Ludlam and Taylor, 2003: 733).

11. The GPMUs merged with AMICUS in 2004, and Dubbins became Deputy General Secretary. Dubbins was also Chairman of the TULO from 2003 until 2008.

12. UNISON's national executive council approved recommendations of a two-year review of the union's political funds, which included rejecting a fund for alternative political parties ahead of its June 2003 Conference. The review was originally approved by the 2001 Conference on a "tide of hostility towards the government" (Labour Research Department, May 2003).

13. In 1985–86, the average turnout for workplace ballots was 69 per cent, but for postal ballots, it was 39 per cent (Leopold 1986 cited in Leopold, 1997: 29).

14. Matt Carter was General Secretary of the Labour Party from 2004 to 2005.

15. The retirement age for local government workers was to be raised on 1 April 2005, from 60 to 65, to reduce public sector pension costs. The strike was scheduled to go ahead on 23 March, just weeks before the general election. The strike action was called off following the decision of Deputy Prime Minister, John Prescott, to withdraw amended regulation to introduce pension changes.

16. Johnson proposed that unions' voting strength at Annual Conference should be reduced from 50 per cent to the proportion at the NPF (i.e. around 16 per cent).

17. The GMB would decide not to merge with the TGWU and AMICUS to create Unite in 2007.

18. Sections 257 and 258 of the Pensions Act 2004 provide pension protection for certain employees involved in a transfer to which the Transfer of Undertakings (Protection of Employment) Regulations 2006 (TUPE) apply. The protection applies to employees who, before the transfer, had rights in an occupational pension scheme, or a right (including a future right) to join an occupational pension scheme.

19. Green—pledges implemented or current progress to completion satisfactory to government and the affiliated trade unions. Yellow—areas of substantial concern amongst affiliated unions regarding the implementation or delivery of that pledge. Red—those policies and priorities where there is a disagreement between affiliates and the government over interpretation or delivery.

20. The Swedish Derogation, according to ACAS (2013), applies to the following: "For it to come into play, the temporary work agency offers an agency worker a permanent contract of employment and pays the worker between assignments. It has to be made clear to the worker that entering into the contract means giving up the entitlement to equal pay".

21. At the first Labour Party conference after its election victory in May 1997, the then Home Secretary Jack Straw committed to legislate to bring big companies to account for deaths caused by their actions at the Labour Party conference on October 2. A specific pledge to legislate on corporate manslaughter was contained in the Labour Party's 2001 manifesto on page 33.

22. Lord Monks left the TUC to take up the position of General Secretary of the European Trade Union Confederation (ETUC) based in Brussels from 2003 to 2011.

23. For further reading see Ewing (2005); Heery (2005); Bewley (2006); Leopold (2006); Howell and Kolins-Givan (2011).

24. Labour Party Manifesto (2005: 27) stated: "The Labour Party has agreed a set of policies for the workplace (the Warwick Agreement) and we will deliver them in full".

Bibliography

ACAS (2013). *Understanding Swedish derogation.* Available at: www.acas.org.uk/?articleid=4162 [Accessed 5 Mar. 2016].

BBC (18 July 2002). Profile: Sir Ken Jackson. Available at: http://news.bbc.co.uk/1/hi/uk_politics/2135952.stm [Accessed 2 Feb. 2014].

Benjamin, J. (17 November 2014). Seven things everyone should know about the private finance initiative. *Open Democracy.* Available at: www.opendemocracy.net/ournhs/joel-benjamin/seven-things-everyone-should-know-about-private-finance-initiative [Accessed 4 Feb. 2015].

Bewley, H. (2006). Raising the standard? The regulation of employment, and public sector employment policy. *British Journal of Industrial Relations*, 44(2), pp. 351–372.

Brown, W. (2011). Industrial relations in Britain under New Labour, 1997–2010: A post mortem. *Journal of Industrial Relations*, 53(3), pp. 402–413.

Buckley, C. (14 November 2005). Labour plots to cut power of its union paymasters. *The Times*, London.

Carvel, J. (13 May 2005). Hewitt's £3bn deal to double use of private sector in NHS angers union. *The Guardian*. Available at: www.theguardian.com/politics/2005/may/13/uk.health [Accessed 22 Feb. 2014].

Charlwood, A. (June 2004). The new generation of trade union leaders and prospects for union revitalisation. *British Journal of Industrial Relations*, 42(2), pp. 379–397.

Coates, D. (2005). *Prolonged labour: The slow birth of New Labour Britain*. Houndmills, Basingstoke: Palgrave Macmillan.

Davies, B. (17 May 2006). *Unions election warning to Brown*. Available at: http://news.bbc.co.uk/1/hi/uk_politics/4986118.stm [Accessed 10 Oct. 2016].

EurWork, European Observatory of Working Life (7 November 2004). *Employment Relations Act 2004 begins to come into force*. Available at: www.eurofound.europa.eu/observatories/eurwork/articles/employment-relations-act-2004-begins-to-come-into-force [Accessed 18 Oct. 2016].

Ewing, D.K. (March 2005). The function of trade unions. *Industrial Law Journal*, 34(1), pp. 1–22.

Gennard, J. and Hayward, G. (2008). *A history of the graphical, paper and media union*. Beecles: CPI William Clowes.

Grice, A. and Clement, B. (2 October 2002). Activists and unions accuse labour of 'downgrading' conference. *The Independent*. Available at: www.independent.co.uk/news/uk/politics/activists-and-unions-accuse-labour-of-downgrading-conference-138586.html [Accessed 16 Jan. 2014].

Heery, E. (2005). *Trade unionism under New Labour*. The Shirley Lerner Memorial Lecture 2005. Manchester Industrial Relations Society.

Howell, C. (2005). *Trade unions and the state: THE construction of industrial relations institutions in Britain, 1890–2000*. Princeton: Princeton UP.

Howell, C. and Kolins Givan, R. (June 2011). Rethinking institutions and institutional change in European industrial relations. *British Journal of Industrial Relations*, 49(2), pp. 231–255.

Labour Party (September 2004). *Britain is working*. London: The Labour Party.

Labour Party (2008). *National Policy Forum report to annual conference (2–14 September 2008)*. London: The Labour Party.

Labour Party Manifesto (2001). *Ambitions for Britain*. Sutton: Printed by HH Associates City House.

Labour Party Manifesto (2005). *Britain forward not back*. London: The Labour Party.

Labour Research Department (June 2002). *Unions wait for details of two-tier workforce code*. London: Labour Research Department.

Labour Research Department (September 2002). *Combatting the two-tier workforce*. London: Labour Research Department.

Labour Research Department (May 2003). *UNISON rejects other parties*. London: Labour Research Department.

Labour Research Department (July 2003). *Two new union leaders join independent squad*. London: Labour Research Department.

Labour Research Department (September 2004). *Labour soothes unions with policy promise*. London: Labour Research Department.

Labour Research Department (May 2005). *Unions stump up most of labour cash*. London: Labour Research Department.

Labour Research Department (October 2006). *The unions take stock of Warwick*. London: Labour Research Department.

Leopold, J.W. (March 1997). Trade unions, political fund ballots and the Labour Party. *British Journal Industrial Relations*, 35(1), pp. 23–38.

Leopold, J.W. (2006). Trade unions and the third round of political fund review balloting. *Industrial Relations Journal*, 37(3), pp. 190–208.

Ludlam, S. (2003). Too much pluralism, not enough socialism: Interpreting the unions—party link. In: J. Callaghan, S. Fielding and S. Ludlam, eds., *Interpreting the Labour Party: Approaches to labour politics and history*. Manchester: Manchester University Press.

Ludlam, S. and Taylor, A.J. (December 2003). The political representation of the labour interest in Britain. *British Journal of Industrial Relations*, 41(4), pp. 727–749.

Ludlam, S., Taylor, A.J. and Allender, P. (2002). Indispensable officer corps or embarrassing elderly relatives? Assessing the trade union contribution to Labour's General Election triumph in 2001. Paper presented to the *Annual conference of the Political Studies Association*, Aberdeen, April 2002. Available at: www.shef.ac.uk/politics/unionsinelections [Accessed 12 Dec. 2013].

Maguire, K. (1 October 2002). Leadership defeated on private cash. *The Guardian*. Available at: www.theguardian.com/politics/2002/oct/01/labourconference.labour13 [Accessed 13 Jan. 2014].

Maguire, K., Perkins, A. and Wintour, P. (2 October 2001). Unions hold fire after public sector pledge. *The Guardian*. Available at: www.theguardian.com/society/2001/oct/02/publicservices [Accessed 2 Feb. 2014].

McIlroy, J. (2009). Under stress but still enduring: The contentious alliance in the age of Tony Blair and Gordon Brown. In: G. Daniels and J. McIlroy, eds., *Trade unions in a neoliberal world: British trade unions under New Labour*. London: Routledge.

McIlroy, J. and Croucher, R. (2009). Kills and training: A strategic role for trade unions or the limits of neoliberalism? In: G. Daniels and J. McIlroy, eds., *Trade unions in a neoliberal world: British trade unions under New Labour*. London: Routledge.

Minkin, L. (2014). *The Blair supremacy: A study in the politics of the Labour Party's management*. Manchester: Manchester University Press.

Simpson, R. (2005). Strike ballots and the law: Round six. *Industrial Law Journal*, 34(4), pp. 331–337.

Smith, P. and Morton, G. (2009). Employment legislation: New Labour's neoliberal legal project to subordinate trade unions. In: G. Daniels and J. McIlroy, eds., *Trade unions in a neoliberal world: British trade unions under New Labour*. London: Routledge.

TUC (2004). *TUC annual report of 2004*. London: TUC.

TUC (2005). *TUC annual report of 2005*. London: TUC.

TUC (2006). *TUC annual report of 2006*. London: TUC.

TULO (October 2015). *Affiliated Labour Party membership figures*. Provided by email correspondence.

Undy, R. (2002). New Labour and New Unionism, 1997–2001: But is it the same old story? *Employee Relations*, 24(6), pp. 638–655.

Unite the Union (2008). *Warwick agreement report to Unite Executive Committee—July 2008*. London: Unite the Union.

Waddington, J. (2003). Heightening tension in relations between trade unions and the Labour Government in 2002. *British Journal of Industrial Relations*, 41(2), pp. 335–358.

Wintour, P. (24 December 2001). TUC leak reveals fury at labour. *The Guardian*. Available at: www.theguardian.com/politics/2001/dec/24/uk.Whitehall [Accessed 20 Jan. 2014].

Wintour, P. (7 August 2004). Labour pays the price of union support. *The Guardian*. Available at: www.theguardian.com/politics/2004/aug/07/uk.tradeunions [Accessed 13 Jan. 2014].

Wintour, P. (12 January 2005). Leaked letter reveals labour plea to unions. *The Guardian*. Available at: www.theguardian.com/politics/2005/jan/12/uk.society [Accessed 23 Feb. 2014].

Wintour, P. and Maguire, K. (3 October 2003). We gave them a bloody nose, unions boast. *The Guardian*. Available at: www.theguardian.com/society/2003/oct/03/publicservices.politics1 [Accessed 20 Jan. 2014].

7 Strategy, Influence and Power
Lessons From History

Introduction

The book has been guided by Hamann and Kelly's (2004) four factors which influence trade union decision-making: The book terms these factors as follows: (1) economic and political institutions; (2) union ideology; (3) employer, political party or state strategies; and (4) strategic choices of union leaders. These factors place broad structural, agency and ideational explanations at the centre of understanding and explaining trade union behaviour. Through this framework, it can be clearly demonstrated across the four legislative events that trade unions' decision-making is not determined by structural factors. To compare trade union 'outcomes' during the Labour Governments under analysis—1974–79 and 1997–2010—as equivalents is admittedly problematic. Instead, the book has endeavoured to present the perceptions of the relative success of the 'outcomes' attained in two structurally different environments. This has been achieved principally from analysing the perspective of trade union actors. The ambition of the chapter is to present a conceptually clearer—if far from complete—understanding of the endeavours by British trade unions to attain employment relations outcomes when the Labour Party is in government. These are the junctures at which trade unions are assumed to exercise greater influence and power in the development of the employment relations framework due to the institutional role affiliated trade unions have as a constituent part of the Labour Party.

Structural Context: Shifting Fronts

Trade unions inhabited a dramatically different structural context—politically and economically—during the Social Contract (1974–79) from the employment relations events analysed in the post-1997 period. The collective laissez-faire environment was characterised by a free collective bargaining system, which was ideologically embraced by the largest and most dominant unions in Britain. These dominant unions, principally in the private sector with large industrial and manufacturing bases, were reflective of the economic structure. The share of British manufacturing has since fallen from 36 per cent of the economy in 1948 to around 10 per cent in 2013. Additionally, only 8 per cent of jobs in 2013 were in manufacturing compared with 25 per cent in 1978, which was the juncture of high unionisation (i.e. overall union density at 50 per cent in 1979) (Office of National Statistics, 22 October 2014). The industrial landscape was characterised by an enabling institutional architecture and broad bipartisan acceptance of trade union inclusion in the governance aspects of the economy. The inclusion of trade unions in market relations was characterised by the expansion of collective bargaining in the form of national agreements and statutory machinery such as Wage Boards. However, collective agreements were not legally binding, and trade unions, rather than enjoying enshrined statutory rights, campaigned historically for the restoration of legal immunities.

Howell (2005) identified a process of 'industrial restructuring' during the 1950s and 1960s illustrated by a shift to newer industries such as vehicle assembly, light engineering and oil refining. Accordingly, the postwar consensus came under strain as large employers and employers' associations increasingly questioned the value and relevance of industry-wide bargaining. Therefore, a critical factor contributing to the disintegration of the centrally designed incomes policy component of the Social Contract was the decentralisation arising from fundamental structural changes in the economy. The structural changes were embedded by key sections of the trade union movement including the country's largest union—the TGWU—who supported workplace productivity bargaining as a strategic response to government incomes policies during the 1960s. Undy et al. (1981) opined that irrespective of the strength of the union-party link, it could not override the detrimental structural effects of the decentralisation agenda and the fragmented bargaining system. An additional structural factor attributed to the Social Contract's collapse was that organisational power resided more with individual unions in contrast with trade union confederations in Italy, Spain and Germany. Frege and Kelly (2003: 18) state that in these continental countries, trade unions possessed 'sufficient authority' over members to ensure more coordinated strategies due to structural configuration.

The coordination efforts through the Social Contract and its principal mechanism (i.e. the Liaison Committee) arguably prevented the collapse of the Labour Government at an earlier stage with its minimal majority. From the perspective of Jack Jones, as one of the key proponents of the Social Contract, the Liaison Committee was critical to maintaining 'unity' for as long as possible in light of the economic challenges epitomised by the IMF loan in 1976. A balanced reappraisal, therefore, should view the Social Contract as a political exchange process with significant successes. Lord Monks importantly said that "the process worked but so did the outcomes". The observation is at variance with the dominant academic and political discourse, which perceives the Social Contract as a failure due to the collapse of the incomes policy. Indeed, this view is given partial credence by Lord Monks who conceded that the industrial unrest "ended large trade union influence on the government".

The dominant discourse, which blamed the trade union movement for the Winter of Discontent, obscures the wider achievements in the Social Contract process from its genesis in 1971 to the autumn of 1978. The significant legislative achievements taken in cognisance with the strategic miscalculations by the Labour Government, specifically, the rigidity of the 5 per cent pay policy advanced for 1978–79, should result in the reframing of perceptions that the Social Contract's demise was 'inevitable'. The legislative outcomes should be viewed through the lens of a wider Social Contract, rather than be determined by the incomes policies component, which was having the desired deflationary impact until the collapse of Phase Four in November 1978. The rate of inflation was reduced from 28.1 per cent in the second quarter of 1975 to under 8 per cent during 1978 prior to the Winter of Discontent (Wilkinson, 2007). The legislative successes and voluntary pay restraint coordinated through the Liaison Committee must be considered in the context of significant economic structural tensions (internal and external), the ideological dominance of collective laissez-faireism, greater degrees of heterogeneity in the trade union movement and weak market coordination mechanisms at the height of trade union power.

During the period of economic deconstruction and reconstruction post-1979, a combination of endogenous and external shocks re-shaped the economy. Arguably, the most powerful factor of influence was the actions of successive Conservative Governments. These shocks ended collective laissez-faireism with its supportive employment relations architecture enabled by the state via both Labour and Conservative governments for eighty years (Howell, 2000). The pace of economic, legal and political reform was accelerated by the majoritarian electoral system (i.e. first past the post), which avoids the need for wider consensus through social-pacts as experienced in other European states. The reforms enabled greater opportunities for the state in partnership with employers to deconstruct and reconfigure employment relations regimes to the exclusion of trade unions.

In the liberal market context, the ideological reappraisal by successive Labour leaderships was profound. The internal party reform process was facilitated by leading trade unionists supporting the 'modernisation' programme initiated by Neil Kinnock as Labour Leader. Gennard and Hayward (2008) highlight by the time of the 1987 general election, which saw the return of a Conservative Government for the third consecutive term, trade unions were prepared to accede to internal Labour Party reform due to detrimental economic restructuring and hostile legislation. The political narrative presented to trade unions as an electoral 'reality' was that they had to reduce their institutional role in the Labour Party due to its perceived negative impact on the party's electoral prospects. The party reform process was emboldened by the significant fall in the TUC affiliated membership, which had totalled 12,128,078 members in 1979 but contracted to 9,243,297 members in 1987 (TUC Annual Report of 1979 and 1987).

The Labour leaderships' reforms in the post-1987 period, therefore, would not have been possible or would have been more powerfully resisted if it were not for the institutional concessions from key sections of the party affiliated trade unions. In this context, Leopold (1997: 35) asserts that New Labour perceived the 'loosening of the ties' with trade unions as being central to its electoral popularity. In turn, this process would entail a recalibration of the party's negatively perceived image with the business community. The impact of the Conservatives' neoliberal reforms was devastating for trade unions in Britain, as the total membership fell to 7.8 million by 1998. Labour adjusted to and complemented the reforms as it prepared its legislative agenda for government in 1997. Due to the prevailing strength of these economic, political and ideational factors, leading figures in the trade union movement acquiesced and accommodated the objectives of the Labour leadership in both the unfolding NMW (1998) and ERA (1999) negotiations. As a result, key aspects of both items of legislation were diluted to the dissatisfaction of other trade union leaders and the TUC.

There was a shift in the employment relations model during Labour's period in government away from the continuation of neoliberal market reforms. Undy (2002: 653) identified a more 'benign' environment created by the Labour Government's discourse, which represented a reverse of the 'demonstrative effect' identified by Howell (1998) in relation to the cumulative effects of the Conservative Governments' exclusionary measures. The 'benign' atmosphere is evidenced as trade union density and membership contraction significantly decelerated, which was a significant outcome in light of the trend over the previous eighteen years. The employment relations reforms of Labour modified the existing institutions and practices of labour market relations such as ACAS and Employment Tribunals. The government also created new mechanisms such as the LPC, which were inclusive of trade unions. Partial re-regulation was established in the NMW (1998) and the ERA (1999) frameworks, albeit the statutory focus was on individual rather than collective rights. Therefore, the *regulated individualism* model of employment relations did represent a shift and yielded positive results.

However, as the first term of the Labour Government (1997–2001) progressed, it was accompanied by rising levels of dissatisfaction in relation to the minimalist interpretations of the employment and trade union rights framework. In addition, a number of key policy areas including pensions and the privatisation of public services fuelled intra-union trajectories as trade unions became progressively hostile to the New Labour project as trade union actors such as Derek Simpson (AMICUS/Unite), Dave Prentis (UNISON) and Kevin Curran (GMB) collectively confirm. An alternative strategic response by trade union leaders was considered necessary if the government's control of the agenda was to be shifted towards the interests of trade unions. A structural factor that facilitated the ideational and organisational convergence was further trade union consolidation. By 2006, the Big Four unions constituted 60 per cent of membership out of sixty-three unions affiliated to the TUC.

The new strategy operationalised through the strategic choices of union leaders contributed to legislative success. The Warwick political exchange process contained most notably: the Employment Relations Act 2004, the extension of two-tier workforce protection in local government to public services, the Pensions Act 2004, the Transfer of Undertakings (Protection of Employment) Regulations 2006, holiday entitlement increasing from twenty to twenty-eight days as part of the Working Time (Amendment) Regulations 2007 and the implementation of the European Union Agency Workers Regulations 2010. As Coulter (2014) stated, to 'downplay' these outcomes was "surely to overestimate the room for manoeuvre for centre-left parties and their trade union allies in market-oriented economies with weakly institutionalised trade unions". As such, there should also be a reappraisal of the perceptions of success associated with Warwick. The legislative outcomes must be viewed through a wider political and economic lens. Viewed through this lens, trade unions can be judged to have significantly influenced the *regulated individualism* model of the Labour Government. Moreover, the evidence lends credence to the argument that the Warwick Agreement (2004), from a trade union perspective, can in many respects be contextually judged as a greater success than the NMW (1998) or ERA (1999) in terms of *process* and *outcomes*. Evidently, the successes must be kept in perspective because despite the significant deceleration in trade union density contracting there was no 'trend break' by the end of Labour's tenure in government. The downward trend was partially attributable to the minimalist nature of Labour's employment relations model and weak government support to enable trade union growth despite initiatives such as the Union Learning Fund. Trade union density fell to 27 per cent in 2010 at the end of Labour's tenure in government from 30.8 per cent in 1998. In the private sector, those workers covered by collective bargaining agreements as a proportion of all workers declined from 21.7 per cent in 1998 to 16.9 per cent in 2010. In addition, collective bargaining witnessed a decline as coverage fell from 35.4 per cent (1998) to 30.9 per cent of all employees in 2010 (Visser, 2015).

Degree of Coordination

Trade unions, historically and culturally, had a deep mistrust towards legal 'interference' by the state. The reflexive disposition set the contours to the principle of the division of labour between the industrial and political spheres (Webb and Webb, 1913; Flanders, 1969). The division was greatly influenced by the factors of union ideology and the strategic choices of union leaders, which resulted in unions 'rarely' moving towards coordinated political action (Richter, 1973). The overriding ideology of organised labour, as influenced by the largest affiliates to the Labour Party and the TUC, was support for free collective bargaining in the power dynamics between employers and trade unions as part of a collective laissez-faire employment relations system.

'In Place of Strife' (1969) represented the first major advance by the Labour leadership into 'closed' areas (i.e. industrial sphere) (Minkin, 1974). Despite the proposed legislation producing a negative reaction, it was also the catalyst for a new group of trade union leaders after the 1970 general election defeat. The Liaison Committee was the structural manifestation of the trade union strategic response. A. Taylor (1987: 10) described the Liaison Committee as a 'major step forward' for trade unions because the process presented a "coordinated view-point for the movement as a whole". The process symbolised the industrial and political wings of the labour movement working in a coordinated and cooperative fashion. The most influential factor in the creation of the Liaison Committee was the strategic choices of trade union leaders. Jack Jones, as leader of the country's largest union the TGWU, advocated a process of greater 'liaison' that would "work out a clear programme" (Jones, 1986: 237).

Crucially, the Liaison Committee would incorporate the TUC rather than Labour Party affiliated unions exclusively to maximise coordination. The inclusion of the growing size of non-Labour Party–affiliated unions such as NALGO with a significant presence in the TUC's structures was considered a strategic necessity to the success of any social-pact. Lord Whitty noted that the inclusivity of the process helped to provide a 'solid centre' through the TUC as the channel of influence. The alternative position was one which would have exclusively involved the trade unions affiliated to the Labour Party who were in the words of Lord Whitty 'becoming increasingly polarised' at this juncture.

The underlying factor of personal relationships has significantly shaped the strategic choices of trade union leaders and the shared interpretative extent of the opportunities available. The dynamic has correspondingly influenced the degree of trade union coordination. Dorfman (1983) supported the centrality of personal relations among trade union leaders by highlighting that after the departures of both Jack Jones (TGWU) and Hugh Scanlon (AUEW), trade union cohesion disintegrated. The aforementioned point should not to be confused with suggesting that the voluntary incomes component in Phase Four of 1978 had not reached its peak. The weight of factors such as union ideology, structural weaknesses, strategic miscalculations by the Labour Government and an improving inflation position all indicate that the incomes policy had *probably* reached its culmination. It most certainly had on the basis of a 5 per cent pay policy.

Rather, in one of the labour movement's greatest 'what ifs', the findings do indicate that the subsequent unravelling and the scale of the Winter of Discontent could have been reduced through different strategic choices. The process would have been aided if there had not been leadership changes occurring at the Social Contract's most critical juncture in the largest trade unions. The retrospective conjecture is based on the literature, archival material and data obtained from actors. The average increase in earnings from August 1977 to August 1978 came out between 14 and 15 per cent. The inflation figure had, in fact, hit 7.4 per cent by June 1978, despite the TGWU Conference in July 1977 demanding an immediate return to free collective bargaining. There were considerable coordination efforts through the strategic choices of union leaders to sustain the Social Contract. The outcomes of the social-pact process are evidenced by TULRA (1974), the Health and Safety at Work Act (1974), Employment Protection Act (1975), Industry Act (1975), the Aircraft and Shipbuilding Industries Act 1977 right through to the collapse of the incomes policy (Phase Four) in November 1978. The outcomes achieved through the Liaison Committee coordination should be viewed as even more significant in the context of structural weaknesses and economic turbulence.

In Labour's first term (1997–2001), ideational, agency and organisational differences prevailed among trade unions. Trade unions such as UNISON promoted a minimum wage formula, whereas the AEEU was evasive on any pre-defined rate based on its ideological embracement of the Labour Government's social partnership approach. As the negotiations developed over the NMW (1998), the passivity and accommodation by certain trade unions aided Labour ministers wishing to dilute its scope in relation to the exemptions, tiered age rates and overall level. The most striking example of trade unions lacking coordination across the legislative events is the ERA (1999). The coordination problems associated with the legislation can be traced to the fault lines in advance of the 1997 general election. Due to an absence of effective coordination mechanisms in the economy and internally within the structures of the Labour Party, these factors contributed towards significant policy dilution. This is symbolised by the divisions between trade unions over the size of the bargaining unit eligible for trade union recognition. In parallel with the NMW (1998) negotiations, trade union leaders and Labour ministers, however, contend that if forms of coordinated political action were not in situ, principally through the TUG and the TUC then there would have been further dilution in the ERA (1999).

The NPF at Exeter in 2000 is identified as a turning point for many leaders of the affiliated trade unions. The episode shares similarities to the coordination efforts launched by trade union leaders in the aftermath of 'In Place of Strife', except in the case of the latter it was in a cooperative not adversarial manner with the Labour leadership. Trade union leaders and Labour ministers (Dave Prentis, Liz Snape, Tom Watson, Tony

Dubbins, John Edmonds and Sir Ian McCartney) all identified a lack of trade union coordination at Exeter by drawing attention to the individual organisational basis in which trade unions approached the policy-making process. Due to the progressive centralisation of power in the Labour leadership, greater union-party detachment and an absence of strong coordination mechanisms, it was structurally easier for the Labour leadership to manipulate the policy-making process.

The catalyst for the Warwick Agreement (2004) from the trade union perspective was the leadership changes in the largest trade unions—AEEU section of AMICUS, GMB, TGWU and UNISON. The successive leadership changes "confirmed the general trend to more radical leadership of the affiliated unions" (Ludlam and Taylor, 2003: 738). The coordinated political action was operationalised inside the structures of the Labour Party. This was in contrast to the Social Contract process where trade union coordination efforts were channelled through the TUC (Ludlam and Taylor, 2003; Charlwood, 2004; Gennard and Hayward, 2008). A two-strand strategy emerged which focused on maximising trade union institutional influence inside the party's structures. The first strand involved the reform of TULO, which involves all trade unions affiliated to the Labour Party, after the 2001 general election. The second strand was a complementary process involving the new leaders of the largest four trade unions—the 'Big Four'—all Labour Party affiliates. Dave Prentis (UNISON), Kevin Curran (GMB), Jack Dromey (TGWU) and Derek Simpson (AMICUS) identified the policy divisions and the centralisation of power in the Labour leadership as compelling greater trade union coordination in order to offset environmental constraints. From a strategising perspective, the reform of TULO and the creation of the Big Four is a fascinating development. It supports the assertion in the academic literature that any given structural environment does not exclusively determine trade union behaviour, albeit the scope for manoeuvre is more constrained in a liberal market (Child, 1972, 1997; Boxall and Haynes, 1997). Therefore, illuminating how trade union actors interpret the opportunities available and accordingly design strategies to attain employment relations outcomes is of significant research value.

Lord Collins, Jon Cruddas, Sir Ian McCartney and Lord Whitty lamented the marginalisation of the TUC as the trade union centre for policy-making influence which stemmed from the new strategic approach.

The trade union leaders involved in the Big Four process contend the TUC being marginalised was not a deliberate exclusionary strategy. Rather, it emerged due to institutional objectives converging. Individual trade unions came under increasing pressure to evidence outcomes deriving from affiliation to the Labour Party and the associated political levy financial contributions to the party. Sir Brendan Barber, General Secretary of TUC during this period, did acknowledge that the strategic development was partly attributable to the 'absence' of any 'appropriate collective mechanism'. In this context, Sir Brendan Barber, Jon Cruddas and Lord Monks judged the Warwick Agreement (2004) as delivering 'mixed' results and drew attention to the new approach limiting the potential for a more comprehensive deal. In addition, Lord Collins observed the following:

> I think people now who are arguing that TULO has achieved more are deliberately ignoring the facts because I think the policy-making process in the lead up to the 1997 manifesto was terrific and if you look at the record of that first Labour Government in terms of workers interests and issues they were incredibly positive and lot was achieved out of it. Then there is the second and third term. So, where is the evidence that TULO taking common positions has achieved more—I don't think so!
>
> (Extract from Lord Collins, Interview 22)

However, Labour Government ministers such as Gerry Sutcliffe and Sir Ian McCartney, in conjunction with trade union actors, assert the Warwick Agreement (2004) was a relatively successful outcome from the trade union perspective. Despite the contestation over the extent of progress, the agreement produced positive outcomes in an era of weaker trade unionism characterised by low levels of union density and collective bargaining coverage. Interestingly, an ideological and experiential fault line emerges between trade union leaders themselves; and in turn with the Labour leadership. The new set of trade union leaders post-2001 were more favourably disposed towards reforming institutions like TULO and to adopting adversarial positions with respect to the Labour leadership. In contrast, an accommodative relationship between the leaders of the largest trade unions and the TUC in conjunction with Labour leaders existed prior to 1997, and to a lesser extent the first term (1997–2001). The leaders of the labour movement during this period had developed close working relationships over the long period in political opposition and worked collaboratively to varying degrees to reform the Labour Party in order to make it 'electable' as Chapter 3 on Employment Relations Reform under New Labour substantiates.

Transition to Informality

The book has sought to trace the usage of informal processes and spaces, which were designed to influence formal processes and legislative outcomes. Jack Jones (1986) highlighted an unproductive private meeting in relation to 'In Place of Strife' at Chequers in May 1969 with fellow trade unionists Hugh Scanlon (AUEW) and Victor Feather (TUC) along with Prime Minister Harold Wilson and the Secretary of State for Employment and Productivity, Barbara Castle. The lack of progress in these informal

spaces was in stark contrast with the success of formal mechanisms utilised by trade unions such as the TUC and the TUG in parliament to
force the government to abandon the White Paper. In this context, Jack
Jones emphasised that the existing processes in 1970 had not delivered
unity or mutual understanding. As such, a semi-formal mechanism was
advanced (i.e. the Liaison Committee) through the TUC due to the strategic choices of union leaders. This represented a shift away from the
Labour Party Annual Conference and the NEC into other spaces that
were not formally within the constitutional structures of the party. The
liaison process was considered a significant element in the continuation
of the Social Contract beyond expectations given the prevailing economic
circumstances during 1974–79.

The Liaison Committee maintained personal and organisational relations up until 1978 when the incomes policy component of the wider
Social Contract collapsed. The 'less securely founded' status of the Liaison Committee deriving from its non-constitutional status in the Labour
Party's structures, which was a factor identified as a virtue of the process,
would, in fact, accelerate its demise in the post-1979 period (A. Taylor,
1987: 27). Successive internal Labour Party reforms such as the PRP in
1987 fostered new processes designed to strengthen the centralisation of
policy-making in the Labour leadership. The process was supported to
varying degrees by the strategic choices of union leaders and the ideological reorientation of trade unions in an attempt to offset environmental
constraints. The by-product of these shifts was the increasing importance
of informal processes.

Lord Monks noted that the creation of the informal Contact Group
in the 1980s was in an era where the institutions and mechanisms of the
Labour Party were undermining the party leadership's policy preferences.
The process included the TUC leadership and the largest affiliated trade
union leaders in conjunction with the Labour parliamentary leadership.
The Contact Group meetings progressively replaced the Liaison Committee equivalents, as the latter forum ceased to effectively operate by
1989. The prominence of informal processes mirrored the shift towards
a more individualised and decentralised employment relations model.
Regini (1995: 133) interestingly observed that in periods of company
restructuring the formalised institutions of employment relations could
diminish in significance leading to the increasing importance of "indirect
and therefore less visible mechanisms".

One of the most important underlying dynamics influencing the strategic choices of union leaders is the strength of personal relationships. This
is implicitly if not explicitly acknowledged. In an era of greater centralisation in the Labour leadership, informal processes became more important as certain institutional routes were closed off. In the transition under
successive Labour leaders, informal processes were of significant value
to both trade union and Labour leaders under the leaderships of Neil

Kinnock and John Smith. The strength of these informal processes, however, came under significant strain when Tony Blair became leader. In the transition from Smith to Blair, previous understandings and agreements were either diluted or reneged upon such as the minimum wage formula policy. As such, Rodney Bickerstaffe concluded that although informal processes were useful, at the same time, they "weren't about firm agreements between the union and the party".

Further internal party reforms, in particular, the creation of the NPF, continued to dilute the power of trade unions in the Labour Party's institutional structures. The policy-making reform was introduced in an era of weaker personal relations between trade union leaders, and in turn with the Labour leadership. Lord Monks drew attention to a central issue, which is if the principal actors are neither politically converged nor have strong personal relationships, the opportunities to attain positive outcomes through informal processes significantly diminishes. Lord Sawyer specifically commented upon the centralisation of power in the Labour leadership and the weakness of collective decision-making mechanisms during his tenure as General Secretary of the Labour Party under Blair. Moreover, Sir Brendan Barber and Lord Monks both confirmed that despite their repeated efforts to open up regular dialogue with the Prime Minister, the efforts proved largely unsuccessful. In this context, Jon Cruddas opined that the 'reorientation strategy' post-2001 was a strategic response to the lack of progress from the first term (1997–2001), and in turn the perceived ineffectiveness of the TUC leadership with the Labour leadership.

As the negotiations unfolded over the details of the NMW (1998) and ERA (1999), the leadership of specific trade unions and the TUC correspondingly focused their strategy on applying leverage upon the formal mechanisms that were available. For example, Gerry Sutcliffe, Frank Doran, Tony Dubbins and Jon Cruddas all state that the use of the TUG in parliament and TULO to varying degrees were central to exercising political pressure on elements of the Labour leadership. Formal processes were critical to preventing further dilution in key elements of both the NMW (1998) and ERA (1999). The emphasis on these processes was representative of the diluted role of informal processes and also a by-product of the associated bureaucratic machinery accompanied with the legislative process. However, the previous point should not to be confused with suggesting that informal processes did not perform a pivotal role. Through these informal processes, the General Secretary of the AEEU is identified as conceding an important element on the size of the collective bargaining unit eligible for recognition at variance with the TUC policy line. The decision rendered the established collective position ineffective, sowing the seeds of further policy dilution. The observation is complemented by the reflections of John Edmonds and Tony Dubbins in relation to the role of other trade union leaders, specifically those at the

MSF and USDAW trade unions. Accordingly, John Edmonds described the Labour leadership management approach in the following terms:

> The idea of collective discussions designed to reach a conclusion which everybody could agree with, which was John Smith's style. This was replaced by a pretty obvious attempt by the party leader to use which ever contacts were important for a particular issue in order to produce the outcome he wanted. It became essentially manipulative.
>
> (Extract from John Edmonds, Interview 6)

Tony Blair was widely criticised for operating a 'sofa-style' government. Lord Butler, who led the Review of Intelligence on Weapons of Mass Destruction in the aftermath of the Iraq invasion, stated Blair's style excluded members of the government from the decision-making process. In a damning indictment of Blair's use of informal processes, Lord Butler's report concluded: "The informality and circumscribed character of the government's procedures which we saw in the context of policy-making toward Iraq risks reducing the scope for informed political judgment" (Wheeler, 2004). The observation could equally be applied to the trade union movement in regard to engaging individual trade union leaders in the ERA (1999) and to a lesser extent the NMW (1998) to deliver Labour leadership objectives.

The most significant factor of influence in the institutional reconfiguration of TULO derived from the strategic choices of trade union leaders. The general secretaries developed a shared interpretation of the opportunities available in a liberal market economy. The reform of TULO arose from informal conversations among trade union leaders due to the minimal progress on employment relations matters at the Exeter NPF in conjunction with the rising dissatisfaction associated with the NMW (1998) and ERA (1999) outcomes. The emergent strategy post-2001 produced several policy victories at the Labour Party Annual Conference. This included UNISON successfully tabling a motion calling for a moratorium and review of PFI deals at the October 2002 conference. Kevin Curran (GMB), Derek Simpson (AMICUS) and Dave Prentis (UNISON) confirm that the initiation of the Big Four process was informal in origin. Curran specifically identified the influence of warm personal relationships as being central to delivering greater coordination. The latter dynamic was missing between the leaders of the largest unions during 1997–2001.

The usage and effectiveness of informal processes for the purposes of developing coordinated political action is directly correlated with the personalities involved along with the extent of ideological convergence. The key point from the perspective of the book is the ability to attain employment relations outcomes from these informal processes. The evidence supports the view that informal outcomes performed a detrimental role to the collective trade union position in the NMW (1998) and ERA (1999) to varying degrees. Informal processes had deliberately displaced formalised processes, which were correspondingly manipulated by the Labour leadership to facilitate accommodative positions by individual trade union leaders through bilateral dialogue. As part of a complex matrix of interests, trade union leaders, Labour ministers and a Prime Ministerial advisor simultaneously disclose an alliance through informal and formal processes, which prevented further policy dilution. The *group contestation* involved government actors more sympathetic to trade union objectives who initiated efforts to 'outflank' (McCartney) other ministerial colleagues in the internal debates over the NMW (1998) and ERA (1999). In contrast, the positive role of informal processes for the purposes of maximising trade union outcomes was critical to the preparatory work for Warwick and the endeavours thereafter to hold the Labour Government to account. As such, informal processes designed to influence formal processes can be judged to have been the dominant process to the extent that they provided the strategic foundations for trade unions to act collectively to deliver the Warwick Agreement (2004) outcomes.

Concluding Observations

The impact of the four factors of influence as proposed by Hamann and Kelly (2004) at different junctures has been latent or active. Trade unions arguably faced greater structural, ideational and agency constraints in relation to the NMW (1998) and ERA (1999) than the Warwick Agreement (2004). The context of Labour's first term was one whereby the government enjoyed a substantial parliamentary majority along with inheriting a marketised economy. The Labour leadership in this context prioritised positive relationships with the business community. There was an absence of strong coordination mechanisms and weak informal processes prevailed between the respective leaderships of the largest trade unions and the TUC and, in turn, with the Labour leadership. These elements combined to limit the ability of trade unions to exercise constraint.

Union ideology can be more or less influential as was experienced across all the legislative events. Ideational accommodation is positively associated with the Social Contract process through a *collective cooperative* approach by trade unions with the Labour leadership. The approach was coordinated by the TUC through the Liaison Committee due to the strategic choices of union leaders. It is also negatively associated with the demise of the Social Contract. Alternatively, ideational accommodation with the Labour Government's social partnership approach by individual union leaders *(individualised accommodation)* had negative associations with the NMW (1998) and ERA (1999) outcomes. The observation derives from Labour ministers using informal and bilateral processes with individual trade union leaders to dilute key aspects in both aforementioned items of legislation. Conversely, there was the law of unintended consequences deriving from informality. Upwards pressure was applied upon the NMW (1998) and ERA (1999) frameworks through *group contestation* involving an alliance of trade union leaders, Labour ministers and advisors. The strategy was orchestrated through a number of mechanisms including the TUC, TULO and TUG in parliament. A parallel group of trade union leaders and Labour ministers simultaneously exerted downwards pressure on the frameworks in sync with the attempts of business organisations to externally apply pressure to limit the strength of the frameworks.

In relation to the Warwick Agreement (2004), the strategic choices of union leaders and union ideology would mutually reinforce each other to strengthen coordination. The Big Four developed a *collective adversarial* approach towards the Labour Government based on a shared assessment of the viable escape routes available in a liberal market economy. The leaders of the largest four unions operationalised this approach initially through strategising in informal spaces. The strategic reappraisal was initiated after the Exeter NPF (2000), whereby policy divisions and weak coordination among trade unions was exploited by the Labour leadership in order to constrain trade union policy objectives. The Warwick Agreement (2004) clearly has stronger parallels with the Social Contract as a political exchange process, specifically union ideology and trade union sectionalism were to a greater degree constrained as a result of trade union leaders utilising strong coordination mechanisms (i.e. Liaison Committee and TULO/Big Four).

Admittedly, it is problematic to identify which factor is the most important in each legislative event. However, it is clear that the strategic choices of union leaders are pivotal to employment relations outcomes. These choices have become even more significant in the context of a liberal market economy. Nonetheless, the strategic choices of union leaders as a factor of influence remains comparatively under researched, in contrast with the other three factors of influence. The strategic choices of union leaders were the most important factor in the Social Contract's initiation and operation through the creation of the Liaison Committee. The factor is also negatively associated with its demise in 1978, which coincided with key trade union leaders retiring (i.e. Jack Jones and Hugh Scanlon). In Labour's first term (1997–2001), the *group contestation* strategy is positively associated with constraining the Labour leadership's objectives to a degree, but the strategic choices of individual union leaders ultimately facilitated the minimalist outcomes in the NMW (1998) and ERA (1999) frameworks. In contrast, the *collective adversarial* approach arising from the strategic choices of union leaders helped to deliver the successes in

Table 7.1 Trade Union Strategy, Influence and Power during Labour Governance

	Social Contract (1974–79)	NMW (1998)	ERA (1999)	Warwick (2004)
Employment Relations Regime	Collective Laissez-Faire/Corporatist	Social partnership/Regulated Individualism	Social partnership/Regulated Individualism	Regulated Individualism
Dominant Process	Formal	Informal/Formal	Informal/Formal	Informal
Trade Union Leadership Strategy	Collective Cooperative	Individualised Accommodation/Group Contestation	Individualised Accommodation/Group Contestation	Collective Adversarial
Mechanism(s) for Policy Influence	Liaison Committee	Individual Unions and TUC	Individual Unions and TUC	Big Four/TULO
Channel of Trade Union Policy Influence	TUC	Labour Party and TUC	Labour Party and TUC	Labour Party
Degree of Policy Coordination between Trade Unions	Strong	Weak	Weak	Strong

Note: Italicised words denote correlation between categories.

the Warwick Agreement (2004). Therefore, strategic choice is central to the channel, mechanisms and process used for policy influence; the degree of trade union coordination, and the approach adopted by trade union leaders—collective, group (not inclusive of all major unions) and individual. Accordingly, the book presents in Table 7.1 a new analytical framework for capturing trade union strategy, influence and power during periods of Labour Party governance in the post-1970 period. The framework contrasts with Coulter's (2014) recent work which identified three methods of influence: (1) political exchange, (2) party institutions and (3) insider lobbying by the TUC.

Despite the book being limited to junctures of Labour governance, the findings can provide valuable insights and inform strategic reappraisal by trade unions operating in liberal market economies, or in nations increasingly exposed to neoliberal measures. The experiences of the Labour Governments (1974–79 and 1997–2010) can also offer a number of key lessons for trade unions and the Labour Party leadership in advance of the next Labour Government. At the time of writing (March 2019), a general election could be imminent in the context of the unfolding Brexit negotiations. Sir Ian McCartney reflected on his period as one of the lead ministers with responsibility for enacting employment relations legislation. McCartney, in doing so, challenged both trade unions and prospective Labour ministers to strategically prepare for government:

> However, the biggest lesson is the need to sit down before an election and achieve clarity and what the work programme should be. I remember saying to the TUC that there was a new union on the block called HMG, that being Her Majesty's Government, because we were performing a role that quite frankly the unions should have been doing themselves. There used to be a day when people like Jack Jones would tell the government to 'stay out of it' in the workplace and for all sorts of reasons, many of them legitimate, whereby they {trade unions} now rely too much on the government. Collective bargaining in the private sector has largely gone and public bodies don't recruit for trade unions. So, there needs to be a strategy and what that strategy would result in and how do we need to do it and campaign for it.
>
> (Extract from Sir Ian McCartney, Interview 18)

The Conclusion will reflect upon this challenge and will draw out the implications of the book's findings by considering practical and policy implications for various actors but particularly for trade unions. The limits of the claims made within the book are reflected upon as well as future areas of research that need to be addressed.

Bibliography

Boxall, P. and Haynes, P. (1997). Strategy and effectiveness in a liberal environment. *British Journal of Industrial Relations*, 35(4), pp. 567–591.

Charlwood, A. (June 2004). The new generation of trade union leaders and prospects for union revitalisation. *British Journal of Industrial Relations*, 42(2), pp. 379–397.

Child, J. (1972). Organisational structure, environment and performance: The role of strategic choice. *Sociology*, 6(3), pp. 1–22.

Child, J. (1997). Strategic choice in the analysis of action, structure, organisations and environment: Retrospect and prospect. *Organisation Studies*, 18(1), pp. 43–76.

Coulter, S. (27 February 2014). *Insider lobbying: New Labour and the TUC*. Available at: http://blogs.lse.ac.uk/netuf/2014/02/27/insider-lobbying-new-labour-and-the-tuc/ [Accessed 11 July 2016].

Coulter, S. (2014). *New Labour policy, industrial relations and the trade unions*. Houndmills: Palgrave Macmillan.

Dorfman, G.A. (1983). *British trade unionism against the Trades Union Congress*. London: Macmillan.

Flanders, A. (1969). *Trade unions and the force of tradition*. The Sixteenth Fawley Foundation Lecture. University of Southampton.

Frege, C. and Kelly, J. (2003). Union revitalization strategies in comparative perspective. *European Journal of Industrial Relations*, 9(1), pp. 7–24.

Gennard, J. and Hayward, G. (2008). *A history of the graphical, paper and media union*. Beecles: CPI William Clowes.

Howell, C. (1998). Restructuring British public sector industrial relations: State policies and trade union responses. *Policy Studies Journal*, 26(2), pp. 293–309.

Howell, C. (June 2000). Constructing British industrial relations. *British Journal of Politics and International Relations*, 2(2), pp. 205–236.

Howell, C. (2005). *Trade unions and the state: The construction of industrial relations institutions in Britain, 1890–2000*. Princeton: Princeton University Press.

Jones, J. (1986). *Union man: Autobiography*. London: Collins.

Leopold, J.W. (March 1997). Trade unions, political fund ballots and the Labour Party. *British Journal Industrial Relations*, 35(1), pp. 23–38.

Ludlam, S. and Taylor, A. (December 2003). The political representation of the labour interest in Britain. *British Journal of Industrial Relations*, 41(4), pp. 727–749.

Minkin, L. (1974). The British Labour Party and the trade unions: Crisis and compact. *Industrial and Labour Relations Review*, 28(1), pp. 1–37.

The Office of National Statistics (22 October 2014). *UK continues to be a manufacturing nation, says ONS*. Available at: http://webarchive.nationalarchives.gov.uk/20160105160709/www.ons.gov.uk/ons/dcp29904_381700.pdf [Accessed 20 Feb. 2017].

Regini, M. (1995). *Uncertain boundaries*. Cambridge: Cambridge University Press.

Richter, I. (1973). *Political purpose in trade unions (1973)*. London: George Allen and Unwin.

Taylor, A. (1987). *The trade unions and the Labour Party*. Burrell Row, Beckenham, Kent: Room Helm Ltd. (Provident House).

Undy, R. (2002). New Labour and New Unionism, 1997–2001: But is it the same old story? *Employee Relations*, 24(6), pp. 638–655.

Undy, R., Ellis, V., McCarthy, W.E.J. and Halmos, A.H. (1981). *Change in the trade unions: The development of United Kingdom unions since 1960*. London: Hutchison.

Visser, J. (October 2015). *ICTWSS database*. version 5.0. Amsterdam: Amsterdam Institute for Advanced Labour Studies AIAS. Open access database available at: www.uva-aias.net/nl/data/ictwss [Accessed 31 Dec. 2016].

Webb, S. and Webb, B. (1913). *Industrial democracy*. Printed by The Authors for the Trade Unionists of the United Kingdom. London: Longmans Green and Co.

Wheeler, B. (15 July 2004). Curtains for Blair's 'sofa cabinet'? *BBC* Online. Available at: http://news.bbc.co.uk/1/hi/3895921.stm [Accessed 2 Feb. 2017].

Wilkinson, F. (2007). Neo-liberalism and New Labour policy: Economic performance, historical comparisons and future prospects. *Cambridge Journal of Economics*, 31(6), pp. 817–843.

8   Conclusion

The presentation of the reflections of trade union leaders on the successes of the Social Contract (1974–79), the importance of informal processes in the initiation of the Liaison Committee and the rationale for the TUC as the channel of influence is of significant strategic value. The legislative achievements achieved through a *collective cooperative* approach allow for a more circumspect and positive reflective lens of the period. The observation remains valid despite the industrial unrest in the winter months of 1978–79, which stigmatised the Social Contract as a political exchange process. The NMW (1998) and ERA (1999) legislative events revealed a complex matrix of labour movement interests epitomised by weak market and internal party coordination mechanisms, ideological differences and weaker personal relationship among labour movement leaders. The context contributed towards trade union leaders individually accommodating the Labour leadership's policy objectives. In parallel, through *group contestation* an alliance of trade union leaders and Labour ministers utilised formal and informal processes in order to contest policy dilution with varying degrees of success. In contrast, the successes attained through the Warwick Agreement (2004) from the trade union perspective were achieved through a *collective adversarial* strategy. The approach was facilitated by ideological convergence, warmer personal relationships and stronger coordination mechanisms as a result of strategising in informal spaces via the Labour Party channel.

Leadership and Strategic Choice

The observations in the book are anchored in the reflections of those actors who strategically influenced the behaviour of trade unions in the legislative events. This permits the book to make informed judgements rather than to infer how trade union leaders frame the opportunities and constraints from their organisational vantage point and thereafter to strategically act. There may be a degree of optimism bias shared among actors that laud outcomes to have been more successful than can be empirically justified, primarily due to their own personal roles. Trade union leaders also criticised—implicitly and explicitly—the role of predecessors based on ideational and personal differences. Yet the legislative events reveal trade union leaders and Labour ministers critically reflecting on their own roles—and the role of their peers. Dave Prentis (UNISON) stated trade unions, in relation to the Warwick Agreement (2004), could have 'pushed harder', and the successes had to be kept in 'perspective'. Various actors critically reflected on the lack of coordination and divisions within the trade union movement as contributing to policy dilution in relation to the NMW (1998) and ERA (1999). Lord Monks and Sir Brendan Barber further highlighted their repeated efforts as the respective heads of the TUC to persuade both Tony Blair and Gordon Brown to have a different process for engagement with the trade union movement without success. This in turn fermented trade union dissatisfaction. Moreover, Sir Ian McCartney reflected on the role of the Labour Government during its third term (2005–2010), describing it as having 'completely lost its way' before the global financial crisis in 2008.

Nonetheless, the weight of evidence substantiates the proposition that there is a dividend deriving from Labour Party affiliation in terms of the attainment of positive employment relations outcomes. Understanding why political action has performed a progressively more important functional role in Britain, and crucially how it differs from the 1974–79 period, is brought to the fore with important contemporary implications. After the election of Jeremy Corbyn as Leader of the Labour Party in September 2015, there has been comprehensive ideational re-convergence between the leaderships of trade unions and the Labour Party.[1] The process initially emerged following the election of Ed Miliband as Labour Leader in 2010, whereby trade unions were critical to his successful leadership election contest under Labour's electoral college system.[2] Miliband's leadership led to a series of successes through the Labour Party's policy-making structures characterised by the 2015 general election manifesto 'Britain Can Be Better'. The manifesto pledged to ban 'exploitative' zero hours contracts, to close the 'loophole' allowing firms to 'undercut' permanent staff by using agency workers, and to raise the minimum wage level to more than £8 per hour by October 2019.[3]

The Corbyn leadership has presided over the welcome re-emergence of formal collective policy-making structures from the trade union perspective; principally the NEC and the Labour Party Annual Conference as the sovereign bodies of the party. The *collective cooperative* approach under Corbyn has resulted in the reaffiliation of the Fire Brigades Union in November 2015 to the party and led to discussions by the Public and Commercial Services Union to consider affiliating in the post–New Labour era (Labour List, 2016). The Labour Party's manifesto 'For the Many Not the Few' (June 2017) consolidated the ideological re-convergence, despite a further general election loss.[4] The manifesto in the employment relations arena pledged to redress the perceived weaknesses of the *regulated individualism* model, as evaluated in the book. Labour pledged to roll-out sectoral collective bargaining (a Warwick Agreement pledge), ban zero hours contracts to ensure a guaranteed number of hours each week, review the rules on union recognition, guarantee trade unions a right to access workplaces to speak to all employees with an aim to recruitment and to raise the minimum wage to the level of the Living Wage for all workers aged 18 or over. Moreover, Labour pledged to repeal the Conservative Government's Trade Union Act (2016), similarly to the IRA (1971), which enacted a series of measures primarily designed to further constrain the ability of trade unions to conduct industrial action.[5]

The new *collective cooperative* approach contrasts with the Social Contract era, which positioned the TUC as the primary channel of union influence. Whether the present strategy remains the dominant process if Labour does enter government or whether this is channelled through the TUC involving non-affiliated Labour Party unions remains to be established. It will be interesting to monitor in the event of a Labour victory if the TUC leadership is reintegrated into the informal and formal processes involving the largest trade unions and the Labour leadership in an era of stronger party mechanisms. If so, it could involve the reintroduction of a Liaison Committee type policy-making mechanism, perhaps with a view to a new Social Contract process. The channel and degree of trade union coordination will be indicative of the underlying organisational, ideational and leadership dynamics in operation. In the event of the Labour Party not winning the next general election, this could once again induce strategic reappraisal (ideational and procedural) to move beyond the narrower organisational focus on the Labour Party channel by the largest trade unions. The strategy could involve re-positioning the TUC to be the primary channel of policy influence in order to engage a wider array of key stakeholders. Some strategic differences have also emerged between the largest trade unions (GMB, UNISON and Unite) over the direction of the Labour Party, as the GMB did not back Corbyn in the 2016 contest at variance with UNISON and Unite. Tensions in the wider labour movement also continue over the party's position in relation to the current Brexit negotiations.

Political Action and Electoral Reform

A key factor that influences the ability of trade unions to attain policy objectives in Britain—and across advanced industrial economies—derives from the role of the state, the principal political parties and employers. Baccaro and Howell (2011) contest that it is the functionality and purpose of institutions that reveal the 'common' trajectory of economies, therefore, one must also focus on the functionality of trade unions endeavouring to offset environmental constraints. It appears reasonable to speculate that there is currently underway the same progressive reliance on political action by trade unions as a method for change as experienced in Britain. Admittedly, the ability to institutionally influence a Left political party inclusive of financial contributions is not an 'opportunity structure' open to trade unions in the majority of advanced industrialised nations. However, Hyman and Gumbrell-McCormick (2010: 318) highlight the progressive focus by German unions operating through the trade union centre—the Deutscher Gewekschaftsbund (DGB)—on 'political campaigning'. Similarly to Britain, the German unions have also undergone a process of 'conversion' in relation to supporting the minimum wage.[6] These developments come in the context of trade union density declining to 17 per cent (2016) from 27 per cent (1997) and collective bargaining coverage from 74.9 per cent to 56 per cent over the same time span (Visser, 2015; ILOStat, 2018).

A structural factor facilitating the shift towards political action can be traced in the pace of trade union consolidation. The DGB in Germany had sixteen unions affiliated in 1970 and eight in 2005—three of which represented 80.9 per cent of all members (ver.di, IG Metall and IG BCE). The TUC had one hundred and forty-two trade unions affiliated in 1970 down to forty-nine in 2018; the Irish Congress of Trade Unions (ICTU) had seventy-four trade unions affiliated in 1970 and forty-four in 2017; and the SAK confederation in Finland dropped from thirty-one trade unions affiliated in 1970 to eighteen in 2018 (Waddington, 2006; Moody, 2009).[7] The book's findings may facilitate strategic reappraisal by trade unions facing common economic convergence pressures to develop coordinated forms of political action. Theoretically, coordination should be easier to achieve through greater concentrations of trade union power.

Political action through worker mobilisation in France, Spain and Italy, for example, remains a critical dynamic to challenging and offsetting environmental constraints. The industrial unrest in France arising from the labour reforms introduced by President Emmanuel Macron in 2017 illustrates this point.[8] Trade unions in advanced industrialised nations are not immune to patterns of convergence among political and employer interests even if the pace and form of change is constrained by institutional path dependencies. Blanton and Peksen (2016: 12–14) found that there was a 'trade-off' between market-liberalising policies and labour rights, whereby the "decline in the respect for workers' rights appears to be higher for the freedom to trade and the government size variables". The extent of the relationship was correlated with the party in government as Left political parties were 'less likely' to promote free market policies.

The findings presented in the book may inform strategic change by trade unions to work more closely with political parties after a significant period of union-party detachment induced by neoliberal policies, as experienced in Britain (Hamann and Kelly, 2004; Hyman and Gumbrell-McCormick, 2010). Working more closely with political parties may include increased direct financial contributions to candidates or political parties where the law permits. It may also involve increased financial and organisational resources being directed towards campaigning on specific issues in alliance with political parties. Moreover, trade unions could accelerate the process of building strategic relationships with social movements or seek new relationships with alternative parties to the main social democratic parties in an endeavour to seek viable 'escape routes' (Waddington and Kelly, 2003; MacDonald, 2014). These options as part of the political action process are not necessarily mutually exclusive; rather, they can reinforce each other.

LMEs such as Britain and the United States who have majoritarian systems inhabit a more constrained opportunity structure (Doron and Sened, 2001). In contrast, the opportunity for trade unions to attain employment relations outcomes or to challenge detrimental legislation is increased in political systems where coalition and minority governments are more frequent. Baccaro and Howell (2011) supported this proposition by identifying tripartite agreements in Italy signed by trade unions with both centre-left and centre-right governments who required trade union cooperation in the management of economic change. Hassel (2013: 138) further argued that political systems characterised by proportional representation "allow for a variety of different groups access to the policy-making process and are hence generally biased towards centre-left governments". Therefore, trade unions in Britain could potentially revisit electoral reform as a strategic response to offsetting environmental constraints. In the British referendum of May 2011 on an alternative voting system, two of the largest trade unions—GMB and Unite—recommended its members reject the more proportional voting system. The proposal was overall rejected by 67.9 per cent of all those voting (*BBC*, 2011). In this context, a comparative analysis of the devolved institutions and governments across Great Britain and Northern Ireland regarding the potential for variegated employment relations regimes is worthy of further examination. The Welsh Assembly, Northern Ireland Assembly, London Assembly and the Scottish Parliament operate under more proportional electoral systems. The devolved administrations in Wales and Scotland have also periodically involved the Labour Party as the largest party with coalition partners.[9] Admittedly, the potential for a different employment relations regime being fostered is constrained by employment law and large sections of the private sector economy falling under the present remit of reserved powers.

New Structural Pressures

The structural pressures confronting trade unions arising from lower levels of density more often than not in sync with contracting collective bargaining coverage are magnified in the context of a new economic challenge. Automation, artificial intelligence, cloud technology and the gig economy present the greatest structural challenge to trade unionism since its birth from a position of relative weakness. The structural challenge is particularly acute for those trade unions with large private sector memberships where overall union density is lower than in the public sector. Private sector density currently stands at 13.5 per cent and the public sector at 51.8 per cent in Britain (2017). Trade unions also have a significantly stronger organisational presence in larger workplaces, as 71.4 per cent of employees who are trade union members had jobs in workplaces with fifty or more employees. Workplaces with more than fifty employees constituted 53.6 per cent of the total workforce, whereas those with fewer than fifty constituted 46.54 per cent.[10] These structural and organisational challenges occur in tandem with the exponential rise in self-employment, which is partially being driven by companies in the gig economy. Self-employment increased from 3.3 million people (12 per cent of workforce) in 2001 to 4.8 million (15.1 per cent of workforce) in 2017.[11]

Accordingly, the ability of trade unions to influence the employment relations model is increasingly tied to the position adopted by the state and political parties. Deliveroo, for example, won the right in November 2017 not to pay its couriers the minimum wage or holiday pay following a key legal ruling by the CAC.[12] As such, political action can be considered the most important method for delivering change to the employment relations framework. It is not dramatic to suggest that the receptiveness of trade unions towards political action strategies across advanced industrialised nations will determine their levels of power and influence in the new economy. The strategic lessons presented in the book are designed to inform and nurture a climate of hope for trade unions, but making the correct strategic choices will mean everything.

Notes

1. Under Ed Miliband's leadership, One Member One Vote was introduced for the future election of Labour Leader and Deputy Leader contests following a special conference on 1 March 2014. The three largest unions—GMB, UNISON and Unite—supported the new format. Through the new system, Jeremy Corbyn was elected, with 59.5 per cent of first-preference votes. Andy Burnham came second, with 19 per cent followed by Yvette Cooper (17 per cent) and Liz Kendall (4.5 per cent). 422,664 votes were cast out of an electorate of 554,272 constituting a turnout of 76.30 per cent. Tom Watson won the Deputy Leader contest. The GMB, UNISON and Unite all backed Corbyn. Corbyn would win re-election on 24 September 2016, gaining 61.8 per cent of the vote over Owen Smith's 38.2 per cent following a period of parliamentary unrest over his leadership.

2. Ed Miliband won the support of the three largest trade unions—the GMB, UNISON and Unite. In the trade union and affiliates section of the electoral college, the decisive lead of Ed Miliband in this section ultimately facilitated

his victory over his brother, David, by 50.65 per cent to 49.35 per cent of the total vote. David Miliband 49.35 per cent (17.812 from MPs and MEPs, 18.135 from members, 13.40 from unions and affiliated societies) and Ed Miliband 50.65 (15.522 from MPs and MEPs, 15.198 from members, 19.934 from unions and affiliated societies).

3. Labour lost the general election in 2015 as the Conservatives won 36.9 per cent of the vote with three hundred and thirty-one seats opposed to Labour's 30.4 per cent and two hundred and thirty-two seats.

4. Labour gained 40 per cent of the vote (two hundred and sixty-two seats) as the Conservatives lost their majority but emerged with 42.4 per cent of the vote (three hundred and one-seventeen seats) to lead a minority government with command and supply support from the Democratic Unionist Party.

5. Industrial ballots must meet a 50 per cent +/- turnout threshold in order for the results to be legal and those workers delivering 'important' public services are additionally required to reach a 40 per cent support threshold among all workers eligible to vote.

6. The German national minimum wage was introduced on 1 January 2015 and set at 8.50 euros (£6.80) per hour.

7. ICTU (2018), SAK (2018) and TUC Directory (2018).

8. Businesses in France with fewer than fifty workers—95 per cent of French companies—are able to negotiate specific deals directly with employees and without trade union representatives on areas such as working hours, pay and overtime. Larger companies are also permitted to negotiate 'ad hoc' agreements with trade unions instead of sector-wide agreements. The minimum pay-out for two years' employment was six months' salary, which is now limited to three months' pay for two years of work, and twenty months' pay for thirty years.

9. Members of the Scottish and Welsh devolved institutions are elected by the Additional Member System.

10. Statistics provided by the Department of Business, Energy and Industrial Strategy (May 2018).

11. Statistics provided by the Office of National Statistics (7 February 2018).

12. The CAC stated that the delivery firm's couriers were self-employed contractors due to having the right to allocate a substitute to perform for them. The case was brought on behalf of Deliveroo couriers by the Independent Workers Union of Great Britain (IWGB). Despite the decision being contested by the IWGB through the courts, the High Court has upheld the CAC ruling.

Bibliography

Baccaro, L. and Howell, C. (2011). A common neoliberal trajectory: The transformation of industrial relations in advanced capitalism. *Politics and Society*, 39(4), pp. 521–563.

BBC (11 March 2011). AV referendum: Union stance 'depressing', says Johnson. Available at: www.bbc.co.uk/news/uk-politics-12706074 [Accessed 31 July 2018].

Blanton, R.G. and Peksen, D. (February 2016). Economic liberalisation, market institutions and labour rights. *European Journal of Political Research*, Early Online Version, pp. 1–18.

Department of Business, Energy and Industrial Strategy (May 2018). Trade union membership 2017: Statistical bulletin. Table 3.1: Characteristics of union members and non-members, 2017. Available at: www.gov.uk/government/collections/trade-union-statistics [Accessed 15 Oct. 2018].

Doron, G. and Sened, I. (2001). *Political bargaining: Theory, practice and process*. London: SAGE Publications.

Hamann, K. and Kelly, J. (2004). Unions as political actors: A recipe for revitalization? In: C.M. Frege and J. Kelly, eds., *Varieties of unionism: Strategies for union revitalization in a globalizing economy*. Oxford: Oxford University Press, pp. 93–116.

Hassel, A. (2013). Chapter 8: Employment relations, welfare and politics. In: C. Frege and J. Kelly, eds., *Comparative employment relations in the global economy*. London: Routledge Publications.

Heery, E., Kelly, J. and Waddington, J. (2003). Union revitalization in Britain. *European Journal of Industrial Relations*, 9(1), pp. 79–97.

Hyman, R. and Gumbrell-McCormick, R. (2010). Trade unions, politics and parties: Is a new configuration possible? *European Review of Labour and Research*, 16(3), pp. 315–331.

ICTU website (2018). Available at www.ictu.ie/about/affiliates.html [Accessed 15 Oct. 2018].

ILOStat (2018). *Collective bargaining and trade union destiny statistics*. Available at: http://laborsta.ilo.org [Accessed 31 July 2018].

Labour List (26 May 2016). *PCS' praise for Corbyn as it considers labour affiliation*. Available at: https://labourlist.org/2016/05/pcs-praise-for-corbyn-as-it-considers-labour-affiliation/ [Accessed 18 May 2018].

Labour Party (2010). *Britain can be better*. London: The Labour Party.

Labour Party (2016). *For the many not the few*. Available at: https://labour.org.uk/wp-content/uploads/2017/10/labour-manifesto-2017.pdf [Accessed 15 Oct. 2018].

Macdonald, I.T. (December 2014). Towards neoliberal trade unionism: Decline, renewal and transformation in North American Labour Movements. *British Journal of Industrial Relations*, 52(4), pp. 725–752.

Moody, K. (2009). The direction of union mergers in the United States: The rise of conglomerate unionism. *British Journal of Industrial Relations*, 47(4), pp. 676–700.

The Office of National Statistics (7 February 2018). *Trends in self-employment in the UK*. Available at: www.ons.gov.uk/employmentandlabourmarket/peopleinwork/employmentandemployeetypes/articles/trendsinselfemploymentintheuk/2018-02-07 [Accessed 13 Oct. 2018].

SAK website (2018). Available at: www.sak.fi/en/trade-unions/sak-affiliated-unions [Accessed 15 Oct. 2018].

TUC Directory (1 January 2018). Available at www.tuc.org.uk/publications/tuc-directory-2018 [Accessed 15 Oct. 2018].

Visser, J. (October 2015). *ICTWSS database*. version 5.0. Amsterdam: Amsterdam Institute for Advanced Labour Studies AIAS. Open access database available at: www.uva-aias.net/nl/data/ictwss [Accessed 31 Dec. 2016].

Waddington, J. (2006). The trade union merger process in Europe: Defensive adjustment or strategic reform? *Industrial Relations Journal*, 37(6), pp. 630–651.

Appendix A
List of Interviews as Introduced

1. Jack Jones—General Secretary of the TGWU (1968–78). Date of interview, 21 May 2008.
2. Lord David Lea—Assistant General Secretary of the TUC (1978–99) and Joint Secretary of Liaison Committee. Date of interview, 12 October 2011.
3. Lord John Monks—General Secretary of the TUC (1993–2003) and President of European Trade Union Confederation (2003–11). Date of interview, 26 January 2009.
4. Lord Larry Whitty—General Secretary of the Labour Party (1985–94) and Labour Minister (1998–2001). Date of interview, 8 May 2009.
5. Geoffrey Goodman—Industrial editor, columnist and assistant editor of the *Daily Mirror* and founding editor of the *British Journalism Review*. Goodman also headed the counter-inflationary unit for the Labour government (July 1975–August 1976). Date of interview, 22 May 2008.
6. John Edmonds—GMB General Secretary (1986–2003). Date of interview, 8 May 2009.
7. Lord Bill Morris—General Secretary of TGWU (1992–2003). Date of interview, 7 May 2009.
8. Tony Dubbins—General Secretary of the National Graphic Association (1984–90), Graphical Paper and Media Union (1990–2004), and Deputy General Secretary of AMICUS (2004–07). Date of interview, 8 February 2010.
9. Gordon Brown—Prime Minister, Chancellor of the Exchequer and Leader of the Labour Party (1997–2010). Date of interview, 15 September 2010.
10. Rodney Bickerstaffe—General Secretary of National Union of Public Employees (1982–93) and UNISON (1996–2001). Date of interview, 14 September 2009.
11. Lord Tom Sawyer—Deputy General Secretary of NUPE and UNISON (1981–94) and Labour Party General Secretary (1994–98). Date of interview, 18 October 2010.

12. Sir Brendan Barber—General Secretary of the TUC (2003–12). Date of interview, 27 January 2015.
13. Charlie Whelan—Political Director of Unite (2007–10) and Spokesperson for Chancellor, Gordon Brown (1992–99). Date of interview, 9 September 2010.
14. Sir Ian McCartney MP—Labour Minister (1997–2007) and Chair of the Labour Party (2004–05). Date of interview, 7 May 2009.
15. Tom Watson MP—Former Political Officer of the AEEU union, former Labour Minister and Deputy Leader of the Labour Party. Date of interview, 8 July 2015.
16. Dave Prentis—General Secretary of Unison (2001 to present) and Liz Snape—Assistant General Secretary at UNISON. Joint Interview. Date of interview, 2 March 2015.
17. Frank Doran MP—Parliamentary Private Secretary to the Minister of State at the Department of Trade and Industry Ian McCartney (1997–99) and Secretary of the Trade Union Group of MPs. Date of interview, 14 October 2009.
18. Sir Ian McCartney MP—Labour Minister (1997–2007) and Chair of the Labour Party (2004–05). Date of interview, 8 August 2018.
19. Jon Cruddas MP—Prime Ministerial advisor on trade unions as Deputy Political Secretary (1997–2001). Date of interview, 1 February 2010.
20. Gerry Sutcliffe—Parliamentary Under-Secretary (Trade and Industry) (Employment Relations and Consumer Affairs) (June 2003–May 2006) and Secretary of Trade Union Group of MPs in Labour's first term (1997–2001). Date of interview, 30 September 2009.
21. John O'Regan—Former Political Officer of GPMU, AMICUS and Unite. Date of interview, 5 August 2009.
22. Lord Ray Collins—General Secretary of the Labour Party (2008–11) and Assistant General Secretary of TGWU and Unite (1999–2008). Date of interview, 17 September 2010.
23. Jack Dromey MP—Deputy General Secretary of TGWU (2003–07) and Unite (2007–10). Date of interview, 29 September 2010.
24. Derek Simpson—General Secretary of AEEU-AMICUS (2004–07) and Joint General Secretary of Unite (2007–10). Date of interview, 6 September 2010.
25. Kevin Curran—General Secretary of the GMB (2003–04). Date of interview, 27 January 2015.
26. Byron Taylor—Secretary of TULO (2002–10). Date of Interview, 15 February 2010.

Appendix B
Key Provisions of the Employment Act 2002

Family-friendly working

- The standard rate of statutory maternity pay and maternity allowance to the lesser of £100 per week or 90 per cent of the employee's average weekly earnings;
- An increase in the period of maternity leave to six months' paid maternity leave followed by up to six months' unpaid leave;
- Introduction of a new right to two weeks' paternity leave paid at the same standard rate as maternity pay in addition to the existing right to thirteen weeks' parental leave;
- Similar entitlements for adoptive parents and amended rules governing employers' handling of parental leave and pay issues; and
- Parents of children under 6 years of age (or children with disabilities up to the age of 18) the right to request flexible working patterns for childcare purposes, and places a duty on employers to give proper consideration to the request.

Employment Tribunal Reform

- The Act enabled the Secretary to state to make regulations authorising tribunals to award costs against a party's representative for conducting the proceedings unreasonably and order one party to make payments to the other in respect of the time spent in preparing for a case (not applied in the case of representatives of 'not-for-profit' organisations, e.g. trade union officers);
- The Act provided the basis for amending employment tribunal rules to introduce a fixed period for conciliation by ACAS and to enable a tougher approach to the handling of 'weak cases'; and
- The Act introduced a new statutory right to paid time off work for trade union 'learning representatives'. ULRs were given time off for training needs of union members they represented, provision of information and advice, arranging training and consulting with employers on these aspects (Section 43).

Workplace Dispute Resolution

- The Act sought to encourage more individual employment disputes to be settled within the workplace without recourse to an employment tribunal.
- Statutory minimum internal disciplinary and grievance procedures for all organisations that employ staff, and measures to promote their use.
- Statutory dismissal and disciplinary procedure and a statutory grievance procedure, each involving three stages (written statement, meeting and appeal).
- Employment tribunals enabled to vary compensation awards by up to 50 per cent where an employer or applicant has failed to use the statutory procedures.
- If an employer fails to follow the statutory dismissal and disciplinary procedures, a dismissal will be automatically unfair. However, the legislation specifies that an employer's failure to follow a procedure other than the statutory procedure will not by itself make a dismissal unfair provided the employer can show that following the appropriate procedure would have made no difference to the decision; and
- The Act expanded the legal requirements on employers to issue employees with a written statement of their main terms and conditions and removed the twenty-employee threshold that applies to the provision of information on disciplinary and grievance procedures.

Equal treatment of fixed-term employees

- The Act included provisions enabling the government to make regulations to prevent pay and pension discrimination against fixed-term employees and implement the EU Directive on fixed-term work. As a result, the Fixed-term Employees (Prevention of Less Favourable Treatment) Regulations 2002 came into force on 1 October 2002 inclusive of the following:
- fixed-term employees to be treated 'no less favourably' than comparable permanent employees on the grounds they are fixed-term employees, unless this is 'objectively justified'; and
- the use of successive fixed-term contracts will be limited to four years unless the use of further fixed-term contracts is justified on objective grounds thus giving employees the right to become permanent after four years.

Appendix C
Key Warwick Agreement Pledges

Fairness at Work

- Four weeks paid holiday for all, exclusive of bank holidays
- Legislation on corporate manslaughter in the next parliamentary term
- Using Anti-Social Behaviour Orders to tackle violence and anti-social behaviour in and around front-line workplaces
- Major roll-out of childcare schemes including Sure Start & Extended Childcare Scheme for lone parents
- Increased statutory redundancy pay
- To work in Europe for the introduction of employment protection for temporary and agency workers
- Protection for striking workers to be extended from eight to twelve weeks.
- New 'Sectoral Forums', for example in low-wage industries to improve pay, skills, productivity and pensions

Pensions

- Protection for pension funds in company transfers or mergers
- Trade unions will gain the right to bargain on pensions
- Training to be introduced for pension trustees, and members to make up 50 per cent of trustees
- Assistance for those who have already lost out on occupational pensions
- An agreement to engage in effective dialogue over the future of public sector pensions
- Legislation, if necessary, to move beyond the current voluntary system of occupational pensions
- A commitment on pensions for same-sex partners

Public Services

- The extension of two-tier workforce protection in local government across the public services

- A review of all NHS cleaning contracts on a test of cleanliness and not just the cost
- Consultation with all stakeholders to monitor PFI including future financial implications
- Steps to develop staff roles, for example health care assistants to receive paid training and possible registration
- A commitment not to transfer out the vast majority of NHS employees
- Agreement to tackle unequal pay in local government
- Measures to promote healthy eating in schools and evaluate the possible extension of the free school meals programme

Manufacturing

- Review and enhance investment funds for manufacturing support with a view to having the best support possible
- Promote a public procurement which safeguards jobs and skills, encourages contracts to be given to UK firms for UK workers within EU law and supports a review of EU procurement policy
- The Bank of England to consider regional and employment information when setting interest rates
- A strong skills agenda, including the expansion of apprenticeships, rolling out Employer Training Pilots, supporting free training up to NVQ2 and action in sectors under-performing on skills, including possible training levies
- Union Learning Representatives trebled to 22,000
- Investment in Research and Development to rise to 2.5 per cent of national income
- Improve credit export facilities
- Ensure Regional Development Agencies produce manufacturing strategies through working with employers and trade unions and assist manufacturers to find new markets

Other Commitments

- The Royal Mail to stay in public hands, with telecom regulation to focus on service choice and reliability as well as network competition
- An immediate review of National Insurance Lower Earnings Limit to help lower paid workers get benefits
- The New Deal to provide help to unemployed over-50s
- Action to tackle unethical labour agencies in the health sector
- Further action to tackle domestic violence and support those at risk
- Legal limits to stop rip-off interest rates for credit
- Stronger company disclosure on social, ethical and environmental issues

Glossary

ACAS   Advisory, Conciliation and Arbitration Service
AEEU   Amalgamated Engineering and Electrical Union
ASTMS   Association of Scientific, Technical and Managerial Staffs
AUEW   Amalgamated Union of Engineering Workers
CAC   Central Arbitration Committee
CBI   Confederation of British Industry
CLP   Constituency Labour Party
CME   Continental Market Economy
COHSE   Confederation of Health Service Employees
CWU   Communication Workers Union
DTI   Department of Trade and Industry
EDE   Ex-Dictatorship Economy
EETPU   Electrical, Electronic, Telecommunications and Plumbing Union
ERA   (1999) Employment Relations Act
ETUC   European Trade Union Confederation
FBU   Fire Brigades Union
GMB   General, Municipal, Boilermakers and Allied Trade Union
GMWU   General and Municipal Workers' Union
GPMU   Graphical, Paper and Media Union
IMF   International Monetary Fund
IoD   Institute of Directors
IRA   (1971) Industrial Relations Act
JPC   Joint Policy Committee
LME   Liberal Market Economy
LPC   Low Pay Commission
MP   Member of Parliament
MSF   Manufacturing, Science and Finance
NALGO   National and Local Government Officers' Association
NCL   National Council of Labour
NEC   National Executive Committee of the Labour Party

NGA National Graphical Association
NME Nordic Market Economy
NMW (1998) National Minimum Wage
NPF National Policy Forum
NUGMW National Union of General and Municipal Workers
NUM National Union of Mineworkers
NUPE National Union of Public Employees
NUR National Union of Railwaymen
OECD Organisation for Economic Co-operation and Development
PFI Privative Finance Initiative
PLP Parliamentary Labour Party
PRP Policy Review Process
RMT Rail, Maritime and Transport workers' union
SOGAT The Society of Graphical and Allied Trades
TGWU Transport and General Workers' Union
TUC Trades Union Congress
TUCC Trade Union Coordinating Committee
TUFL Trade Unions for Labour
TUG Trade Union Group
TULO Trade Union and Labour Party Liaison Organisation
TULRA (1974) Trade Union and Labour Relations Act
TULV Trade Unions for a Labour Victory
ULF Union Learning Fund
USDAW Union of Shop, Distributive and Allied Workers
VoC Varieties of Capitalism

Index

Note: Page numbers in *italics* indicate a figure and page numbers in **bold** indicate a table on the corresponding page.